FARMINGDALE STATE COLLEGE

A sign on Melville Road, facing north, welcomes visitors to the campus, 1924. At extreme right is Hicks Hall, the Horticulture Building. At extreme left is Conklin Hall with smokestack. These original buildings still stand. *FSC Archives*. Unless otherwise stated, all images are from the Archives of Farmingdale State College.

Farmingdale State College

a history

FRANK J. CAVAIOLI

excelsior editions

AN IMPRINT OF STATE UNIVERSITY OF NEW YORK PRESS

Front cover: The memorial oak tree with Thompson Hall in the background.
Back cover: Thompson Hall Cupola

Published by
State University of New York Press, Albany

Printed in the United States of America

EXCELSIOR EDITIONS
is an imprint of State University of New York Press

For information, contact State University of New York Press, Albany, NY
www.sunypress.edu

Production and book design, Laurie Searl
Marketing, Kate McDonnell

Library of Congress Cataloging-in-Publication Data
Cavaioli, Frank J.
Farmingdale State College : a history / Frank J. Cavaioli.
p. cm.
Includes bibliographical references and index.
ISBN 978-1-4384-4367-6 (hardcover : alk. paper) 1. Farmingdale State College—History. I. Title.

T171.F37C38 2012
607.747'245—dc23 2011042035

10 9 8 7 6 5 4 3 2 1

Contents

	Preface	vii
	Introduction	xi
1	Chartering the New York State School of Agriculture on Long Island	1
2	Laying the Foundation	21
3	Albert A. Johnson, 1913–1923	51
4	Halsey B. Knapp, 1923–1956	81
5	The World War II Era	113
6	The Industrial–Technical Division	139
7	The Charles W. Laffin Jr. Years, 1961–1976	165
8	Dr. Frank A. Cipriani Heralds the Future, 1978–2000	193
9	Transition and Transformation	217
10	Into the Twenty-First Century	235
	Notes	257
	Bibliography	279
	Index	291

Preface

THE ONE-HUNDREDTH ANNIVERSARY OF FARMINGDALE STATE COLLEGE, a campus of the State University of New York (SUNY), marks a major development in the history of Long Island and higher education, worthy of a comprehensive chronicle of the individuals and events that have made it a major institution of higher education. Chartered in 1912, it is older than SUNY, which itself was founded in 1948. This carefully researched narrative fills a void in the history of public education during the twentieth century, and later.

I hold the title of professor emeritus of history and political science at Farmingdale State College. I have been drawn to the college's history primarily because it is very much a part of local history, which has been an important interest of mine. Local history has traditionally been left to dedicated nonprofessionals who have nevertheless made valuable contributions to collecting information of community life and its citizens. Without their accomplishments, much of the past would have been lost. Vast amounts of information are now available to the professional historian to record and analyze and to bring the past to light. My commitment to local history and the history of education has led to numerous published articles dealing with the college history in the *Long Island Forum* and the *Long Island Historical Journal*, now the *Long Island History Journal*, as well as other aspects of the history of Long Island.

Additionally, this institutional history presents the evolving relationship between Farmingdale State College and educational establishment in Albany, New York. Scant attention has been paid to this critical relationship. The examination and analysis of an overwhelming amount of factual information will thereby offer the reader a clearer understanding of the special place Farmingdale State College has had in the pre- and post-SUNY era.

Being a mature educational institution of higher learning, the Farmingdale State College Archives, presently in the Greenley Library on campus, contain a rich mine of primary source materials that include rare original documents and images. To the historian, here was a golden opportunity to tap into this mine of materials, most of which has never before been systematically researched or recorded. Endless hours were spent in the archives gathering and analyzing the information. Additionally, interviews with past and present campus personnel complemented the archival collection.

To gain perspective, a century of growth on Long Island and in New York State has generated a fitting background for this volume. I range across the entire spectrum of Farmingdale's history in detailing with the challenges that its leaders and students confronted. In one instance, the institution's very survival was at stake. Little understood and little appreciated by the Albany bureaucracy, the college in the course of its evolution has overcome these issues to emerge as an important public asset. From its humble beginning in a rural-agrarian environment one hundred years ago to its present status as a baccalaureate-granting institution of higher learning in a postindustrial society, Farmingdale State College has taken its place as a respected institution in the twenty-first century. It is now a much appreciated and valuable unit of SUNY within the statewide higher educational system that consists of sixty-four campuses.

From another perspective, the growth of Farmingdale State College has reflected the growth and development of Long Island. Or, conversely, as the demographics of Long Island were altered, along with environmental changes, corresponding developments occurred at the college. Its history is important on its own merit, but also provides a greater understanding of Long Island history and higher education in New York State.

Acknowledgments

Many individuals have contributed to this volume. Most important is Karen A. Gelles who, as college librarian and acting archivist, has guided me to research original source materials. She has been a full participant from the beginning of this historical enterprise as researcher and guide. Her technical skills were indispensable in formatting and organizing vital sections of the manuscript.

Many respected colleagues must be mentioned for their contributions of information based on their experiences and knowledge of the college. President Frank A. Cipriani (1978–2000) was generous in providing a personal copy of his memoir, *Re-Engineering SUNY Farmingdale* (2008), which narrated events during his entire thirty-six-year tenure (1964–2000) on campus as professor, administrator, and president. Many hours were shared communicating directly and through email. He provided an immense amount of assistance and information, and made suggestions where necessary.

Anthony Mastroianni supplied me with insights about the unique leadership qualities of President Charles W. Laffin Jr. and President Frank A. Cipriani. I am indebted to him for sharing his knowledge resulting from more than fifty years with the college as a graduate (class of 1950), alumnus, and member of the College Council for thirty-three years.

Noel Palmer, vice president of the college's Long Island Educational Opportunity Center, was gracious to share his personal memoir, *Let Each Become*, which was written at the time of his retirement in 1991. It covered twenty-three years working for presidents Laffin and Cipriani, offering educational programs and counseling to minority and nontraditional students.

During the 1980s, I conducted formal interviews regarding the college's history with David W. Allee, head of the first technical division, and with professors Michael Abbatiello and Casimir Rakowski. Over the years, through other formal and informal discussions, professors Irving Levine, Ann Senyk, Raynor Wallace, Ed Ore, and Herb Zipper provided details and a general understanding of campus life. At the same time, alumna Betty Mountain shared her understanding of Director Halsey B. Knapp from a student's point of view. Fortunately, all recorded notes were saved.

Other campus personnel who contributed information more recently were professors James Friel, Lou Howard, and Russ Tuthill; and administrators Kathryn Coley, Jonathan Goldstein, James Hall, Eileen Hasson, Kevin R. Laffin, George LaRosa, and Patricia Hill Williams. Mauro S. Zulli provided insightful knowledge of the college from the perspective of professor and acting president.

William J. Johnston, historian of the Village of Farmingdale, responded to requests for information that was not available elsewhere. His knowledge of local history proved to be a valuable asset. The relationship between Farmingdale State College and the Village of Farmingdale, in which it was founded, has been a wholesome one.

A special appreciation is extended to Priscilla Tedesco Hancock for providing excerpts of her father's remembrances as a student at the Farmingdale State Institute of Applied Agriculture covering the years 1929 to 1930. Peter Tedesco benefited from his education there and went on to become a successful educator in the Farmingdale Village School District. His experience was typical of endless student achievements.

A thank you goes to Myrna Sloam of Long Island's Roslyn Bryant Library for granting permission to use the photo of Hilda Ward.

Gratitude is extended to President W. Hubert Keen for his support of this project and his permission to have access to the college archival collection and to include its images in this volume. He follows in the line of dedicated leaders who have committed themselves to the success of Farmingdale State College and who has recognized its historical importance to Long Island and to SUNY.

This book is dedicated to those faculty and administrators whose commitment to educational excellence has contributed to the evolution of Farmingdale State College as a leading institution of higher education.

—Frank J. Cavaioli, PhD

Introduction

THE NEW YORK STATE SCHOOL OF AGRICULTURE ON LONG ISLAND was chartered in 1912 for high school boys and girls from New York City and surrounding counties. The school's origins emerged as part of the "Country Life Movement in America" during a period of growing industrialization and urbanization in the early decades of the twentieth century. Concurrently, educational reform, as part of social reform to advance democracy, became a central part of the era's Progressive Movement. It was an extraordinary idea to train youngsters from the city to become farmers to produce food, help relieve congestion in city schools and neighborhoods, and lay the foundation for social and economic mobility. The school's history has mirrored the growth of Long Island from agrarian to postindustrial. It has evolved into the oldest public college on Long Island. The school's original mission was to provide practical training in agricultural science, but over time, it has been transformed into a comprehensive baccalaureate granting college with emphasis on applied sciences and advanced technology, as well as programs in the liberal arts.

Located on 380 acres at the Nassau and Suffolk county borders, adjacent to Bethpage State Park to the west and busy Route 110 to the east, the school's development followed a flexible path of educational change in keeping abreast of the Long Island's development. Its evolution has led the school to adopt ten different names with the last being Farmingdale State College. The original agricultural program was ended in 1987 as the college focused on technology with a strong humanities and social science component. In 2000, the Broad Hollow Bioscience Park was established on twenty acres of campus land. This venture validated its mission change for the creation of degree programs in biotechnology and production and information technologies, leading to research opportunities for faculty and employment opportunities for students. The Biotechnology Park is an economic–educational collaboration of New York State, Farmingdale State College, and the Cold Spring Harbor Laboratory, known for its award-winning research scientists from around the world.

Its beginnings go back to the early part of the twentieth century, a time of educational progress and democratic expansion. Politicians, educators, agricultural, and business and community leaders lobbied for an agricultural school on then rural Long Island, some of whom were Franklin W. Hooper, Hal B. Fullerton, John M. Lupton, James Cooley, Frederick Cox, C. H. Howell, Dennis J. Harte, George L. Thompson, Elwood V. Titus, and Ezra Tuttle. Hooper, a leading educator and the director of the Brooklyn Institute of Arts and Sciences Institute (Brooklyn Museum), was the driving force behind the movement. There was no farm school downstate at this time when three similar institutions existed at Canton, Alfred, and Morrisville, as did the State College at Cornell. Delhi and Cobleskill joined this group. The original farm schools would share a similar development, although Farmingdale, because of its geographical location, experienced distinct differences.

Albert Aaron Johnson became the first director. He was mainly responsible for laying out the physical configuration of the campus and for developing the original curriculum. The first students, sixty in all, entered in March 1916 and the first graduation took place April 4, 1919. Students and faculty actively participated in World War I by joining the armed forces, producing food, and receiving military training on campus. A World War I memorial oak tree was planted 1921 in soil donated by the American states, the territory of Alaska, and the victorious Allied nations. The memorial oak tree flourishes today between Whitman and Thompson halls and is a living memory of an era long gone.

In the early years, the school witnessed many challenges: lack of funding, inconsistent enrollments, questionable standards, low number of graduates, problems of establishing permanent educational programs, a New York State investigation leading to the resignation of Director Johnson; and attempts by Gov. Alfred E. Smith to close the school. All these issues were eventually resolved.

Halsey B. Knapp (1923–1956), became the longest-serving director. His strong educational and administrative leadership helped the school through difficult times. He worked with community leaders, agricultural societies, and New York State legislators to achieve credibility for the school. He motivated the faculty to create innovative programs and to reach out to the community, especially through the annual open house program, which was started by his predecessor. Hard times emerged during the 1930s Great Depression and the World War II era. In 1937 the

School of Horticulture was established and became one the most successful curriculums. New Deal programs of the 1930s during the Franklin D. Roosevelt administration helped the school to continue normal operations with special funding. New York State appropriations were secured for the construction of Knapp Hall (1936) and Thompson Hall (1938) in this period of economic hard times.

Attendance at the upstate agricultural schools remained fewer than one hundred per year up to the 1930s, with the exception of Downstate Farmingdale, which more than doubled that number. In 1939 there were 359 students in attendance. Several studies in this period called for establishing technical education at all of the agricultural institutes. Knapp was committed to agricultural education, but he established the Industrial–Technical Division in 1946 under the guidance of David W. Allee. This initiative contributed to Farmingdale's successful educational transition following World War II.

In 1941, there were 286 students enrolled in regular programs. During the next four years attendance declined sharply in the regular programs. World War II effected campus life as attention turned to supporting the war effort through special courses in aeronautics, camouflage, mechanics, and food production, among others. These course offerings helped the school to survive the war emergency. Immediately following the war, large numbers of veterans enrolled under the GI Bill of Rights. For ten years (1946–1956) there was a "Campus Village" on the premises that housed student veterans and their families. Thirty-five barracks-type structures, near where Thompson and Whitman halls now stand, served as their living quarters.

Major changes occurred under the leadership of Dr. Charles W. Laffin, Jr. who served as president from 1961 to 1976. He guided the institution, now titled Agricultural and Technical College at Farmingdale, to a total enrollment of more than 14,000 students at its peak in the next decade. The evening college also expanded to meet the demands of part-time students. At this time, there were thirty-four two-year programs leading to degrees of associate of applied science, associate in science, and associate in arts. Laffin's tenure occurred at the time of student unrest, war in Vietnam, civil rights revolution, and women's movement, all of which impacted the campus. An aviation program was initiated with a fleet of airplanes at nearby Republic Airfield. The campus possessed the first Urban Center administered by a unit of SUNY to educate nontraditional students and minorities. Laffin hired faculty with advanced degrees and publications who were active in professional associations. His efforts to advance Farmingdale as a leading institution of higher learning were cut short by his sudden death in 1976. Until 1961, the chief executive officer had the title of "director." Laffin was the first to assume the title of "president."

Under the leadership of Dr. Frank A. Cipriani, president from 1978 to 2000, Farmingdale completed its transformation to a full-fledged four-year college, noted for applied sciences and technology. The agricultural program ended in 1987. "The Call of the Farm," a verse published in the 1920 Yearbook, no longer was heard on Long Island. The college responded as its new mission change was achieved with the support of faculty and staff. Cipriani believed if Farmingdale were to survive, it had to transform itself, a similar goal of President Laffin. "If we are not the architects of change we will surely be its victims," he warned. Another of his achievements was the establishment of a collaborative venture with the Cold Spring Harbor Laboratory that led to the construction of the Broad Hollow Bioscience Park on campus. All the previous leaders had been either new to the campus or new to the region, or both. The exception was Dr. W. Hubert Keen who served as campus provost before becoming president. Cipriani was the first president to have spent his previous fifteen years at the college in key administrative positions such as vice president of administration and assistant to President Laffin; this experience prepared him to lead the college into the future. All together, his service to Farmingdale, including professor, totaled thirty-six years (1964–2000). The transition to advanced technology allowed the college to assume its rightful place in the SUNY system and guarantee its future.

Jonathan C. Gibralter became the seventh president June 1, 2001 and built on the policies put in place by Laffin and Cipriani. Additionally, he initiated a major gifts campaign and developed a comprehensive strategic plan that focused on increasing the academic profile of the College, using new marketing techniques and implementing a student retention program. He continued cooperative ventures with the business community. During his tenure, new bachelor degree programs were launched in bioscience, technology studies, applied mathematics, and computer programming and information systems. The school assumed the new title of Farmingdale State College in 2006, the last of ten titles in its history. Dr. Gibralter resigned in 2006 to become president of Frostburg State College in Maryland.

Dr. W. Hubert Keen was appointed eighth president January 11, 2007. Under his leadership, the college added academic programs, increased support for scientific research, and made important infrastructure improvements. He instituted programs in applied economics, applied psychology, and software technology. He emphasized improving student services, and expanded alumni affairs, community outreach, fundraising, and campus construction and renovation. Dr. Keen extended ties with the business community to benefit the college's academic programs. His leadership style has earned him the respect of faculty, staff, and students. As a unit of SUNY, Farmingdale is the only college of technology on Long Island to offer a comprehensive base of programs in applied sciences and technology. It has a strong foundation of the liberal arts and humanities, emphasizing ethics, and esthetics, as well as promoting a diverse student population. The college has established itself as one of the fastest growing campuses within the SUNY system. The student enrollment head count was nearly 7,000 in 2010.

Following World War II, mainly as a result of the GI Bill of Rights and broadening equal opportunity, demand for higher education compelled New York to establish the SUNY system—in 1948 under Gov. Thomas E. Dewey. New York was the last state in the nation to do so. The long-held monopoly of the private colleges and universities, excepting the high-caliber City University of New York, had to yield to a more competitive economic and democratic system. Ironically, the agricultural–technical colleges and teachers colleges predated SUNY and possessed traditions of their own. To recognize recent interest in SUNY and to validate its history, a 2009 scholarly conference was held in Albany to celebrate its 60th anniversary. Fifty-six papers were presented, most of which were published in *SUNY at Sixty, The Promise of the State University of New York* (SUNY Press, 2010), edited by John B. Clark, W. Bruce Leslie, and Kenneth P. O'Brien. A comprehensive bibliographical list of publications on the history of SUNY and its campuses was included. Stony Brook Professor Emeritus Joel Rosenthal's essay offered a concise narrative, "Pride and Identity: The College Histories of the SUNY Campuses," in which he analyzed the reasons for recording campus histories. He acknowledged "many components of SUNY had been going about their business in an efficient and admirable way for almost three-quarters of a century before 1948, proud of their traditions and well ensconced in their own communities." Such was the case of Farmingdale, and the process of writing its history has been a personal and professional commitment to this act of "memorialization."

The author of this official history has chronicled and analyzed one-hundred years of historical events, personalities, and change. It is chronological in approach with emphasis on leaders who shaped the institution. He has attempted to apply faithfully the tools of his profession.

—Frank J. Cavaioli, PhD

ONE

Chartering the New York State School of Agriculture on Long Island

Physiography, climate, and location have all combined to make Long Island a farming country.[1]

Through its one-hundred years of existence, Farmingdale State College, a campus of the State University of New York (SUNY), has adapted to the demographic changes of Long Island's transition from rural to suburban and from agriculture to high technology in its development as an educational institution. It has been a microcosm of local history. More than 80,000 alumni have joined the public and private sectors of American society, and beyond. Chartered in 1912, at a time when William Howard Taft was president and the population of the United States was 92,228,496, as recorded in the 1910 census, its original name was the New York State School of Agriculture on Long Island and its mission was to provide agricultural training to high school boys and girls from New York City, and the counties of Suffolk, Nassau, Westchester, Dutchess, Rockland, and Putnam. At the beginning of the twentieth century, in the southeastern section of the state, an attempt was made to preserve a lifestyle of the past, and to benefit from the prevailing economic and social conditions. Today, in the twenty-first century, Farmingdale State College has established itself as the oldest public college on Long Island, and is older than SUNY itself, which was established 1948. The college has contributed to the present high socioeconomic status of the combined population of Nassau and Suffolk counties, which counted 2,832,882, according to the 2010 U.S. Census.

Since it's founding, change has been a constant factor in how the college has met the needs of an evolving society. This can be seen in the various names the college has assumed throughout its history. The following list reflects the official titles used in the official college bulletins and catalogues, which are held in the College Archives:

New York State School of Agriculture on Long Island, 1912
State Institute of Applied Agriculture on Long Island, 1920
State Institute of Applied Agriculture, 1924
State Institute of Agriculture, 1939
Long Island Agricultural and Technical Institute, 1946
SUNY Long Island Agricultural and Technical Institute at Farmingdale, New York, 1953
Agricultural and Technical College at Farmingdale, 1966
SUNY College of Technology at Farmingdale, 1987
SUNY Farmingdale, 1993
Farmingdale State College, 2006

The drive for an agricultural school on Long Island did not emerge out of a vacuum. Even before 1912, leaders stepped forward to provide the impetus for organization and planning to achieve that goal. They possessed the knowledge and experience to preach, publicize, and promote the need for a school. They used their political expertise to lobby effectively. As early as May 3, 1909 in a letter to *The New York Times*, Frederick H. Cox, a congressman from Queens County who was to serve as a trustee for the Farmingdale school, had called for an agricultural school on Long Island. Cox pointed out that in addition to the State College of Agriculture at Cornell University, there were three similar farm schools existing at Canton, Alfred, and Morrisville, but none in the downstate area where the majority of the population resided. Because of this "unfairness to our part of the State," he demanded that an agricultural school be established on Long Island.

Among the other outstanding leaders were Hal B. Fullerton, special agent of the Long Island Railroad (LIRR), who also advocated for a downstate school of agriculture and who served as LIRR director of its Agricultural Department; Franklin W. Hooper, director of the Brooklyn Institute of Arts and Sciences (the Brooklyn Museum); John M. Lupton, state assemblyman from Mattituck; George L. Thompson, state assemblyman and later senator from Smithtown and Kings Park; Dennis J. Harte, state assemblyman from New York City; Dr. James S. Cooley, superintendent of schools in Nassau County; Charles H. Howell of Riverhead, district superintendent of schools; Elwood V. Titus, pioneer in the cooperative movement among farmers and sponsor of the Nassau County Farm Bureau; Ezra Tuttle, a leading Long Island lawyer and expert in agriculture; Benjamin F. Yoakum, railroad executive who had a farm in Farmingdale; and Austin Corbin, William H. Baldwin, and Ralph Peters, all presidents of the LIRR who had a vested interest in transportation expansion.

The LIRR is one of the oldest railroads in the nation, and its development was an important part of the expansion of the region's transportation infrastructure that would inevitably influence the establishment of an agricultural school in Farmingdale. As Edwin L. Dunbaugh has stated regarding the railroad's original transportation goal:

> Probably few of us who have ridden it would be surprised to learn that the Long Island Railroad was not built with any thought of servicing the people on Long Island. The Long Island Railroad was in fact originally conceived solely as a major link in a combined rail and water route between New York and Boston.[2]

The LIRR was chartered in 1834 to transport passengers originally from Manhattan by ferry to Brooklyn, eastward through Long Island, then to Greenport-Orient Point, and by ferry to Stonington, Connecticut, where they would board another train to reach their destination in Boston. (A ferry was used until 1910 to cross the East River to reach the LIRR.) It was intended to use this route to reduce travel by five hours between New York City to Boston, the two major cities on the north east coast. Initially, the route achieved profitability carrying passengers and mail during the years 1844 to 1847. However, a competing all-land route was soon completed that extended from Charleston, South Carolina to New York City to Boston, rendering the Long Island connection to Boston unprofitable.

The LIRR turned to developing traffic at the local level, eventually merging various short trunk lines. Austin Corbin, the railroad's president from 1881 to 1886 even attempted to expand a large bay at the southern tip of Long Island called Fort Bay Pond to be converted to a transoceanic seaport. This venture for an American harbor at the east end of Long Island was unable to raise capital and it failed. In 1902, the LIRR became a part of the Pennsylvania Railroad and in 1910 was connected directly to New York City via a tunnel under the East River to the newly constructed Pennsylvania Station. As a result, the LIRR was relegated to local interests, concentrating on expanding local travel. Because Long Island was primarily an agricultural region, food products also would be shipped to the city, thereby sustaining its population while the city developed into a manufacturing, corporate, and financial center. It became obvious to the railroad leadership that lobbying for construction of an agricultural school would generate business and hopefully profits.[3]

The vision of Hal B. Fullerton (1857–1935) contributed significantly to the development of Long Island. In 1897, the LIRR appointed him to the position of special agent, and in 1905 assigned him the title of director of its Agricultural Department. His photographs—upward of 10,000—writings, and lectures made the public aware of Long Island as a growth extension of the New York City metropolis, as a place that could foster seaside resorts, recreation, tourism, suburban population growth, and agriculture, which in turn could influence the local demand for a school that specialized in farming. Fullerton's goal was to secure a profitable environment for the railroad. For more than thirty years he guided the railroad's promotional activities that emphasized Long Island "as an ideal vacation destination, a recreational paradise, an ideal home for commuters, and a fertile land for agricultural pursuits."[4]

As the head of the railroad's agricultural department, Fullerton guided the successful experimental farms in Suffolk County at Wading River from 1905 to 1910, named "Peace and Plenty," and at Medford from 1907 to 1927, named "Prosperity Farm," containing eighty acres, whose purpose was to demonstrate that fruits, vegetables, flowers, and foliage plants could be profitably grown and marketed from Long Island's less productive soils. The area was considered a wasteland. LIRR President Ralph Peters justified the program by pointing out the most undesirable parcel of Long Island land could be made fertile to produce every species of vegetables, fruit, and flowering plants. The success of the Wading River experiment was then extended to Medford where "scrub waste" was cleared and converted into productive agricultural soil. Long Island's experimental stations for years proved that farming could succeed through proper cultivation and fertilization. *The New York Times* commented in 1912 that because agriculture was largely responsible for Long Island's prosperity in the past, it would "become a more potent influence in the future."[5]

Fullerton combined his enthusiasm with staging publicity events to achieve his goals. As a friend of former President Theodore Roosevelt of nearby Oyster Bay, Fullerton organized a media extravaganza on August 10, 1912 by inviting him to the Medford farm. The LIRR set up a special train, with accompanying reporters and photographers. The event was well publicized. In all his endeavors, his talented wife, Edith Loring Fullerton, assisted him at fairs, expositions, trade shows, and public lectures. She produced a popular account of the Wading River experimental farm venture in a book, *The Lure of the Land, A Call to Long Island* (New York: Long Island Railroad, 1906), later revised and expanded into several more editions. The book included her husband's photographs. This successful husband–wife team established close connections with editors, publishers, and journalists who willingly cooperated in publishing articles extolling the benefits of agricultural and country life on Long Island.[6]

Theodore Roosevelt voiced support for the farmer. He believed that the future of the nation rested on conserving natural resources and the quality of rural life. Each was interdependent. In a speech he delivered to the State Grange during an August 1910 picnic at Oriskany, New York he stated, "In any great nation the prime physical asset—more valuable than any other—is the fertility of the soil." He went on to say that cities drain the nation of its resources. He admitted that the growth of cities may bring prosperity, but it must not be at the expense of the country. "Cities prosper and the men decay." The rural life problem is to make the career of the farmer as "attractive and remunerative as corresponding careers in the city." Roosevelt asserted that the great industrial leaders employed "expert and technical knowledge" to succeed, while farmers lagged behind. Farmers, therefore, also should benefit from technical advances. He called for an educational system "more turned toward the farm and the shop." Fully aware of the experimental farms on Long Island, he praised the work of Fullerton and the LIRR for cultivating farmland, using modern methods, and adding value to the soil. The Grange attendees were pleased with the former president's remarks that advocated the preservation of country life in a growing industrial society. The expansive Roosevelt personality provided creditable support for agriculture in general and specifically for an agricultural school on Long Island.[7]

From 1907 to 1914, Hal and Edith Fullerton wrote and published the *Long Island Agronomist*, an influential monthly publication boasting 14,000 readers that was used to promote local farming. The publication praised the well-attended agricultural educational programs in Riverhead during the 1911–1912 years. On numerous occasions it made reference to the "Long Island Agricultural University" and the "Long Island Agricultural College" even before the school was chartered. The *Long Island Agronomist* highlighted achievements of local farmers proudly stating that Long Island products had won high honors in every important competition at the 1912 State Fair in Syracuse. Gold medals were won for butter; milk earned the highest award. Long Island's fruit and grapes won thirty-eight prizes, while its vegetables won forty-one. Additionally, the local fairs at Huntington and Riverhead demonstrated progress resulting from the application of modern methods on Long Island farms.[8]

FIGURE 1-1. Melville Road, then called Sweet Hollow Road, captures the rural nature of Long Island in this pre-1912 image. The horse and carriage are having difficulty traversing this unpaved road. The New York State School of Agriculture was built on land to the north.

Fullerton seized every opportunity to advance his goal. In fact, he was such an enthusiastic booster for Long Island that the contemporary term *Fullertonize* entered the vocabulary. For example, he promoted bicycling at a time when cycling was a very popular sport in geographically flat Long Island. He conceived the dramatic "Mile-A-Minute-Murphy" promotion in 1899, the result of his friendship with Charles R. Murphy (1871–1950), who was a champion bicyclist. Fullerton arranged the construction of a two-mile plank "roadway" between the tracks on a stretch of the LIRR east of Farmingdale. The plan was for Murphy to ride a mile on this level plank in less than one minute. Fullerton controlled the publicity, organizing special excursion trains, highlighting Murphy's training program and practices, and generating interviews. Journalists and photographers were invited. After a preliminary run, Murphy successfully bicycled the mile in 57.8 seconds on June 30, 1899, at the appropriate time when the League of American Wheelmen was meeting at Patchogue.[9]

Throughout his busy and creative life, Fullerton maintained the vision that agriculture would continue to play an important part of the economic and social life of Long Island. In 1927, the year he retired from the LIRR, in an interview at his home in Medford he clung to this vision. A reporter from the *Brooklyn Eagle* recorded his vision in this way:

> [Fullerton] foresees a tremendous residential growth for Long Island, with New York working its way eastward at a rapid gait and the many villages becoming more and more urban in character. But tilling the soil is to be the main industry . . . "God, Providence, or whatever you may call it, put Long Island here to feed New York, and it has to carry out that purpose . . ."[10]

Despite the advances in transportation, suburbanization, and recreation on Long Island, so evident toward the end of his life, the agricultural ideal prevailed in the mind of this romantic-progressive leader. His "blessed isle" reflected the Jeffersonian ideal of an agrarian society that he believed was conducive to democratic civic virtue, sustained by unencumbered farmers, superior to a less free life style in urban-industrial society. In this view, farmers were regarded as the chosen people of God. Fullerton was conscious of the high tide of immigration covering the period from 1880 to 1920 when 18,638,406 immigrants entered the United States, most having settled in the cities and providing the labor for an expanding industrialized society.[11]

Changes were occurring rapidly in America. From 1870 to 1930 the nation's rural population had declined from 80 percent to less than 40 percent of the total population. For Nassau County

FIGURE 1-2. The Mott House in 1916 was part of the original farm purchased by New York State for the Agricultural School on Long Island. It faced Melville Road. Mott House served as an office, dormitory, and classrooms in the early years.

alone estate and real estate expansion had reduced the 1,658 farms in 1900 to 618 in 1950, and to 55 in 1977. Similarly, in 1900, in Suffolk County there were 3,277 farms, in 1950 there were 2,187, and in 1977 there were 311. In 1950, New York State boasted 124,977 farms on 16,016,721 acres; by the end of the century the number of farms had declined to 31,757 on 7,254,470 acres. The New York State 2000 census figures counted 54,372 (.06 percent of the labor force) working in agriculture, including forestry and mining. Despite a very different future that lay ahead, Fullerton enthusiastically promoted his pristine vision of Long Island as an agrarian society that dated back to the nineteenth century.[12]

Franklin W. Hooper (1851–1914), educator, scientist, and civic leader, was just as important as Hal B. Fullerton in setting the agenda for a Long Island school. As a respected educational reformer, he heralded the benefits of scientific farming and the need for an agricultural school. He, along with local leaders, recognized the importance of Long Island in the context of the region's overall economic and social development. It was Hooper who was the driving force in the struggle to establish an agricultural school at Farmingdale.

Hooper was known throughout the scientific world for his achievements as a scientist and educator. Born in Walpole, New Hampshire, on February 11, 1851 he grew up on his parents' farm. He was educated in common schools in a rural environment. At the age of seventeen he entered Antioch College in Yellow Springs, Ohio. After two years there, he enrolled at Harvard where he completed his studies under such scholars as Asa Gray, Louis Agassiz, and Josiah Cook, and he received a bachelor of arts degree in biological studies. In 1872, he attended the Agassiz Summer School of Natural History at Penikese Island off the coast of Massachusetts. Swiss American Louis Agassiz had started a school for natural history at this time. In 1876, Hooper was an agent for the Smithsonian Institution studying algae and coralline formations on the Florida coasts. Hooper married Martha Holden of Augusta, Georgia, whose father was an abolitionist during the time of slavery. This marriage produced three children. From 1877 to 1880, he served as principal of a high school in Keene, New Hampshire. He then accepted a professorship of chemistry and geology at Adelphi Academy in Brooklyn from 1880 to 1889. In 1889, Hooper was appointed curator at the Brooklyn Institute, which he helped reorganize to make it the newly established Brooklyn Institute of Arts and Sciences. He had served there as a fellow. His work earned him the right to be appointed as the first general director in 1899, holding this position until his death in 1914. The Brooklyn Institute of Arts and Sciences became the forerunner of the prestigious Brooklyn Museum of Art (1897) and included the Brooklyn Academy of Music, as well as the Brooklyn Children's Museum and the Brooklyn Botanic Garden. The institute had been founded in 1823 to provide a library for working boys as the Brooklyn Apprentices' Library Association. Two years later, on July 4, 1825, the great Frenchman who had served the American revolutionary cause, Gen. Marquis de Lafayette, while visiting Brooklyn, laid the cornerstone of the first building for the Apprentices' Library. The institute evolved into one of the most important cultural and educational institutions in the United States. Hooper provided the leadership in expanding the functions of the institute because of his keen interest in education, horticulture, botany, and civic responsibility.[13]

Hooper also served as a member of the Board of Education and as a trustee for the Brooklyn Public Library. As an important educator, leading citizen, and director of the institute, he assumed a prominent position in the community. He was aware of the emergence of new schools and courses developing toward the end of the nineteenth century. The agricultural high school was first established in 1888 at the University of Minnesota. By 1898, ten such high schools were in existence in the United States. After 1900, the development of agricultural high schools was more rapid than any other previous type of secondary school. The number of these agricultural high schools had reached sixty by 1909. Moreover, 346 other secondary schools were offering agricultural courses. Hooper would have been amazed, had he lived past 1914, by the number of secondary schools offering agricultural instruction. By 1934 the number had surpassed ten thousand.

The Brooklyn Institute of Arts and Sciences was nearly seven decades old when Hooper became director, and from this vantage point he worked to broaden the democratic base through educational reform. He extended the reach of the Institute by quadrupling its membership. He developed a philosophy of education that would have an important societal impact during the Progressive Era. He merged this philosophy of education with his influential leadership position to lobby effectively for the agricultural school in Farmingdale.

Toward the end of his life, having accomplished so much in public service, Hooper refined and articulated a philosophy of which he considered to be an advanced American educational system. In a paper he presented at a conference in Philadelphia, in 1913, his position was made clear when he stated, "Our educational ideals and institutions have been undergoing a very great change and that change has not at any time been more rapid or far reaching than at present."

He pointed out that the American system of public and private education had been greatly influenced by colleges and universities. According to his educational philosophy, the old system prepared students for postsecondary education, rather than for life, in a chiefly agrarian society. Hooper termed it *artificial* because it focused on the classics and it had little relation to life. This put boys and girls living in the city at a disadvantage. He said nearly all American statesmen, painters, poets, and industrial leaders had come from a farm, a hamlet, or had country origins. He continued:

> The life of the boy or girl on the farm or in the village workshop was a liberal education in itself superior to any substitute that could be devised. . . . The youth on the farm learned more of botany than the city-trained college professor of botany. . . . Our schools need to be revolutionized that each boy and girl has a real training—industrial, intellectual, and moral.

Hooper called for the formation of industrial and vocational schools; more high schools should focus on manual training and technical skills. He praised such contemporary educational institutions as Pratt Institute in Brooklyn, Drexel Institute in Philadelphia, Armour Institute in Chicago, and the Carnegie Industrial School in Pittsburgh. Although there were those who would disagree with this viewpoint, it did influence the growing trend of American education and helped guide the establishment of an agricultural school in Farmingdale.[14]

The interest in scientific farming to reclaim farms had been supported by agricultural societies in New England since the eighteenth century, while interest in the South had declined since the invention of the cotton gin because virgin land was more accessible and profitable. Agricultural societies flourished in the northeast and were some of the most prominent of the rural organizations. By 1867 there were more than nine-hundred such societies in existence. Famous Americans as Benjamin Franklin, George Washington, Thomas Jefferson, James Madison, and John C. Calhoun were members of agricultural societies. *The American Farmer*, issued in Baltimore in 1819, became the first journal devoted to farming. In 1860, there were fifty farm newspapers being published primarily in the North as progressive farmers sought new ways to reclaim and protect the land. The Department of Agriculture was created in 1862, allowing the federal government to broaden its support for farming. It is clear that the institution of farming played an important role in the development of the United States. This trend continued into the twentieth century when the need, indeed the demand, for an agricultural school on Long Island emerged.

The passage of the national Morrill Land-Grant Act of 1862 became the most important piece of agricultural legislation in American history as it applied to education. The law appropriated public land to the states for the establishment of agricultural and industrial colleges. Congress enacted the Hatch Act of 1887, which further subsidized farming by providing agricultural experiment stations in every state of the Union. Thus, by the turn of the twentieth century, scientific farming had been established as public policy with the goal of eliminating plant and animal diseases, overcoming natural obstacles, adapting plants to American conditions, and applying science to improve production.

At the same time, in the middle of the nineteenth century in New York State, the legislature established the official State Fair. Huge crowds came to see the exhibits. *The Rural-New Yorker* and *The American Agriculturist* were several of the leading publications that promoted the agricultural fair and spread knowledge extolling the benefits of scientific farming. In 1832, the New York State Agricultural Society was founded and the *Cultivator* became its official voice. Other periodicals such as the *Plough Boy* (Albany, 1819), *Genesee Farmer* (Rochester, 1831), and *American Agriculturalist* (New York, 1842) gained readership in the tens of thousands by informing its readers of fairs, rural life, farming conditions, and methods of improvements. The first New York State Fair was held in Albany in 1841 with endorsement and support of the state government. Huge crowds have traditionally attended the event. Since 1890, the State Fair was held in Syracuse. In 1841, the Queens County Agricultural Society was founded with Nassau and Suffolk counties. As one of the oldest agricultural organizations in the nation, the society has sponsored an annual fair since 1842. Now known as the Long Island Fair, it has been held at the Old Bethpage Village Restoration since 1970. In 1865, under the Morrill Land-Grant Act of 1862, New York State chartered Cornell University with a small agricultural department, and it became the New York State College of Agriculture in 1904, now the New York State School of Agriculture and Life Sciences. An experiment station was set up in Ithaca, in 1879, and it became affiliated with the Cornell Agricultural College. The following year, a second experiment station was instituted in Geneva and placed under the Agricultural College in 1923. The college sponsored New York State's first Farmers Institute in 1886. These were among the major developments that led to the formation of agricultural schools at Canton (1906), Alfred (1908), Morrisville (1908), Farmingdale (1912), Delhi (1913), and Cobleskill (1916).[15]

Thus, such widespread interest in promoting farming set the stage for aggressive lobbying activity to achieve this goal. Other leaders who joined with Fullerton and Hooper in this endeavor were John M. Lupton, Ezra A. Tuttle, Elwood V. Titus, George Lincoln Thompson, Dennis J. Harte, Frederick Cox, Charles H. Howell, James C. Cooley, and those executives representing the LIRR. The press also voiced support. As a result, twenty-one bills establishing agricultural schools were passed in the New York State Legislature in 1908. Gov. Charles Evans Hughes (1907–1910), however, vetoed all of them because they were considered too numerous and too costly. In 1909, Assemblyman Lupton introduced a bill that would create a school under the general education law. It was passed by the legislature, but vetoed this time by Gov. John Alden Dix (1911–1912). In 1910 and 1911, similar bills were passed, and Dix vetoed them as well. Nevertheless, Dix accepted an alternative bill that authorized him to appoint a committee to develop a specific plan for the formation of agricultural schools. The committee gathered the relevant information and recommended that two schools be established: one in the Finger Lakes district and the other in the southeastern part of the state.

Opposition to a downstate school remained, especially from upstate interests. For example, the editor of *The Rural New Yorker* argued that such an agricultural school in the southeastern region of the state was not needed. With Canton, Alfred, and Morrisville already chartered, the New York State government also was reluctant to increase the number of schools. Congressman Cox had warned of such opposition. Now, more than ever, effective lobbying was imperative. On April 6, 1912, Franklin W. Hooper (president), Frederick Cox (secretary), and John M. Lupton (treasurer) organized the Agricultural Education Association at the Brooklyn Academy of Music Building to further the goal of promoting agricultural education in the New York City metropolitan area and to assist in the establishment of a farm school. This development coincided with the emergence of the Harte-Thompson bill in the state legislature to create a farm school on Long Island. On April 9, Agriculture Education Association (AEA) president Hooper and secretary Cox sent letters to officers and members of agricultural organizations, boards of trade, and civic groups to urge Dix to sign the Harte-Thompson Bill into law, which he did on April 15. A week later, at a meeting at the Brooklyn Academy, Hooper and Cox asked all members of the AEA to promote the welfare of the new farm school and to inform local citizens of its importance. The AEA Nassau County branch officers were Elwood V. Titus (Glen Cove), president; Adolph Bausch (Farmingdale), vice president; Dr. James S. Cooley (superintendent of schools), secretary. Titus also served as vice president of the main organization. A special committee was formed to recommend trustees for the school while invitations were sent out to prominent community leaders, including former President Theodore Roosevelt, to assist. The Queens and Nassau County branches of the AEA went even further by offering a Free Winter School of Agriculture and Allied Subjects in Jamaica during the winter of 1913. The AEA continued to maintain close ties with their legislative representatives.

In addition to the work of the AEA the New York State Advisory Board on Agricultural Education and Country Life, created in 1911 by the legislature for the purpose of studying this entire issue, reported to the governor and the legislature in March 1912 and recommended the chartering of a farm school. Responding to this official report, State Assemblyman George L. Thompson, Republican from Smithtown, introduced a bill in the same month for the creation of a state school on Long Island. The bill was co-sponsored by Senator Harte, Democrat from Long Island City. Hooper had actually written the bill with the assistance of Queens Congressman Cox, Fullerton, Nassau County Superintendent of Schools Cooley, and District Superintendent of Schools Howell of Riverhead. Following passage by the legislature, Dix signed the bill into law on April 15, 1912. Babylon's newspaper, *The South Side Signal*, praised Thompson for his leadership. Superintendent Howell, representing the sentiments of his colleagues, stated his support.

> An agricultural school on Long Island is an institution to which southeastern New York has long been entitled. . . . Some Long Island fathers' sons have taken advantage of agricultural schools [in northern and central New York State] but they have been too far away from the average farmers' sons. Then, too, these [upstate] institutions cannot specialize along lines, which are engaging the attention of Long Islanders most extensively.[16]

Even the influential *New York Tribune Farmer*, which described itself as "A National Illustrated Agricultural Weekly for the Farmer's Home," reversed its earlier opposition to the school. In a letter to Gov. John A. Dix, the editor of this weekly publication now supported the agricultural school because "this section of the State has been neglected and that it has not been treated fair." Since the agricultural problems of the New York City area were different from other areas in the state, he asserted, "there should be an institution provided by the State to work specifically on these problems."[17]

The Harte-Thompson Act became Chapter 319 of the Laws of New York of 1912 and stated in its opening paragraph that the act's purpose was to amend the education law in relation to the creation of the new school, and to provide for its control, management, and to provide an appropriation. The following are excerpts from the new law:

> *Section 1185*. . . . There shall be established on Long Island an institution to be known as the New York State School of Agriculture on Long Island. *Section 1186*. . . . Such

school and the property shall be under the immediate supervision, care and management of a board of nine trustees, of whom the governor shall appoint one from each of the five boroughs of the city of New York, two from the county of Nassau and two from the county of Suffolk. They shall be so appointed that the terms of office of three trustees shall expire each year. All trustees shall serve without pay. . . . Students bona fide residents of the state shall have free tuition.

Section 1187. . . . Such school shall furnish instruction and training in agricultural science, manual arts and domestic science; courses for public school teachers and others; winter courses for farmers and others, and such other operations as may be approved by the trustees and the commissioner of education.

FIGURE 1-3. The Director's Cottage was one of the original buildings and cost, with garage, $15,89.00. Completed in 1915, it housed all the directors, including President Charles W. Laffin, Jr. who moved to a home in nearby Dix Hills. Today it is used for administrative purposes.

FIGURE 1-4. Dormitory I, under construction in the distance, was renamed Ward Hall in 1962 in honor of service rendered to the school by Hilda Ward as student, alumna, and member of the College Council.

The Harte-Thompson Act mandated the governor appoint a board of trustees within thirty days after the act took effect. Furthermore, land was to be acquired in either Nassau or Suffolk counties, "suitable for the purposes of such school." Fifty thousand dollars was appropriated to carry out the act. The sum of $10,000 was added to acquire school lands, and "the remainder of such fifty thousand dollars for constructing and equipping a suitable school building and minor structures."[18]

Based on the philosophy of those leaders who lobbied for the school, a year-round calendar was to be established enabling students to acquire the science and practice of agriculture under real farm conditions. Instead of hiring employees to do the gardening and farming and care for the livestock, students were to do the work as an essential part of their education. The plan was to organize the course of study to emphasize a maximum amount of fieldwork, supplemented

FIGURE 1-5. Newly enrolled students in the agricultural program gather for a 1921 group photo in front of the Horticultural Building, now Hicks Hall. As one of the original buildings on campus, Hicks Hall is closed and awaits renovation.

by study of the theory of agriculture and its underlying sciences. This goal intended to assure students of a thorough training in practical and scientific farming. Thus, the original mission of the school was to train high school boys and girls from New York City and surrounding counties in agricultural training. The principle of instruction and learning in agricultural science, with hands-on experience, was to predominate. Theory was to be subsidiary to practical education and training. Additionally, courses in English, history (citizenship), economics, and mathematics (arithmetic) were planned to round out the educational program.

With the official chartering of the agricultural school, new challenges lay ahead. An official site had to be located, buildings had to be designed, and an infrastructure constructed. Would the campus be in Nassau County or Suffolk County? Would enough funds be appropriated? Community leaders had to be appointed by the governor to serve on the board of trustees. Administrators and faculty had to be chosen.

Local publications praised the establishment of the new agricultural school. For example, in the issue of September 9, 1914 *The Long Islander* expressed great satisfaction by noting one of its most important goals had been achieved for the advancement of the Long Island region and the agricultural industry. It articulated its sentiments in noteworthy fashion:

> The Island is coming a-running all right. We have proof of this fact. It took many a year and innumerable hard fights to get the original appropriation for the establishment of the much-needed agricultural college on Long Island, but we got it right. It is going to be the real thing. It won't be an emporium for the distribution of fancy initials for the attachment to the end of somebody's name. It won't be a place where someone will poll-parrot year after year the words of some agricultural dreamer of the past. It won't be a sacred edifice for the development of fads and fancies. It will be a practical, vitally necessary institution for the turning out of competent, capable, self-supporting out-door men and women. Theories will be put to the practical test and if they don't make good will be handed back to the laboratory investigator for embalmment, amendment or revampment. Say-sos will not be accepted as facts. Prophets, soothsayers, wizards and know it alls will have to make good in the open before a jury of disinterested and closely observed unsubsidized men and women.

Now that an agricultural school had been chartered on Long Island, its social and economic impact was expected to be immense. High expectations abounded.[19]

There could be little doubt the southeastern region of New York State needed such an institution in this period of local history. None had existed to serve the vast metropolitan area. The seed was planted for the growth of a new practical agricultural school that aspired to train young boys and girls for the future. There were few models to follow. The New York State School of Agriculture on Long Island would experience unprecedented change in its early years to the extent that its survival would be at stake. Problems arose that appeared insurmountable. In fact, its very existence would be challenged.

The Farmingdale School's origins arose as part of the "Country Life Movement in America" and the "Back to the Soil Movement" during a reformist era in American history. It was an "extraordinary idea to train urban young people to become farmers and homemakers . . . [and] would relieve overcrowding in city neighborhoods and schools, and thus benefit both urban and rural interests." The school matured into an institution of higher learning, offering degrees in applied arts and sciences at the associate and bachelor levels, and it became a microcosm of Long Island's growth. The transition was complete when the agricultural program ended in 1987. The early history of Farmingdale State College, as it is known today, illustrates an aspect of Long Island, which has all but vanished.[20]

TWO

Laying the Foundation

> Recognizing that all wealth comes of development of natural resources, we have begun to realize that the soil is great in its potential wealth.[1]

Two years before the New York State School of Agriculture (NYSSA) on Long Island was established, the U.S. Census of 1910 recorded 96,138 people living in Suffolk County and 83,930 people living in Nassau County. Basically agrarian, the 1910 Long Island (Suffolk and Nassau) official population totaled 180,068. Ten years later, in 1920, the census count for Suffolk County reached 110,246, while Nassau County surpassed this number with 126,120. The two counties in 1920 totaled 236,366 people.[2] Eight years earlier, President William Howard Taft served his last full year in office, and the following year, 1913, Woodrow Wilson ascended to the presidential office to initiate his New Freedom program. It was a time of fundamental reform at the state and national levels. Historians have identified this early twentieth-century movement as the Progressive Era, a time when reformers campaigned to root out political and economic corruption, regulate business, expand democracy, and broaden the educational and social process.

Of course, Long Islander Theodore Roosevelt of Oyster Bay, having preceded Taft as president, had been a catalyst for reform from 1901 to 1909. In a speech to the New York State Grange in Oriskany, in August 1910, Roosevelt joined Hal Fullerton, Franklin W. Hooper, and others urging farmers to create careers that were as remunerative and productive as those people living in the city. By combining education and science, Roosevelt believed agriculturists would achieve greater success in the future, leading to advances in productivity. Such appeal coincided with the movement to found a farm school at Farmingdale. But World War I (1914–1918) served as a counterweight to this spirited era. The Great War, as it was then called, produced devastating destruction, causing millions of deaths and casualties. The United States entered the war April 1917 and helped to turn the tide in favor of the Allies. These events served as the background for the fledgling agricultural school on Long Island.[3]

With the passage of the 1912 legislation, the agricultural school was finally a reality. However, much work would be needed to make it a viable institution. A sum of $50,000 was originally allocated, of which $10,000 was to be used for the purchase of school lands and the remaining $40,000 was for "constructing and equipping a suitable school building and minor structures." This work would be executed by the school's Board of Trustees (often referred to as Board of Visitors and later as the College Council) with the "advice and assistance" of the state architect, commissioner of agriculture, and commissioner of education, "acting together as a board." The appropriation proved to be insufficient, and more funds would follow.[4]

Dr. Franklin W. Hooper played a direct role during the organizing years that followed the creation of the school, maintaining close contact with educational leaders in Albany. Following one of his overnight trips from Brooklyn to the State Capitol, he submitted an expense account of $11.60 on February 28, 1914. He listed each individual item: $5.75 round trip railroad ticket; $3.75 Pullman Parlor seat; $.60 for supper in Albany; $.70 for breakfast in Albany; $.50 for lunch in Albany; $1 for dinner on return train; $.30 railroad fares on Albany trolleys; and $2 for room at Hotel Ten Eyck. In his important role as Board Secretary, he recommended to the governor individuals who were to serve as trustees. The men who were appointed had been actively working for the establishment of the school. Their backgrounds in agriculture, business, and education qualified them to serve. The Board of Trustees was appointed by Gov. Dix and held its first meeting May 2, 1912 at the Brooklyn Academy of Music. Ezra A. Tuttle (Suffolk County) was elected chairman, Henry A. Reeves (Suffolk County) vice chairman, and Franklin W. Hooper (Brooklyn) secretary. The other trustees were Frederick H. Cox (Brooklyn), John F. Murray (Bronx), William A. Shortt (Staten Island), Berthold Flesch (Manhattan), James Byrne (Nassau), and Frederick B. Pratt (Nassau). Byrne declined to serve because he was a trustee on the board of City College of New York. He was replaced by James Malcolm (Nassau). Pratt also resigned because he had many other commitments. He was replaced by John A. Carll (Nassau). When Malcolm died soon after his appointment, Gov. Dix appointed Benjamin F. Yoakum (Nassau), who owned property in Farmingdale. Yoakum (1859–1929), a prominent corporate executive with the St. Louis & San Francisco Railroad, had a farm consisting of 1,100 acres on the northern border of Farmingdale where he raised prize cattle, fruit, and vegetables. Yoakum's estate, along with three-hundred acres of the Joseph Botto farm, became Bethpage State Park, which abuts the campus. The governor thus was empowered to appoint nine trustees, two each from Suffolk and Nassau counties, and one each from Queens, Brooklyn, Staten Island, Manhattan, and the Bronx. The five trustees from New York City amounted to one more than the combined four from Suffolk and Nassau counties because the school's mission was to provide agricultural training to the boys and girls of the city (and surrounding counties).[5]

The Board of Trustees began its work by identifying specific responsibilities among themselves. Former State Assemblyman John M. Lupton headed the committee to select a site for the school. Hooper led the committee to find an experienced educator who would be appointed as the first director. The entire Board of Trustees prepared to establish educational policies to guide the school. The board members were entering untested waters as there were few models to follow, and many of them had no previous experience in the work of founding a school.

Would the school be placed in Nassau or Suffolk county? With such a large land area from which to choose, certain localities were discussed and recommended. Once a site was chosen, it would produce obvious benefits for the economy of the surrounding communities, as well as local pride. Lupton, chairman of the site committee and chairman of the Long Island Educational Association, wanted to locate the school in eastern Suffolk County, which was more distant from New York City but thought to be more adaptable to farming. Born in 1856 in Mattituck, Lupton was a Republican, president of a Long Island seed-growing company, and president of a bank. He had represented New York Assembly State District 1.[6] During the selection process other sites emerged: Riverhead, Holtsville, Yaphank, Manorville, Babylon, and places along the Nassau–Suffolk border. Lobbying surfaced for and by the respective communities. It became obvious that certain criteria had to be met, such as proximity to transportation, cost per acre, expense of clearing the land, and quality and availability of land with running water and electrical power components.[7]

The Board of Trustees discussed sites for the schools. Local leaders had sent communications to the board extolling the advantages of their communities. Of all the groups that lobbied, the Farmingdale Board of Trade was the most direct and effective; it invited members of the Board of Trustees to be its guests at a meeting of businessmen at Brown's Hotel on Main Street in Farmingdale. The invitation was accepted and the meeting took place there on June 29, 1912.

Following an early dinner, the trustees were escorted to local farms on a tour of the area. They were impressed with the area and its facilities. Other advantages emerged for Farmingdale as further investigation continued.[8]

At the conclusion of evaluating all the sites, Farmingdale was chosen because it met all the important prerequisites. Located on the border of Nassau and Suffolk counties, it was near the cross-island trolley that ran between Huntington and Amityville. The trolley connected the north shore with the south shore of Long Island and contributed directly to the prosperity of the area. Paul Bailey, prominent resident of Amityville and founder and publisher of the *Long Island Forum* from 1938 to 1959, vividly remembered this form of transportation:

> In 1911 the Huntington cross-island trolley ran down Broadway, past our door, on its devious way to the foot of Richmond Avenue. One block north of the *[Long Island] Sun* office, the Babylon trolley had its westernmost terminal on Union Avenue. I used both lines frequently, my only means of transportation, besides the LIRR, being a bicycle.[9]

Organized as the Huntington Rail Road in 1887, the line began service three years later between Huntington and Halesite, eventually expanding to Melville, Farmingdale, and Amityville. From Halesite to Melville the line followed New York Avenue, down to Route 110 (Whitman Road) at the Lower Melville Church and cemetery, continuing on the east side of Route 110 to Conklin Street, Farmingdale to the village line where 160 feet from the southeast corner of Secatogue Avenue the track turned north and merged into Depot Road to run one block to the station platform. The track continued south at Main Street, crossing the Central Extension Branch of South Farmingdale. The cross-island trolley went on its southward path to its final destination in Amityville. The entire line was divided into six fare zones, each costing $.05. Service was discontinued in 1927 because of a decline of riders.[10]

The school site was also close to the LIRR station at Farmingdale, providing easy, inexpensive access to New York City, from which most of the student population was expected to originate. It was convenient for students to attend religious services in town, and parents could more easily visit their children at the school. Adequate water and power facilities were available. There were buildings on the Farmingdale site that represented value and could be used immediately for instruction, housing, and office space. Also, studies made by the State Departments of Education and Agriculture, and Cornell University soil expert Professor E. O. Flippen, concluded soil at the Farmingdale site was ideal for an agricultural school. More than half of the land was already cleared and under cultivation. Farmingdale was therefore recommended over Pinelawn, Babylon, Riverhead, Wyandanch, Holtsville, Manorville, Huntington, Northport, Smithtown, and Port Jefferson, which had all been studied and considered.[11]

The only apparent disadvantage was the high cost of $300 to $325 per acre for the land. But most of the land was already under cultivation and could be farmed immediately upon the opening of the school. If less-expensive land were acquired, the cost of clearing and preparing the land would have been prohibitive. Hooper explained the Farmingdale requisition in this way:

> The Board of Trustees entered into a contract for the purchase of three farms on the Farmingdale road [Melville Road], one and one-quarter mile northeast of Farmingdale, comprising altogether 290 acres of land. These farms are so situated as to be on the borderline of Suffolk and Nassau counties, about 40 acres in the town of Oyster Bay and the balance divided between the towns Huntington and Babylon, or altogether forming a compact area. Of the 290 acres, approximately 200 acres are now under cultivation, and the balance is pasturage and woodland. The titles of these three farms purchased have been searched by the Attorney General and have been proven. The State Comptroller will pay for the farms during the month of December at the rate of $300 an acre for two of the farms and $325 an acre for the third for the latter farm being on the average of higher value per acre than the other two.

Hal Fullerton, already an expert on Long Island farming, agreed with Hooper that the land was "ideal" for an agricultural school.[12]

Thus, New York State had actually acquired 308.5 acres of land at this time from Ezekiel K. Smith, Judson F. Ruland, Richard S. Mott, M. M. Lazarus, J. K. Hendrikson, and M. A Seaman. The total expenditure, including surveys, came to $96,205.65. The school was located on Broad Hollow Road (Route 110) and Sweet Hollow Road, now named Melville Road. The latter name was also referred to as Farmingdale Road. The bulk of the land on which the school would be established comprised 200 acres of the Mott farm. Smaller parcels of land were added later to bring the campus total to 380 acres. Until the time when the school became a reality by occupying the buildings, William A. Weiners moved into the Mott House to serve as caretaker. The Mott House was used later as a dormitory, classrooms, and offices.[13]

Students' travel expenses also were factored into the decision to locate the school in Farmingdale. It was argued that if the school had been placed twenty-five miles farther east on Long Island, the round-trip ticket fare for each student would have been increased by $1. Considering that students would go home five times a year (Thanksgiving, Christmas, mid-year, Easter, summer) an additional $5 would be added to students' costs. Parents also traveling to visit students on campus would have to bear the extra cost.[14]

More savings in travel expenses would benefit students who did not live on campus. In early 1916, the monthly cost of a student commutation ticket from New York City to Farmingdale on the LIRR came to $7.10. A taxicab ride from the Farmingdale station to the campus cost $.25. As an alternative to riding, it was a pleasant twenty-minute walk to the campus along the new concrete road. Finally, the cross-island trolley made hourly trips to the campus for $.05. Of course, there were many other special advantages being located approximately one-hour's ride from New York City. Parks, museums, libraries, educational institutions, resorts, theaters, and many more amenities were available in the metropolis.

The respected *Long Island Agronomist*, published by Hal and Edith Fullerton, firmly supported the selection of Farmingdale as the location of the agricultural school, pointing out that Yaphank, for example, to the east in Suffolk County, was inadequate because it did not meet stated criteria. The publication went further in conceding the "original Agricultural school has for two years held sessions in Riverhead, but Farmingdale is preferred because of accessibility to larger numbers of students and better transportation. Riverhead had the further disadvantage of being at a greater distance from the Nation's greatest city." Even though reference was made to an "Agricultural school" and classes were held in Riverhead, there was no formally established agricultural school or college under the auspices of New York State before 1912 on Long Island.[15]

Board members of the new farm school made every attempt to keep expenses as low as possible. As with other public institutions, free tuition was provided for New York State students, while those from out of state were charged $150 per year. In all other respects they would be treated equally. Additional expenses included an estimated $15 for books and stationery; the cost for students' room and board was calculated at $30 per month. The school intended to reduce the last mentioned expense if farm-grown food could be used. Students were expected to give service on and off campus. In these early years, the tradition of welcoming visitors to the campus was begun and continued throughout the school's history. Student guides were available to assist visitors by showing them the buildings and grounds, and demonstrating agricultural cropping systems, and farm practices.[16]

An examination of the population of the Village of Farmingdale during the early part of the twentieth century revealed the rural nature of the community, a condition that characterized all of Long Island. This fact produced a belief that was conducive to farming and a bias toward agriculture. It provided a lingering appeal for an idyllic image of rural life that advanced agricultural interests. The figures shown in Table 2.1 for the first half of the twentieth century, however, revealed the Farmingdale Village population trend that paralleled the growth of the new school during the next four decades.

While the location for the school was being decided, the search for an educational leader was being conducted. Hooper led the search for a prominent educator in agriculture to organize the school and initiate its educational programs. He contacted state education departments and colleges around the country, the U.S. Department of Agriculture, and appropriate professional associations for recommendations. Three directors of agricultural schools and two university department heads were recommended, and they were interviewed during summer 1912. The Board of Trustees settled on Albert Aaron Johnson at the end of the year, offering him the directorship of the new school. He was highly regarded by government officials and educational leaders. His credentials were impressive.

Albert Aaron Johnson (1880–1963) was born in South Dakota and spent his youth on a farm near MacFarland, Wisconsin. His father died when he was twelve months old and his family relocated to a farm in Webster, South Dakota. After serving as a foreman on a ranch in South Dakota, he attended the South Dakota Agricultural College at Brookings. While there, he earned income as a student-instructor. He enrolled in the College of Agriculture at the University of Wisconsin where he received a bachelor's degree in science in 1907. Following his graduation,

Table 2.1. Farmingdale Village Population Trend

YEAR	POPULATION
1910	1,567
1920	2,091
1930	3,373
1940	3,524
1950	4,492[17]

FIGURE 2-1. Director Albert Aaron Johnson, third from left in front row, poses with his faculty in front of the Horticultural Building, Hicks Hall, in 1920. Johnson was assumed the directorship in 1913 and resigned ten years later.

Johnson secured the position of professor of agriculture and biology at the University of North Georgia Agricultural College, in Dahlonega, Georgia. In 1919, he married Ellen Glen. He returned to Wisconsin and headed the Marinette County School of Agriculture and Domestic Economy. Johnson next became principal of the La Crosse County School of Agriculture and Domestic Economy in Onalaska, where he was responsible for planning, equipping, and directing.

The last educational position Johnson secured during this period of his career was superintendent of the Milwaukee County School of Agriculture and Domestic Economy in Wauwatosa, Wisconsin. While there, he assumed overall control of planning the construction of buildings, selecting faculty, and equipping the institution, which was at the secondary level. Most of the students came from the city. The curriculum emphasized farming, domestic skills, community welfare, and the practical aspects of education rather than the theoretical. The specific subjects taught were soil fertility, farm crops, horticulture, poultry science, farm mechanics, animal husbandry, and such academic subjects as music, arithmetic, general science, civics, and English. His success in organizing two county schools made him a prime candidate for the newly chartered Farmingdale institution. His service in the Spanish American War of 1898 and ensuing insurrection in the Philippines further enhanced his distinguished career.

Johnson's educational background conformed to Hooper's educational philosophy. In fact, Johnson was an important part of progressive agricultural educational movement at the beginning of the twentieth century. He was influenced by, and supported, such organizations as the National Grange and Farmers Institutes in Wisconsin Institute in demanding the reform of rural and agricultural education at all levels. He was committed to the agenda of the Association of American Colleges and Experiment Stations, which had created a uniform agricultural curriculum. He was therefore highly recommended to serve as director of the school. The Farmingdale Board of Trustees agreed that he was an ideal choice and offered him the position on December 23, 1912. After considerable negotiations, Johnson's salary was eventually settled at $5,000 in February 1913 and took effect January 1914 when he assumed full time duties. The Board of Trustees of the Milwaukee County School of Agriculture and Domestic Economy granted Johnson's request to resign January 1, 1914. He expected to receive $1,000 more in salary from Farmingdale, but was persuaded to accept the $5,000 when free housing, utilities, and farm produce were added. Before he began full-time work on Long Island, a period when he was completing his contract in Wisconsin, he was given a subsidy of $300 per month starting in 1913 and an expense account. During this time he maintained communication with New York State officials preparing for his new duties as director. He made several trips to New York.[18]

From January to December 1913, a long correspondence was exchanged between Johnson and Hooper, secretary of the Board of Trustees, in the preliminary planning for the school. It was a difficult time because of geographical distances. Johnson himself was busy writing catalogues, completing work at his Wisconsin agricultural school, and participating in the Wisconsin State Fair, thus postponing his arrival on Long Island. In the exchange, blueprints, sketches, buildings, dormitories, landscaping, capital expenses, maps, salary, personal expenses, and other matters were discussed. Finally, on December 27, 1913, he notified Hooper that he would leave Wisconsin three days later and meet with Hooper and the New York State architect in Albany to review the design for the campus and its buildings. His official start of work in New York would be January 1, 1914 although much preliminary work had been done the previous years.[19]

Based on his previous experience as a chief educational administrator, Johnson submitted a personnel list necessary for the opening of the school. The Civil Service Commission requested the list of positions and a copy was forwarded to Board Trustee Hooper (see Table 2.2). Johnson put considerable thought into planning. His experience prepared him well to be precise in submitting initial proposals, and he was determined to exercise the authority given to him.[20]

Table 2.2. Positions and Salary for Personnel

POSITION	BEGINNING DATE	ANNUAL SALARY
Director	Jan. 1, 1914	$5,000, plus subsistence
Secretary	Jan. 1, 1914	$1,200
Bookkeeper	Jan. 1, 1914	$1,020
Stenographer	Aug. 1, 1914	$720
Extension Department head	July 1, 1914	$2,700
Department head of market/gardening	Aug. 1, 1914	$2,400
Gardner	July 1, 1914	$900
Department Head of horticulture	Aug. 1, 1914	$2,400
Department Head of agronomy	Aug. 1, 1914	$2,400
Department Head of poultry	Aug. 1, 1914	$1,900
Department Head of dairying/animal husbandry	Aug. 1, 1914	$2,400
Farms caretaker	Jan. 1, 1914	$1,560

Many of the original buildings of Georgian architectural style continue to grace the campus today. The credit for such design goes to several individuals. The Board of Trustees' minutes of December 14, 1912 indicate that state architect Herman Hoefer began the work. He sent his representative, Mr. McPherson, to meet with the board and discuss plans with Johnson. Two weeks later, Hoefer mailed preliminary sketches for a block plan for the buildings, including floor plans for the proposed horticultural building. Present at this meeting of December 18, representing Hoefer, were Mr. McPherson and Mr. Manning to discuss the submitted plans. The board accepted the plans, with some modifications. In the board minutes of January 4, 1913, Hoefer's letter dated the previous day outlined cost estimates for additional buildings. On January 20, Hoefer indicated he would be forwarding blueprints. The board's minutes of February 8 state that correspondence from Hoefer now reflected a revision of the general block plan for the campus buildings. At this point, Louis F. Pilcher, who became state architect, suddenly replaced Hoefer. In Pilcher's first visit to the Board of Trustees in June 1913, he stated he was deeply interested in Long Island because he was born in Brooklyn and would commit himself to the project. He returned to Albany and guided his staff to complete the design of the buildings. Director Johnson was involved in these proceedings, offering suggestions. It may be concluded that Hoefer, Pilcher, and Johnson were primarily responsible for the campus layout and architectural design. Pilcher later served as the architect for Sing Sing Prison and other state prisons. He later became professor of architecture at Pennsylvania State University.[21]

Johnson continued with his participation in planning the infrastructure of the campus. He submitted more specific proposals:

> First: Provide a central Heat, Light and Power plant in which, from burning coal, to generate steam power with which to pump cold water into tanks for diverse uses; to pump and to heat, with steam, besides water for general domestic uses, sufficient water to heat all buildings of the school; to generate electricity with which to operate both electric fans (for ventilating buildings) and some of the laboratory apparatus and farm machinery, also electricity for indoor and outdoor lighting. From this central plant underground conduits for electricity and diverse water pipes were to be laid in advance of making foundations even for those buildings not to be erected with such control plant; the exact locations of all buildings to be at one time.

Figure 2-2. The Institute of Applied Agriculture on Long Island offered special courses of varying length. Here students are studying and participating in a hands-on "Bee" class during the summer of 1920.

FIGURE 2-3. Seventeen-year old Nellie Buff poses in front of the Agronomy Building, Cutler Hall in March 1916. She was the first female student to enroll at the new farm school. She and her mother moved from Switzerland to Huntington to be within commuting distance of the school. She planned to return to her country to practice modern farming and dairying, but soon withdrew without giving a reason.

FIGURE 2-4. An instructor, center, examines turf demonstration plots that were created and organized by students in 1919. In the distance is the Director's Residence/Cottage with garage in front. The vista captures an agrarian campus as part of rural Long Island.

> Second: Up-to-date school buildings, minor structures, barns, gardens, orchards, fields—the laboratories for students—should be equipped with first-class tools, laboratory apparatus, farm machinery, animals, and other facilities for really practical teaching and farm practice or work. The law requires free tuition to citizen students, and they should not be paid for their work.

> Third: Such buildings and other school facilities should ultimately cost over a million dollars; instruction should be furnished to 1,000 resident students—at least 200 regular students to be accommodated in each of the four year classes—in addition to "extension" teaching elsewhere; such facilities to be provided as fast as State appropriations allow.[22]

Actual work began in 1913 when temporary wells were sunk, along with temporary living quarters for workers. The land was broken up by a series of deep trenches for sewer, water, and heating systems. Roads, walks, and landscaping were laid out. Construction began in 1914 on the power plant and was completed a year later at a cost of $190,000; this structure was later named Conklin Hall and used for academic purposes. In 1914 the same year construction began on the following: director's residence and garage (The Cottage), $15,889; agronomy building (Cutler Hall), $63,629; horticulture building (Hicks Hall), $63,629; and dormitory 1 (Ward Hall), $43,379, as indicated in the College Archives. (In 1936, local artist Frederick Marshall painted WPA murals in Cutler and Hicks halls, which today are closed and require restoration.) Ward Hall was used as a dormitory for more than forty years and later for instructional purposes. Cutler Hall has columns that are set flush with the façade, while the front of Hicks Hall has a portico. These majestic structures still stand today.

Because the original appropriation for the school was inadequate, the state provided more money as needed. Director Johnson moved as quickly as possible to enroll students. During his tenure as director, which lasted to 1923, he guided other construction projects with the original estimated costs, as shown in Table 2.3.

Table 2.3. Additional Construction Projects and Cost Estimates

PROJECT	ESTIMATED COST	YEAR OF COMPLETION
Sewage disposal plant	$35,387	1915
Dormitory 2 (Hooper Hall)	$10,000	1916
Dormitory 3	$27,000	1919
Dormitory 4	$75,900	1921
Dairy barn and silos	$12,500	1920
Rural engineering building	$29,000	1922
Gym and lockerroom	$24,000	1922[23]

There was great expectation when the NYSSA on Long Island prepared to open its doors. According to the *Amityville Record* of December 13, 1915, the planned opening was set for September 1915, but was delayed because Gov. Charles S. Whitman (1915–1918) vetoed a $69,000 appropriation bill that sought to maintain the school for the first year. Whitman asserted the requested funds lacked specific details. Only after satisfactory negotiations was the money released the following December. Delays in hiring faculty and construction work also postponed the actual opening to March 1, 1916 with an enrollment of sixty students. Two-thirds of the student body came from New York City, the rest from Nassau and Suffolk counties. One student was a woman. Student ages ranged from 15 to 45 years.[24]

Advocates argued that for the first time, a public agricultural school would attempt something new: to prepare high school boys and girls to become practical farmers. Minimum educational requirements for matriculating had to equal an eighth-grade level. The Farmingdale School was not a preparatory school for college, but a finishing school. Previously, it was assumed that the students from farms were already equipped with the techniques of farming. They were then merely taught the theoretical side of farming. Now the majority of students would be drawn from an urban environment and it would be necessary to train them in the practical side of farming. The system would engage students in all aspects of hands-on agriculture, such as plowing; testing and cultivating seeds; gathering and marketing crops; feeding and milking cows; and care of horses, pigs, and chickens for egg and meat production, as well as classroom studies of scientific aspects of agriculture. It was assumed that scientific and practical study of plant and animal life was consistent with the educational needs of the period.

Johnson, having moved from Wisconsin to New York, sought to create something new by combining an academic program with the practical aspects of agricultural education. He stressed his vision in this way:

> Students are taught to plow by plowing, to garden by planning, planting, and managing a garden; to milk by milking morning and evening, until proficiency has been attained; and so with pruning trees, picking and packing fruit, operating tractors, threshing machines, road machinery, and so forth.[25]

The philosophy of pragmatism of William James (1842–1910) and John Dewey (1859–1952) greatly influenced the development of the school and society's beliefs in general. James, for example, rejected absolute truth and believed that the validity of an idea or action is in its practical results. Ideas are changeable and can be validated by their consequences. Dewey taught that education is more than just acquiring a body of information; students "learn by doing." Progressive education, as it was identified, taught that individuals in a democracy could transform society and improve their status as constructive citizens. Progress was paramount. The agricultural school at Farmingdale reflected this promise by providing boys and girls a practical education through the benefits of a healthy working environment away from the negative aspects of urban life. To make access more affordable, students would pay no tuition and education would be within the reach of all. Even though private elite institutions of higher education predominated at the turn of the twentieth century, there were trends in New York to foster an upper-level educational system funded by the public and open to all. Horace Mann (1796–1859) and his successors provided a rationale for public education in an industrial age. This revolutionary movement, coupled with a sense of egalitarianism, contributed to the forces leading to the establishment of the Long Island agricultural school.[26]

The first *Bulletin* of the NYSSA on Long Island, dated February 1916, presented a composite picture of those who would lead the educational program. Johnson was mainly responsible for the selection of the faculty. John Michels, MSA, was in charge of the Extension Service and Dairying and Animal Husbandry Department. Michels was a recognized expert and author in his field. He actually replaced A. B. Graham as head of the Extension Service when the former resigned the year before to take a position with the U.S. Department of Agriculture. H. F. Button, BSA, led the Farm Crops and Soil Fertility Department. He was a farmer and graduate of Cornell, with seven years experience as a teacher of agriculture. Walter B. Nissley, BS, a farmer from Canastota, New York, was put in charge of vegetable gardening and fruit growing. With experience in this area, he achieved success in a similar position at Pennsylvania state colleges. U. J. Marra, BA, chaired the Academic Subjects and Elementary Sciences Department. Possessing a Phi Beta Kappa Key, he left New York University to join the Farmingdale academic staff. The academic credentials demonstrated that agricultural studies were a serious field of study.

Other faculty included L. M. Cole, MA, instructor in farm mechanics; David B. Greenberg, MA, extension instructor in poultry husbandry; E. L. Chase, BS, laboratory instructor in farm management; J. C. Hungerman, BSA, extension instructor and assistant in dairying and animal husbandry; and Grace A. Taylor, instructor in library methods and in charge of the library. Three other individuals filled out the school staff: Louis Orgelfinger Jr., Ssecretary; F. L. Whitman Jr., chief engineer; and William Andrews, school carpenter. Johnson availed himself of the highly trained personnel located in the New York City region.

The 1916 *Bulletin* pointed out that when the first teachers were hired in August 1, 1914, the school began to provide extension service in the region. In seventeen months, faculty from the school visited 1,207 farms, delivered 246 lectures and demonstrations, and addressed nearly 25,000 people. Advice was given in 12,614 letters to help settle various farming and home economics problems. Practical assistance was provided to farmers' wives through 23 cooking classes and 103 canning demonstrations. The cost of these extension programs amounted to $15,949.24. It was clear that Johnson and his staff, by detailing their early accomplishments, were proud of their record and were out to prove that the establishment of the agricultural school on Long Island was wise public policy. In the near future, electrification would transform rural life. During the World War I era farmers began to mechanize their farms and install their own generating systems. General Electric and Westinghouse, for example, began installing rural electrification in the next decade. About one-fifth of GE's advertising in its magazine was devoted to the rural market in 1925.[27]

The extension service became an important part of the school as it promised to share the recent growth of farming methods with the general public. The federal government assisted in this area. Before leaving office, President Theodore Roosevelt had appointed the County Life Commission in early 1909 to study the needs of people living in the country. The commission recommended efforts to improve the quality of life for men and women on farms. Congress passed the Smith-Lever Cooperative Agricultural Extension Act in May 1914. It established the general principle of federal aid for vocational education. A national system of agriculture and home economics was hammered out, allowing for federally "assisted agricultural extension programs." It helped to promote adult education along the lines of improving rural home living. The Smith-Lever Act allocated funds to the states for "the diffusion among the people of useful and practical information on subjects relating to agriculture and home economics. . . ." As World War I progressed, vocational education was considered an aspect of national preparedness. President Woodrow Wilson included this idea in his 1916 address to congress. The Smith-Hughes Act, passed in February 1917, laid down the principle of federal aid to vocational secondary schools. The U.S. Agricultural Department and agricultural colleges in each state implemented this educational function to persons not attending college. The program resulted in future improvement of advanced efforts toward improving crops, stocks, and home life in rural regions. Farmingdale's educational system, which was very much a part of the progressive movement, was considered vocational at this time and benefited from these events.[28]

The extension service at Farmingdale concentrated on the people of lower New York State who were unable to attend school in distant upstate New York. In this way, extension services, through correspondence, circulars, bulletins, lectures, and demonstrations were delivered to various organizations and individuals, reaching 25,540 individuals in the period from July 1, 1916 to July 1, 1917. The leaders of the school acknowledged that the farmer's cause extended beyond the individual farmer's interest. "It is recognized today, as never before, that upon the prosperity of the farmer depends quite largely the general prosperity of all classes of people." It was believed that the economic value of agriculture was tied to the growth of American democracy and its prosperity. Enthusiasm and commitment of the school to achieve its goals appeared limitless.[29]

The 1916 *Bulletin* specified general entrance requirements for the agricultural school at Farmingdale, based on its original mission as a secondary school. Although the minimum requirement for admission was completion of an eighth-grade education, students with a high school education and others interested in general phases of education of agriculture could find additional opportunities at the school. This broadened the range of student body interest and allowed for unconventional students to enroll regardless of age and other requirements. In describing the course of study, the school will "teach Agriculture itself through the farm, the garden, and the live stock." It was admitted in the *Bulletin* that books and schools offered much knowledge about farming, but the charge of "book farming" could never be made against the school at Farmingdale. Basic to its educational philosophy was the belief that the best way to learn was by doing. Benefiting from these policies, Farmingdale planned to operate for twelve months of the year and the course of study would follow the changing seasons, focusing on modern agricultural life though "diversification" while "narrow specialization" would be avoided.

Requirements for graduation included four years, consisting of nine months each, in the classroom and laboratories; students with agricultural experience and special ability may graduate in a shorter period of time. Those who lacked practical experience would be required to spend at least one summer on the school farm, which consisted of 380 acres, counting the campus itself. Plans were being prepared for teaching homemaking to female students who were expected to live in houses, giving them practice in actual housekeeping, gardening, and flower raising, as well as other skills. As with the male students, they will "learn by doing."

A unique program related to World War I was military training. Discipline and military drill played an important role during the early years. Although it was not a military preparatory institution, the 1916 *Bulletin* emphasized the value of "military preparedness, and that every citizen should experience the rudiments of military training." This program was under the direction of an officer of the U.S. Army. Throughout the school, military discipline was enforced. In this period of patriotic fervor, faculty and students accepted such paramilitary training. Johnson

FIGURE 2-5. During the World War I era paramilitary procedure prevailed. In addition to regular class and laboratory study, they followed rigorous physical training on campus. This group posed in front of Hicks Hall in full military dress, 1918. The practice ended after the war.

FIGURE 2-6. Students stand at attention during retreat as they train to be soldiers and farmers. Cadet camps were established at the school and functioned during the war months of July, August, and September. The Women's Land Army in New York City sent women to Farmingdale for agricultural work and instruction. They resided at Mott House.

and his assistants were guided by events of World War I, which had started in August 1914. The United States entered the war in April 1917. The program was instituted that year at the school with male and female students wearing uniforms and taking training together.

By 1918, military discipline, drill, and instruction had become "an established factor in the school system" on a daily basis, except weekends. Daily exercises were included for the "student cadets." Students wearing uniforms could be seen doing exercises at 6 a.m. on the grounds opposite Cutler Hall, at the circle near the area where Thompson Hall now stands. Inspection of students' quarters, clothing, and physique took place on Saturdays, and the commandant inspected rooms daily. The October 1917 *Bulletin* laid out the formalized daily routine (Table 2.4).

The importance of the military program is obvious during the early growth of the school. The schedule allowed little time for relaxation for the "student cadets," as they were then called, except during late afternoons and weekends. Additionally, special farming cadet camps were established for high school students during the summer months of 1917 and 1918, and they were an important factor in food production. To enhance school spirit and student camaraderie, the social committee and faculty planned weekly dances and "impromptu" entertainment in the barracks.[31]

Table 2.4. Formalized Daily Routine

5:45 a.m.: First call for Reveille
6 a.m.: Reveille
6–6:20 a.m.: Setting up exercises
6:20–7 a.m.: Care of quarters
7 a.m.: Mess call for breakfast
7:30–8:30 a.m.: Drill
8:30 a.m–12:30 p.m.: Class work
12:30 p.m.: Mess call (dinner)
1:30–3 p.m.: Class work
5:25 p.m.: First call for Retreat
5:30–6 p.m.: Retreat (evening parade)
6 p.m.: Mess call (supper)
9:30 p.m.: Tattoo (quiet in quarters)

The 1916 and 1917 *Bulletins* made special reference to the women's role at the school. Careful preparations were instituted to teach actual homemaking for women, gardening, and flower production. Female students would learn by applying themselves to their tasks, just as male students would in their endeavors. Women had made great strides in agricultural pursuits in America and Europe. There was even a Women's Land Army of 32 Fifth Avenue, New York City that recruited women for farm work at the school during the wartime summer months. They resided at the Mott House and Dormitory Two. Women demonstrated that they could perform all the work of a modern farm. The principle of equal opportunity was practiced from the school's beginning. Women and minorities were represented on campus since 1916 and in the graduating classes from 1919 forward. However, actual numbers for gender, nationality, and race are lacking for these early years. The October 1917 *Bulletin* stated:

> Since the opening of the school, there have been many women students who have shown that they can perform, without undue strain, all of the work of a modern farm where machinery is extensively used. The courses of the school are open to men and women on equal terms and the attention of all women is called to the opportunities here offered. During the summer of 1917 over seventy-five women took special courses in Agriculture, with special work in Horticulture, Soil Fertility, Field Crops, Dairying and Poultry Husbandry. The way in which these women have entered into the work, and the excellent work which they have performed, demonstrate conclusively the ability of women in farm work of all kinds.

Even before the principle of equal opportunity was promulgated as late as the 1960s, the practice of nondiscrimination based on sexual orientation, age, ethnicity, and race had become a part of the agricultural school's inception.[32]

There also were student activities. The *Furrow* was the name of the school's monthly publication. Its first issue appeared August 18, 1916, covered two sheets of white paper, and expanded later. The first editor-in-chief was Edward Hegman, and the faculty advisor was Mr. Marra, who was also head of the Literary Society. In a letter published in the first edition, Johnson congratulated them on this new undertaking. The student publication was considered so important that the first issue was included in the special "Anniversary Number," Volume III of *The Furrow* three years later. By this time, the school had been assigned a new name, State Institute of Applied Agriculture on Long Island.

FIGURE 2-7. Students relax on the porch of Dormitory I, Ward Hall, as they view the campus sites in the early 1920s. Schoolwork required regular class study, physical effort on the farm and in dairy and poultry laboratories. They assumed other tasks such as shoveling snow, barnyard duty, and fire squad duty.

FIGURE 2-8. The 1921 football team poses in front of Ward Hall. Sports assumed an important part of the curriculum at Farmingdale, and the football program was one of the strongest on Long Island. The sport was dropped in 1963 because of low game attendance, budgetary reasons, and lack of competition.

The 1916 *Bulletin* recognized the importance of sports and spelled out the athletic program even though there were no established leagues or conferences. Farmingdale competed against high schools, club teams, colleges, and even the faculty. With the permission of the faculty, students organized an Athletic Association. Mostly men participated during these early years. Students paid a $5 fee to join the Athletic Association to participate in competition, to use the athletic equipment, and to receive reduced rates to home games. The attempt to run the sports program on voluntary fees failed, and athletic fees were collected immediately upon entrance to the school. Teams were established immediately at the time the school began to function: baseball (1916), football (1916), basketball (1917), and track (1918). The baseball team's record in 1916 was nine wins and two losses, including two victories over the faculty. Members of the baseball team constructed the playing field. The basketball team achieved a record of nine wins and five losses in 1917. The football team was not so successful in its first year of competition, winning one game and losing three. The victory occurred over Freeport High School with an impressive 18 to 0 score. One newspaper reported, "Visitors to Farmingdale may see these husky farmer lads going through a snappy signal drill or rushing a ball down the field . . ." For many years, Farmingdale was the center of Long Island football. In 1919, Farmingdale's thirteen players defeated the Mitchel Field Aviators, 28 to 0. Jerry Allard arrived on campus 1929 and soon became athletic director. He remembered the stunning 86 to 0 loss to George Washington University at Griffith Stadium in Washington, DC, in 1930. For that game, Farmingdale athletic program earned $1,000 to play the superior football team. The Farm Mechanics Department built a double tennis court that was available for use by all members of the Athletic Association. Students had access to a swimming pool and made use of the "Farm Beach" less than one mile from the school. A swimming team was organized. Physical training also became a part of the curriculum.[33]

As early as November 22, 1916, the Farmingdale campus was visited by fifty-three people representing legislators, public officials, trustees, and reporters. State Sen. George L. Thompson (Kings Park) and Assemblyman Henry A. Murphy (Huntington) were in attendance. The new farm school proudly provided guided tours and student demonstrations. Students Freda Lane and Kathryn Freeman demonstrated a gasoline tractor that was hitched to a plow. Other exhibits included students butchering and dressing a hog, pruning fruit trees, and planting vegetables. Johnson announced scholarships would be awarded to needy students. Trustee William M. Baldwin, a Garden City resident, stated that he would donate money for five of the scholarships, each in the amount of $100. The school hosted a luncheon served by students to the guests. In keeping with agricultural tradition and early school policy, a branch of the Patrons of Husbandry

FIGURE 2-9. The Poultry Science curriculum was a very successful program and popular with students in the early years of the school. This 1924 image shows poultry-laying sheds near Hicks Hall, not shown.

(Grange) was organized in December 1916 with fifty-three students guided by faculty sponsors. The Grange was a national society for farmers that advanced the welfare and ideals of farm life.[34]

An unbounded pioneer spirit for agricultural education prevailed in the formative years at Farmingdale. An item in the budget for 1917–1918 revealed this optimistic faith:

> If Horace Greeley were living today, he would, without doubt, change his advice from "Go west young man, and grow up with the country" to "Remain east, young man, take hold and develop the worn-out land and undeveloped lands of the east."[35]

Those who organized and laid the foundation of the NYSSA on Long Island were filled with energy and idealism. The vision focused on farming and rural life. The belief that the land was the basis of all wealth predominated in a society that was in transition during the early part of the twentieth century. The mission to train young boys and girls with an agricultural education sought to open opportunities to all leading to productive citizens. The emerging philosophy of progressive education began to reshape society from static learning to a dynamic democratic system. The quality of farm life would inevitably benefit rural folk, and economic prosperity would result. "Learning by doing," or "hands-on learning," was put into practice. Three decades later, the farm school expanded to include industrial and technical education, but retained its agricultural curriculum. Farmingdale's educational system would be tested as challenges developed to force the institution to adapt to the needs of a changing society. Change, then, would be a constant factor in the school's long history. Indeed, an understanding of the agricultural basis of the Long Island school offers a clear vision of its legacy and the foundation on which it was built.

As early as January 1917, the *Furrow* mused on the school's accomplishments since the start of classes in March of the previous year: "The year just past was one that will long be remembered by every loyal Aggie." Students persevered, it continued, to build "a sound foundation for future progress." The *Furrow* printed the original "Alma Mater song" in this issue. It listed no composer. It would be replaced with a new composition later in the twentieth century. It signaled a typical uplifting spirit that all alma maters expressed:

Alma Mater Song
Far above the noisy city,
Out in Farmingdale,
Stands the school Agriculture
That we proudly hail.
New York State School Agriculture
Devotion true we'll serve,
When we've left these Halls of Learning
On our farms to live.
Refrain
Hail, Alma Mater
To thee we homage pay!

Hail to the glorious green,
Of the N. Y. S. S. A.
Life now stretches out before us,
Wondrous dreams will reign,
Soon its battles we'll be fighting
With our might and main.
Loyally let's stand together.
Comrades true are we,
Memories of this Aggie School
Ever dear shall be.

In the 1950s, professors C. Dick Thomson, Edwin F. Ore, and Raynor Wallace, acknowledging the inherent changes the institution was experiencing, replaced the words of the Alma Mater, which was based on a traditional hymn. It now expressed an enduring perennial quality:

On the land between the waters,
Where the wind blows from the sea,
Stands our noble Alma Mater
For everyone to see.
We will raise her name to glory,
As the years go rolling by,
Her precepts before us now
Like stars up in the sky.
We salute thee Alma Mater,
As we gather here today,
All thy sons and all thy daughters
Will honor thee alway.
As our voices swell the chorus,
We will hold on high your light,
Fling wide your banner over us,
Fair hues of green and white.[36]

THREE

Albert A. Johnson, 1913–1923

> The New York State Institute of Applied Agriculture at Farmingdale, L.I., N.Y., is thirty-three miles from the city of New York, and may be reached by train on the main line of the Long Island Railroad or by motor over the finest state roads.[1]

The leadership of Albert A. Johnson as director of the NYSSA on Long Island at Farmingdale is important for many reasons: He set precedents that were followed in the future; he put in place the physical configuration of the campus; and his vision became a sustaining principle of the institute's educational philosophy. Johnson rejected the kind of elitism that characterized the older, more established specialized schools and colleges. Nevertheless, problems arose immediately during his tenure. Defining and redefining the school persisted. Many issues faced the institute in these early years that might have led to its demise. Enrollments remained low, graduates were few, faculty turnover was high, adequate funding was lacking, the curriculum kept changing, and financial accounting was questioned. Johnson's leadership style was challenged—his defenders and critics clashed. As problems surfaced, investigations were demanded and criticism was directed at him. Johnson himself would be caught up in the spiraling events that eventually led to his resignation in 1923. Decades passed before the institution found its rightful place within the New York State system of higher education. Nevertheless, Farmingdale struggled to provide for the educational needs of a diverse population in a society that was constantly being transformed.

Upon assuming the directorship, Johnson's immediate task was to establish and apply an effective educational program, at a time when he had to turn his attention to World War I (1914–1918). The United Stated entered the war in April 1917. Campus resources contributed to the national effort of winning the war. As indicated earlier, military training was begun. The increased production of food on the campus farm helped to fill a vital wartime need. Nationally, farmers were entering the armed services, and a greater volume of food was being shipped to the allied nations and required on the home front. The institute assisted owners of small plots of land and large country estates on Long Island that were converted into farms. Ornamental gardening played a secondary role in preparing acreage for food cultivation. Formation of the Long Island Food Reserve Battalion was the mainspring of agricultural production. LIRR President Ralph Peters served as the battalion's president, while local clubs, organizations, and public entities lent their support. But it was Johnson, as director general in this patriotic venture, who guided the agricultural plan of the Long Island Food Reserve Battalion. The critical need for food spurred quick action. He organized many groups, instructing their members on how to apply the most advanced agricultural techniques. The Farmingdale campus had more than fifty resident women performing open-air farming, and another delegation of forty who participated in early May 1917. They were enrolled in short-term courses. Johnson allowed these women to be housed in every available building on campus. In 1917, the campus farm had more than 170 acres under cultivation, producing corn, beans, rye, alfalfa, timothy, clover seed, carrots, cabbage, beets, and parsnips. The ten milk cows, seven heifers, and seventeen hogs were all put to full use. The poultry plant was working at full capacity. Two tractors were being used daily. Elsewhere, Johnson advised real estate owners of idle land how to become successful farmers. The Women's Land Army sent a number of women agricultural workers to assist in food production. By January 1918, twenty-nine students had joined the military service. One student, Jack Bamforth, a nineteen-year-old Marine, was killed in action in France on June 15, 1918. His family emigrated from England to New York City where he was born. Bamforth's body was returned to the United States and was buried at Hillside Cemetery, Westchester County, New York. These events required Johnson's full-time attention.[2]

It was time to turn to the educational enterprise. On a cold day in March 1916, David B. Greenberg of the Poultry Department greeted a small group of students at the Farmingdale railroad station and escorted them to the campus. They comprised a part of the first matriculating class of sixty students. This new class was characterized by its diversity:

> In ages they varied from sixteen to forty-five; in complexion, from fair-haired Berg to dark-eyed Guiliano; in height, from little Thompson to tall Gil Smith; in conversation, from

> the talkative Eddy Bonoff to silent Kemma; in girth, from Sampson to Ballard. In only one thing were they alike, their readiness for business.[3]

One could sense their anticipation. These students considered themselves "pioneers." There were no customs or traditions to follow or to guide them. The faculty was relatively untested. Students' confidence had to be nurtured, but a strong feeling of enthusiasm prevailed. The institute itself had not yet established an identity, and despite an animated spirit, there were concerns that it would survive. The immediate challenge was for the institution to make real farmers out of these students who lacked agricultural experience.

Several of the early students returned to the campus after graduation in a variety of positions. George Franke arrived on campus June 1916 as a student from Brooklyn, graduated in 1920, moved on to Cornell where he graduated, and spent more than four decades as teacher and department head of Animal Husbandry and Agricultural Production at Farmingdale. He remembered picking up the mail on horseback in downtown Farmingdale, which was a small rural village. Eric Patterson was a classmate of Franke, Class of 1920, went on to star in baseball, basketball, and football. After playing professional sports for several years, he was appointed in 1925 farm superintendent of NYSSA and spent his career in this position.[4]

Not surprisingly, the students who had enrolled in 1916 became the Class of 1919—the early programs varied from three to four years. These enthusiastic students expressed feelings of pride and nostalgia for their years of attendance in the following poem:

> Out of the shadows of evening
> As the sun is beginning to set
> The buildings outlined on the campus
> Are those that we leave with regret.
> The broad wide expanse of the farmland,
> The pastures, the orchard and lanes
> Are those that we've tramped in the rain.
> We've seen most of the buildings erected,
> The silo we claim for our own,
> The fields we have plowed and plowed again
> And the grain many times we have sown—

Till we feel that we're planted among them
And held by the strong roots of love
'Mid the glory of Nyssa's green meadows
With the brilliant hued skyline above.
This is our school and we love it.
We've staked out the very first claim.
And though they may add many structures,
In our memory will always remain
The outlined groups on the campus
As the sun is beginning to set
While the moo of a cow and a distant neigh
Are the sounds we cannot forget.[5]

In fall 1917, with Abe Southard as president of his class, World War I continued to make an impact on the school. Many students withdrew to join the armed services or to engage in emergency farm work to increase food production. Students Kelley, Whitelaw, Harris, Owen, Foot, and Hyman were among the first to leave. Others followed. The campus was saddened when the popular Capt. Maguire, who headed the school's military program, suddenly resigned in January 1918; Maj. A. O'Donohoe, formerly of the Canadian Army, replaced him. Soon after, Lt. Baker and Sgt. Baumann arrived to assist with the program. The Army assigned these individuals and maintained supervision of the training. The Army also sent doctors to conduct physical examinations of the cadets. The curriculum, which had been set at four years, was changed to three years and many subjects were revised. Greenberg left the school for a better position, taking with him several other employees. With the signing of the Armistice, November 1918, Bradford K. Southard, Milton Speigel, Alfred J. Kena, and Walter Eidt returned to Farmingdale to complete their education. Support for the Cadet Corps declined and by summer 1919 military training was discontinued.[6]

The Liberty Loan Organization in Washington, DC commended the school for participating in the Liberty Loan drives, a system that allowed citizens to lend money to the government to fund the war. Johnson was chairman of the final two drives. A 100 percent record was achieved among the students, faculty, and staff. During the last drive, one student by the name of Meriwitz, with the encouragement of his wealthy parents, subscribed for $10,000 in government bonds.

FIGURE 3-1. One of the largest campus organizations during the early years was the Grange, an affiliate of the Patrons of Husbandry that was founded in 1867 to advance the welfare of farmers. These students are officers of the Grange at the school.

In 1920, attempting to clearly define the mission of the school, its name was changed to the State Institute of Applied Agriculture on Long Island by a request from the administration and Board of Trustees, with the approval of the New York State Education Department. In another attempt, four years later, it was again changed, this time to State Institute of Applied Agriculture. As the mission of the school continued to be modified, other names would be assigned.[7]

In the middle of 1918, the influenza epidemic struck the campus. Students and faculty were affected. Two students died from this disease, Charles Guiliano from the Class of 1919 and David Wright from the Class of 1921. Johnson's request for an appropriation to build an infirmary on campus was rejected by the state. Although there were only 15 full-time students in 1919, 274 other students were in attendance; many were either part time or in short programs that were conducted at different times of the year.[8]

Other events begun by Johnson helped shape the institute. The annual Farm and Home Equipment Show was started under the auspices of the Mechanics Department in March 1920. The event was well attended; although no official count was made, Johnson and his faculty were pleased. Demonstrations and exhibits were presented of several makes of tractors, pumps, water systems, electric light plants, and other physical equipment. This event became so popular that it was expanded to three days in 1926. Companies brought in machinery for display and demonstrations, and through these contacts, loans of equipment were extended to the school, thereby enhancing the instructional program. In the 1930s, other departments participated and the name was changed to the Country Life Program, and later to Open House. The event was increased to four days in 1940. Two years later, the attendance grew to more than ten thousand over the four-day period, and feature events were a Victory Garden, the Annual Farm and Home Equipment Exhibit, Long Island Baby Chick and Egg Show, and the Farm Machinery and Tractor Adjustment and Repair Exhibit. There were many other attractions on campus. The entire staff and faculty were available to provide assistance and information to people regarding agriculture. This unique annual tradition remained central to the lives of Long Islanders and those in New York City. As the population of the region grew rapidly with the rise of suburbanization, more people would attend this annual event. The combined population of Nassau and Suffolk counties in 1930 was 464,108, or 4.5 percent of the population of New York State. Additionally, the 1940 combined populations of Nassau and Suffolk counties had reached 604,102, or 11.7 percent of New York State's population. Thirty years later, in 1970, the combined county populations had dramatically grown to 2,555,868, or 14 percent of the state population. The evolving changes in the Long Island economy made the Open House program, and all that it involved, an attractive phenomenon.[9]

Another Johnson-era activity that had a long-term impact on the institute was the New York State Egg Laying and Poultry Breeding Contest. Funded by the state beginning in 1920, the purpose of the contest was the elimination of unprofitable, nonproducing hens. The Poultry

Department administered the program. Entries originated from all over the state and from Delaware, Michigan, Ohio, Pennsylvania, and Canada. A special article in the October 1920 issue of the *Long Island Agriculturist*, published in Mattituck, announced the event on its cover, "This contest is attracting the attention of the poultry world, because it is the first one to undertake to accumulate data on breeding records in connection with the egg-laying contest." In the first year alone there were fifty pens entered; by 1926–1927 there were one-hundred pens entered, with ten birds per pen. The institute housed the birds all year, and the contest ran for fifty-one weeks. The eggs from each pen were weighed daily to the nearest quarter of an ounce. Each week, an average weight per egg for all eggs laid by the pullets was calculated. "To obtain the yearly average, weekly averages are added together and divided by 51." A problem arose when some birds died during the year from "roup" (an infectious respiratory disease that affects poultry), bronchitis, and diphtheria. During the 1927–1928 contest alone, 437 birds died. To make up for the lost entrants, each farm sent extra birds that could be used if the original birds died. Three pen houses were located behind Hicks and Cutler halls where Horton Hall now stands. Horton Hall is the present administration building, and was named for D. Hart Horton who headed the Poultry Department from 1927 to 1957. The 1921–1922 catalogue listed four courses of study in the Poultry Husbandry Department: Poultry Management, Poultry Judging, Advanced Poultry Management, and Incubation and Brooding. These events became closely woven into the educational system and generated public and political support. Director Johnson's leadership and the work of the faculty and students made these programs successful.[10]

The school and the Long Island poultry industry got a boost in the 1920 New York State supplemental budget when Gov. Alfred E. Smith signed the bill that appropriated the following funds to the school: $12,000 for chicken houses; $1,500 for completion of the cow barn; an additional $1,250 for the director covering the period July 1, 1920 to June 30, 1921; and $3,000 for personal service and expenses for conducting poultry breeding demonstrations. The Farmingdale poultry program was so rare that only two other similar institutions existed then in the nation, one in Vineland, New Jersey, and one in Storrs, Connecticut. At the same time, the Long Island Poultry Association was formed to promote and manage the private poultry sector. F. D. Brooks, professor of poultry husbandry at the institute, was elected secretary of the association.[11]

The first graduation exercises took place April 4, 1919. Preceding the distribution of diplomas was a concert presented by the 147th Infantry Band. The Rev. Henry H. Mower of

Farmingdale Village gave the invocation. Johnson followed with a short speech praising the work of the school and wishing the graduates success in the future. Kathryn Freeman, who enrolled in 1916, was the first woman to graduate and her outstanding record earned her the honor of salutatorian. She was assistant steward and lecturer of the Grange, class treasurer of 1919, second vice president of the Athletic Association, and manager of the female basketball team. Bradford K. Southard of Freeport was valedictorian. H. W. Collingwood, editor of *The Rural New Yorker*, gave the main address, describing the advances made in agricultural science. Trustee John M. Lupton of Mattituck presented diplomas to fifteen graduates: A. W. Berg, Albert Bullard, Carl Glaesel, Milton Speigel, Alphonse C. Tello, Kathryn Freeman, Abraham Ginsberg, John Nicolais, Bernard Cavallaro, Walter Eidt, Bradford K. Southard, Harry Schoup, Joseph Horak, Scott B. Hutchins, and Alfred K. Kenna.[12]

The second commencement exercise was held May 18, 1920 on the second floor of the newly constructed barn. Col. Theodore Roosevelt Jr., son of President Theodore Roosevelt of Oyster Bay, was the commencement speaker. Twenty-two men and one woman (Maude Schaeffer) received diplomas. In spring 1921, ten men and three women comprised the third graduating class. The Class of 1922 had twenty-two members, and the ceremonies were conducted in the new gymnasium, which later became the campus bookstore. The Class of 1922 had graduates from such backgrounds as Mount Vernon, Jamaica, Manhattan, Brooklyn, Richmond Hill, Pinelawn, Freeport, Glen Cove, Patchogue, Naponach, Mexico, Maine, Connecticut, England, and the U.S. Army. On June 1, 1923, nineteen graduates received diplomas during ceremonies in Machinery Hall. This was to be director Johnson's last academic year in office; he did not attend the graduation.[13]

During this period, interest developed in maintaining ties with graduates and to assist and promote the school. During Christmas week 1921, a group of Aggies, the affectionate term to describe the sports teams, met socially at the Café Boulevard in New York City and recommended an alumni association be formed. The following year, as a direct result of this meeting, the Alumni Association of the State Institute of Applied Agriculture on Long Island was officially established, and the sponsoring group became its charter members. Johnson was a founding member, along with Eric Patterson and Leroy Smith, who would remain with the school in various capacities. Frederick H. Stang was elected president. A constitution was enacted. Patterson assisted Stang in providing the leadership to grow the association in the early years, enriching student and alumni life. In the 1930s, Smith continued the work of the previous leaders. Annual fall meetings and banquets were held, leading to the beginning of Homecoming and Visitation Day in 1929. The Alumni Association provided links with its membership over the years in maintaining an esprit de corps, raising money, and providing service to its Alma mater.[14]

Dan Vairo, born November 1, 1901 the oldest son of a New York City dress designer, was sent by his father to study agriculture at Farmingdale. Dan's parents were impressed with a recruiting bulletin that promoted the school in motivating him to enroll:

> The people of the State of New York have taken a bold step toward the solution of this great problem of providing education for its young producers and homemakers. On Long Island, at Farmingdale, the State has established a vocational educational plant that is exceptional in character and unique in its service . . . yielding a program more practical than the usual agricultural college courses.

Dan spent four satisfying years at Farmingdale, graduating in 1921. He remembered later in life there were few buildings on campus. He attended classes, learned how to feed and breed animals, milked cows, tended horses, and took courses in soil testing, chemistry, and fruits. He worked in agriculture and then in the related field of horticulture, where he managed the grounds of the new Sanitarium where the Nassau County judicial offices were situated at Round Swamp Road. Vairo regarded the four years he spent at Farmingdale as the happiest of his life. His story is one echoed by early alumni.[15]

During the post-World War I era, the institute joined with other public agencies and departments to assist returning veterans to adjust to civilian life. The 1917 Smith-Hughes Act (Vocational Education Act) allocated funds for career programs, which advocated separating vocational education from traditional academic curricula. One of the aims of the new law was to train non-college-bound students to enter the workforce, and a federal Board for Vocational Education was established. This board, working with the Bureau of Rehabilitation, began sending wounded veterans to Farmingdale for agricultural studies. More than 225 former servicemen enrolled to study and resided on campus from 1919 to 1922. At the conclusion of the war, in November 1918, Johnson provided a series of lectures and guided returning veterans at Camp Upton in Yaphank to learn about farming and about opportunities in agricultural employment.[16]

Starting in 1919, the nation witnessed a ceremonial tree-planting movement to honor the dead of World War I. On the Farmingdale campus itself there emerged a special event to memorialize the dead of the war. Mary Peters, the institute's much-loved teacher and wife of campus instructor Clayton A. Peters, suggested to Johnson to invite all Allied nations and the 48 American states, including the territory of Alaska, to send soil to be combined in a bed for a tree to be planted on the Farmingdale campus. Johnson endorsed the project. The purpose of this initiative was to commemorate the sacrifices made by all the Allied forces that fought to "save the world for democracy." It was a demanding task to correspond with all the appropriate foreign governments and the American states to invite them to join in the project, to await a response, and to receive and gather all the soil. Despite the logistical challenge, campus faculty and staff invested time and energy to implement this unique project.[17]

By early 1921, the response from the Allied nations and American states was impressive. Soil was received from Belgium, France, Great Britain, Montenegro, Portugal, Italy, San Marino, Greece, Rumania, Russia, Serbia, Siam, Liberia, Canada, Brazil, Guatemala, Haiti, Nicaragua, Honduras, Cuba, Jamaica, Panama, China, India, Japan, Philippines, Australia, and New Zealand. Soil also was received from all the forty-eight American states and the territory of Alaska. France sent soil that originated under the Arc of Triumph and that was taken from along the line of the march of the victory celebration in Paris. Pennsylvania sent soil from the hallowed ground of the Civil War battleground at Gettysburg. Three Grand Army of the Republic veterans packed the soil around the roots of the twenty-foot oak. Louisiana sent soil form the Agricultural School at Baton Rouge where the house of President Zachary Taylor stood. (Johnson's wife was a direct descendant of President Taylor.) As the soil arrived on campus, the faculty and staff took special care to protect it against danger of disease and insects. Each packet was tested and treated at the campus laboratory.

On June 4, 1921 faculty, staff, visitors, and friends of the institute gathered to attend the ceremony that marked the planting of the historic white oak tree in honor of those who fought in World War I. Some wounded student-veterans were present. All the new soil was combined with campus soil around the base of the tree as it was being planted. As far as possible, representatives of each participating country were selected to deposit the soil. For example, a Filipino-American student whose name was Ponferrada deposited soil from the Philippines and an Italian student by the name of Crisafulli deposited soil from Italy. The military band from Fort Totten, Queens, New York, performed the various national anthems. Johnson and W. W. Cocks, former congressman from the local district, delivered the main addresses. There were other prominent citizens in attendance who spoke: Jesse Merritt, secretary of the Nassau County

Historical Society; nurseryman Henry W. Hicks, of Hicks Nursery and for whom a campus building was named and who donated the tree; Mrs. Arthur Ellis Hamm, representing the Committee for Devastated France; and Charles Lathrop Pack, chairman of the board of *American Forestry* magazine. Pack stated, "In the oak we find sturdiness, steadfastness, strength, all combined as we found it in the characters of those men who asked nothing of themselves, but gave all for others." He had already indicated at the time of the Armistice, on November 11, 1918, that this new form of monument honors the dead of the Great War as a "memorial that lives." Also

FIGURE 3-2. On June 4, 1921 faculty, staff, and friends of the Institute gathered to attend the planting of the Memorial Oak Tree honoring those who fought in World War I. The Memorial Oak today lies between Whitman Hall and Thompson Hall and connects the College's past with the present.

FIGURE 3-3. All World War I Allied nations and the 48 American states plus the territory of Alaska sent soil to be mixed together with the tree's roots. The bags of soil are displayed here before the planting ceremony took place.

present at the Farmingdale ceremony were representatives of the American Legion and Veterans of Foreign Wars. From Washington, DC, President Warren G. Harding acknowledged the event in a letter expressing his complete support of the project. *The New York Herald Tribune* reported the event by commenting, "This memorial will excite unusual interest and its vigor will be the subject of much speculation."[18]

The planting of the Farmingdale Memorial Oak Tree on campus was part of a larger nationwide program commemorating those who served, fought, and fell in the Great War. Towns, cities, American Legion Posts, school children, garden clubs, and other organizations planted thousands of memorial trees across the country. Plaques were placed at the base of each tree. Through the years, however, many of the trees either died or their markers were destroyed. The planting of memorial trees continued after World War II and September 11, 2001.[19]

As a result of proper maintenance and care, the oak tree at Farmingdale today stands proudly at the circle where Thompson and Whitman halls are located. Halsey B. Knapp, who succeeded Johnson as director, stated in the year he retired, 1956, "The tree continues to live and is on the national honor roll of memorial trees. Every Memorial Day appropriate exercises are held under the tree." There is a tablet at the base of the oak tree, which was a gift from the Class of 1927. Conceived by Clayton A. and Mary K. Peters, they and several students placed the tablet on a native stone to remind passersby of the significance of the oak tree. The following inscription on the tablet reads:

> This oak, planted June 4, 1921, commemorates the efforts, sacrifices and achievements of all Americans who gave their lives in the world war. Its roots rest in soil from all the allied nations, from every state and dependency of our country, from the bloody angle of Gettysburg and from the arc de triomph of France.[20]

Knapp (1923–1956) reminisced in his last year in office and explained the campus site on which the Memorial Oak Tree was originally planted. He clarified the transfer of the tree to a new location in this way:

> When I came to the Institute the oak stood in the north end of the panel between the two roads at the main entrance [near Melville Road]. The following year, it was surrounded by a corn crop. (All areas, now lawn and between the Agronomy Building and the Dining Hall, with the single exception of the flagstaff circle, were used for crops—oats, corn, alfalfa, etc.). The Memorial Oak was not doing well, foliage was small and sickly. There was no terminal growth. It was located on a sand gravel bar. Plowing and cultivation were bad for it. I was told that a white oak of the size and so debilitated could not be moved. I felt that from the standpoint of sentiment and as a symbol we should

> attempt to preserve it. The transplanting was successful. Some branches on one side were twisted off by a small cyclone a few years ago, but the symmetry is still good. We added a native boulder and the tablet at a later date, largely through the efforts of Mr. and Mrs. Peters, two much loved teachers.[21]

The planting of the tree symbolized a unique patriotic event in the history of the school and the annals of the United States.

By 1920, Johnson had established himself as a leading educator, but a controversial one. Although his leadership would soon be criticized, his guidance as innovator at the young agricultural school earned him a reputation that was recognized at the local and state levels. He would eventually extend his career beyond the Farmingdale campus. The college archives lists those who supported his leadership and those who charged him with many failures. One of them, Arthur Brisbane (1864–1936), the influential columnist and editorial writer, admired the career of Johnson. In a 1920 editorial in the *New York American*, titled "A school that Creates Farmers and a First-Class Teacher of Farming, Albert A. Johnson, of Farmingdale, Long Island, N.Y.," Brisbane wrote that Johnson "deserves his reputation as one of the best executives and one of the best teachers in the country." Brisbane praised the director for teaching city boys how to "understand and LIKE the green things that grow in the country." Hundreds of city boys have been trained to be productive farmers. During and after the war, Johnson had taken young, wounded soldiers to train them as farmers. He and his staff had taught them to be self-sufficient. Brisbane recommended to parents that their boys and girls enroll at Farmingdale to produce crops that would never have existed without them, and to provide public service. He closed the editorial by stating that New York State should appreciate the "fine institution" at Farmingdale and that the legislature should be "generous in appropriations."[22]

Despite such praise, problems soon arose that challenged Johnson's management style and even the viability of the institute. At the beginning of 1918, there had been a call for a legislative probe of the institute. State Sen. Murphy of Brooklyn had introduced a resolution "to investigate the conduct" of the school and to find out "what results are accomplished by the school" and "the expense of its maintenance." The legislative probe was inconclusive, but doubts continued to swirl over whether educational goals were being pursued, let along being achieved. But Johnson ignored issues that began to surface. Although in office only since 1913, he quickly lost sight between his self-image and the institution.[23]

The early 1920s became a critical time for the school. The attacks on Johnson mounted to the point where they could no longer be ignored. Students and the public lost confidence in Johnson. The majority of the Board of Trustees supported him. Important board members in 1922–1923 were William M. Baldwin, president; William W. Niles, secretary; Irvin J. Long, treasurer; John Angleman, Jacob W. Heineman, Herman D. Nessler, Mrs. Robert Low Pierpont, Henry P. Tuthill, Hilda Ward, Edmund R. Lupton; Carl H. Fowler, Judge Frank S. Gannon, and Wintrhop Taylor. No vice president was listed.[24]

The charges against Johnson were serious. Demands mounted for his resignation, especially when a series of investigative articles were published in the *New York Evening Post*. Freelance reporter Harold A. Littledale, who interviewed individuals close to the situation, which involved allegations of fraud and incompetence, wrote the series that ran from May to December 1922. Littledale acquired access to state documents and Board of Trustees' meetings and produced information not known by the public. The articles were devastating, as each succeeding one added additional charges and repeated earlier ones that provided clarification and emphasis. The result was an official state investigation of the institute, a flurry of charges and counter charges, a student strike, and Johnson's eventual resignation. The allegations against Johnson and the State Institute of Applied Agriculture on Long Island were summarized as mismanagement, wastefulness, and misuse of money. The itemized list follows:

- From its chartering in 1912 through early 1922, more than $1,250,000 had been spent while only 51 students had graduated, and only 137 full-time students were enrolled at this time.
- Not one member of the faculty who had been hired in 1916 remained six years later.
- Surplus money, mainly derived from farm income, was not returned to the state treasury, whereas other farm schools, such as Cobleskill, were returning money to the state.
- The contract between the federal Board for Vocational Education and the institute, dated December 12, 1919, was being violated. Federal money, designated to train disabled veterans at the school, was being misused. The government was paying the institute $25 per veteran, but foreign students and out-of-state students were receiving their education free when only in-state students were legally exempt from paying tuition. Federal funds

were also diverted to ineligible employees and used to purchase a Ford automobile and various services, as well as servants working in the director's cottage.

- Money paid by the federal government to train disabled veterans was spent on a private campus elementary school for the education of Johnson's son and other institute employees.
- Proper accounting procedures were lacking.
- Johnson's base salary of $5,000 was increased by $2,500 from federal money that should have been used for the disabled veterans or turned over to the state treasury.
- Nearly all of the sixty-seven disabled veterans were housed in the federal board dormitory, which was a fire hazard, and physical conditions of extreme cold in the winter and heat in the summer were a "disgrace."
- Johnson developed a close relationship with the Soviet Union after World War I, traveling there to assist their agricultural economy. He placed Russian students at the Farmingdale school without charging tuition.
- Johnson disregarded valuable advice from local agricultural associations. The Long Island Poultry Association Committee complained that it was "frozen out."
- During the 1921 state legislative session, a bill was submitted to make Farmingdale a college and to change the director's title to president. The bill died, but it alleged that it reflected Johnson's ambition at a time when the school did not measure up to collegiate standards.
- Confidence in Johnson's leadership was shaken when students went on strike in October 1922, demanding his resignation.
- The Board of Trustees, appointed by the governor, were not fully informed of conditions on campus and negligent of their legal responsibilities. They allowed the administration to rubber-stamp Johnson's policies.[25]

These public allegations put the young school in a precarious position at a time when it needed all the support it could muster, weakening Johnson's leadership position. The situation involving the veterans was particularly critical, so much so that Col. C. R. Forbes, director of the

Veterans Bureau and others, demanded that Gov. Nathan Miller have New York State conduct an investigation. Forbes insisted that federal payments to the school be stopped. Finally, on November 6, 1922, the Veterans Bureau announced all former military students be withdrawn from the State Institute of Applied Agriculture on Long Island and placed in other institutions "for the best interests of the boys." To soften this move, a Veterans Bureau official said the action was not taken because of its request to have Johnson removed from his position.[26]

The *New York Evening Post*, pursuing its crusade against the Farmingdale farm school, summed up its investigative series by indicating it was no longer viable. In its May 2, 1922 issue the publication stated, "Although correct methods of farming are supposed to be taught at Farmingdale, the farm school there is a tragic failure." Attacks continued. During the regular New York State Federation of Farm Bureaus meeting in Syracuse July 7, 1922 a resolution was adopted. This influential group registered the "belief that the expenditures of State moneys on the New York State School of Applied Agriculture at Farmingdale, L. I. have been and will continue to be a waste of Public Money. . . ." The federation called for a change of management at the school.[27]

Into the center of the controversy entered Roslyn resident Hilda Ward (1878–1950), who became an important player attempting to elevate academic standards of the school. She worked to raise entrance requirements and to prevent readmission of dismissed students. Ward began a long relationship with the Farmingdale institute, first as a student when she enrolled in January 1918, alumna, and later as a trustee from 1920 through the 1940s. Her appointment to the Board of Trustees rested on her lineage, maturity (42 years old), and school enrollment. As a student residing on campus at the Mott house, she made many friends among the faculty and student body. The 1925 *NYSSA* Yearbook was dedicated to her for being "Our respected trustee, esteemed fellow student, and sincerely loved friend." Her father, Aaron Ward, was a graduate of the Naval Academy at Annapolis who rose to the rank of rear admiral and served in various positions throughout the world. She christened a ship named for her father in Kearny, New Jersey, November 22, 1941. Hilda Ward was a successful artist, having exhibited her work at the famous 1913 Armory Show in New York City and at the Art Institute Chicago. She was described as "the first home-grown Expressionist." For some unexplained reason, she stopped painting three years later. Her last exhibit was presented posthumously in 1960 at the New York Pietrananio Gallery. This mutlitalented woman also wrote an illustrated book, *The Girl and the Motor* (Cincinnati: Gas Engine Publishing Company, 1908), featuring the delightful experiences of a skillful girl managing the complexities of motor engines in a boat and several automobiles. Ward

Hall is named in her honor. It was the first dormitory on campus built at a cost of $43,379 to accommodate 56 students; it was originally named Dormitory 1. This building began an expansion of the campus, when it was renovated in 1962 to house the nursing and dental hygiene programs for the next twenty-one years until Gleeson Hall opened in 1983. (Dr. Michael Abbatiello, former student and retired chairman of the Veterinary Science Technology Department, served as faculty supervisor in Dorm 1 in the late 1940s.) [28]

FIGURE 3.4. Hilda Ward (1878–1950), a resident of Roslyn, played a major role in the early history of the New York State School of Agricultural on Long Island at Farmingdale. As student, alumna, and longtime member of the Board of Trustees she worked hard to improve academic standards. From the Bryant Library Local History Collection, Roslyn, NY.

Hilda Ward witnessed the events surrounding the Johnson controversy from both sides of the controversy. She expressed her concerns to board trustee William W. Niles about what she considered the low educational standards at the school. Niles acknowledged Ward's concerns, but no action was taken. Ward sought an appointment to the Board of Trustees, which she received in August 1920, allowing her to become directly involved in ongoing events. An impatient Ward communicated with the New York State Education Department demanding answers and seeking to rectify the situation. On December 6, 1920, she received a response from L. A. Wilson, director of the Department of Education, Division of Vocational and Extension Education in Albany. Wilson reviewed the background of all the state schools of agriculture and concluded that the work at Farmingdale "has been less than college grade" compared to the agricultural colleges at Cornell and Syracuse. The courses at the state schools of applied agriculture at Morrisville, Cobleskill, Alfred, and Farmingdale had set up "entrance requirements considerably less than the college [level]." Those requirements were at an eighth-grade education or sixteen years of age, he wrote. His examination of legislation that established the agricultural schools indicated the education was to be vocational in nature for city boys and girls and others. Wilson admitted that at this level, the agricultural schools delivered excellent training but less was expected because less was required. This somewhat carefully worded opinion did not satisfy Ward.[29]

Not to be silenced, she registered her own assessment of events to the Board of Trustees, pointing out the "deplorable educational conditions" in the academic year of 1919–1920. She focused on student failures and the graduation of nine deficient students. She attempted to stop the graduation of students with deficiencies, to raise entrance requirements that would be enforced, to seek transparent financial reports, and to create new courses in bacteriology and commercial farming. Johnson disapproved of these proposals and the Board of Trustees agreed with him. Ward alleged educational matters were never brought up at board meetings, unless she initiated them. She said members listened courteously while Johnson raised objections, whereupon the trustees voted down her suggestions. The board's meetings were "cut and dried" with seldom more than five of the nine Trustees attending. Ward considered the institute poorly managed financially. She believed Johnson's attempt to make Farmingdale a college was "absolutely preposterous." She withdrew her opposition to the campus elementary school because "little enough" was being done for the faculty. Her first knowledge of the "contingency fund," which she thought was an "emergency fund," came directly from the articles published in the *New York Evening Post*. She firmly believed that this fund was to be used exclusively for veterans.

The board censured Ward for her actions. President William M. Baldwin informed her that she was undermining Johnson's authority. She protested that she had written three letters to Johnson, but they were ignored. Baldwin had instructed Johnson not to answer them. She was further informed that she could not do anything without the cooperation of the board. Fully aware of her situation, she forwarded her resignation from the board to Gov. Miller on May 24, 1922. She was reappointed soon after.[30]

An investigation of the school had been conducted in February 1922. The state comptroller found nothing wrong in its audit of the school's finances and management. This did not quiet the critics who insisted the investigation was not thorough enough. The Veterans Bureau had called for a new investigation in late April 1922, as did the *New York Evening Post* in early May. In Albany, Gov. Miller reviewed the record and agreed that conditions were so bad at Farmingdale that an investigation was needed. Miller appointed Edward G. Zimmer, deputy state comptroller, to investigate allegations of padding the payroll, mismanaging school funds, and actions of Johnson and the Board of Trustees. The governor pursued this action under the Moreland Act, which authorized him to investigate charges against state officials. Frank P. Graves, state commissioner of education, and B. A. Pyrke, state farms and marketing commissioner, were informed of the Farmingdale situation.[31]

The Board of Trustees was aware of the charges and considered them of "grave import." The board and the Institute administration cooperated with Zimmer, who conducted a thorough investigation. Witnesses were questioned and documents examined. In the meantime, Allan Roberts, dean of academic subjects, resigned. Trustee Carl H. Fowler called for a detailed list of salary funds. Johnson declared that the list had been stolen along with eighty cancelled checks. Martin B. Dugan, campus bookkeeper and cashier, was able to provide other relevant documents.[32]

The Zimmer investigation completed its work in late May and released its report at the end of August. It was a strong condemnation of Johnson and the Board of Trustees. The conclusions and recommendations are detailed here:

- Because of low morale at the school, a new director should be appointed.
- The school should be put under a state board or commission because the trustees lacked educational and supervisory skills. Zimmer stated, "Your care and management of said institute has been and is inefficient and improper."

- Questionable expenditures were made of federal monies whose purpose was to train disabled veterans. Johnson added $2,500 to his salary from the Contingency Fund and that money was to be used for veterans.
- Zimmer praised Hilda Ward for exercising "independent judgment" and being "a woman of ability and understanding" who opposed the majority of the Board of Trustees.
- The board was blind to Johnson's shortcomings.
- Non-resident students were not paying the required tuition fee.[33]

The Zimmer Report was supported by prominent citizens who had testified during the hearings: Elwood V. Titus, president of the Nassau County Farm Bureau; Henry R. Talmage, director and vice chairman of the Suffolk County Farm Bureau; Thomas Powell, member of the Executive Committee of Nassau County Farm Bureau; and Morgan Topping, member of the Suffolk County Farm Bureau. They said that there was "no friendly spirit" between the farm bureaus and the institute. They had much to contribute to the institute, but their advice was ignored. Johnson was labeled "unpopular, overbearing, arbitrary" and the investigation concluded, "the school was of no benefit to agriculture on Long Island."[34]

Board president Baldwin disagreed with the conclusions of the Zimmer Report. He stated his experience as head of the board demonstrated he had been "connected" to the school and deeply involved in its affairs before students enrolled in 1916. He served in this leadership capacity because it was a public duty and because of his knowledge of agriculture, and board members had dedicated themselves to implement policies based on "state laws and the official advice of the supervising state departments." Regarding the use of federal funds, Baldwin said the board was guided by opinions obtained from New York State Attorney General Newton and Frank B. Gilbert, legal advisor to the State Department of Education. Letters confirming the matter were then referred to the state comptroller as evidence. The funds were intended to increase Johnson's salary for his work and did not need to be turned over to the state treasury, according to Baldwin. He defended Johnson's use of funds by acting as an agent of the board according to the "written authorization of the attorney general." Some campus employees were employed with different titles because under the civil service law there was no standardization of titles and salaries. No fraud was committed. Baldwin stated he had worked with Johnson for seven years and stood behind him. "I have always found Director Johnson scrupulously honest and a tireless and efficient worker." Baldwin said he had met with Gov. Miller and informed him he refused to resign as president of the Board of Trustees.[35]

Additional support for Johnson did surface. He received high praise in an editorial published by the *Oyster Bay Guardian*. Anyone who had visited the school would realize that the charges against him were malicious, and apparently there was "no love for the Farmingdale School," said the editorial. The newspaper paid tribute to Johnson's ability because he was appointed by President Warren Harding to visit the war-torn European countries following World War I to rehabilitate them with the latest agricultural methods. The Long Island Press Association (LIPA), following an inspection of the institute at Farmingdale, also praised the results attained there and asked that Johnson be retained as director. The visiting members of the LIPA announced, "what once was a wilderness of scrub oak now blossoms as the rose under the direction of the one management, and that without cost to the state." Hal Fullerton, who accompanied the LIPA members, reviewed the history of the farm school, declaring, "everything seen at the School and farm is directly due to Prof. Johnson and that it is without equal anywhere in the United States."[36]

Another damaging incident involving the school's reputation occurred October 19, 1922, when 113 students suddenly went on strike demanding the resignation of Johnson. In an age when established authority prevailed, it was a radical move and a bold assault on the director. The strike dramatized the issues. The 113 striking students, or 84 percent of the campus total, sent a copy of the signed petition, dated October 31, accompanied by a telegram to Trustee Hilda Ward, who was residing at the Hotel Wellington, New York City, calling for the "removal of Director Johnson." The strike would continue until his resignation took effect. The petition summarized the charges against Johnson, and resolved "That we believe full cooperation and complete harmony between the students and the faculty will never be possible until the services of Director A. A. Johnson are completely dispensed with." The students were concerned about the quality of their education, were resentful of unqualified students not paying tuition, and believed that Johnson lacked an understanding of their problems. Harry J. Fisher, chairman of the Student Executive Committee, led the petition's list of signatories and had sent the telegram to Ward. The students placed their confidence in Ward in attempt to lead her board colleagues to resolve the ongoing issues. The petition was also sent to the newspapers.[37]

A special faculty meeting was held in November 11, to discuss what action to take. At the close of discussion, a resolution was adopted to expel the militant student leaders and those guilty of action "subversive of discipline and detrimental to the best interests of the school and the cause of education." Further, the striking students were barred from the dormitories and cafeteria until they relented. On November 22, Johnson presented the faculty resolution to the Board of Trustees, who supported its action. With the exception of two students, all other students who relented were readmitted.

As the controversy grew ever larger, Johnson realized he was in a tenuous position; he had to decide whether to continue or resign. He believed his dedication and hard work had accomplished the goal of establishing a successful agricultural school at Farmingdale, but despite some support for his administration, events were getting out of his control. The student strike was the turning point. It put into question his ability to lead. Thus, in the middle of December he submitted his resignation. It was accepted by the Board of Trustees in executive session at the Manhattan office of Board President Baldwin. No explanation was given for the resignation, but it was obvious his ability to serve effectively had been destroyed. The charges against him had a negative impact on his position as director. His resignation became effective March 1, 1923, but his salary would continue to June 1, 1923. In the open board meeting that followed, Baldwin read the LIPA statement commending Johnson's record. The board also expressed its gratitude to state Sen. George L. Thompson of Kings Park and to Assemblyman Thomas A. McWhinney for their support of the farm school. In its final action, the board passed a motion made by new trustee Winthrop Taylor to audit the federal funds in the school's treasury and submit those funds to the state treasury.[38]

When news of Johnson's resignation was released, Long Islanders joined students to express their approval of ridding Johnson of his position. In December 1922 a crowd of more than one-hundred students and townspeople gathered outside Johnson's campus cottage using automobile horns and other noisemakers to celebrate the event. Johnson was residing in the cottage at the time but did not respond to the demonstration.[39]

The Albert A. Johnson years at the State Institute of Applied Agriculture on Long Island came to an official close March 1, 1923. The last faculty meeting he participated in took place February 23. H. A. Dodge, chairman of the Animal Husbandry Department, was appointed as acting director. A permanent director had to be found to fill the vacancy. The Board of Supervisors of Nassau and Suffolk counties, and other local groups, endorsed popular Sayville Principal Seward S. Travis to lead the Farmingdale institute. Travis was one of the most respected educators on Long Island. Nevertheless, after board deliberations in April, Garland Armor Bricker

FIGURE 3-5. The Open House program invited the community to the campus to see and learn about the educational exhibits created by students and faculty. This elaborate exhibit of 1927 was a typical display of what was taught at the school.

FIGURE 3-6. This collage of campus lighthearted-student activities released the stress of classroom and laboratory work. These images were taken from the 1924 yearbook, *NYSSA*,

FIGURE 3-7. The 1927 basketball team displays the name "AGGIES" on their uniforms. The early teams played against faculty, high schools, clubs, and colleges. Frank Mandato, Class of 1936, named the school mascot "Ram."

was quickly appointed director. Bricker, of Columbus, Ohio, assumed the position of director in May. He was professor of agricultural education at Ohio State and Syracuse universities and author of several books on agriculture, one of which continues to be used by scholars: *Agricultural Education for Teachers* (1914).

Upon assuming the leadership position and after surveying the situation at the institute, Bricker suggested at a faculty meeting that rules be established to guide the actions of the faculty. He pointed out that the director's time should not be taken up signing monthly slips for faculty absences. At another faculty meeting he recommended the heads of departments form a faculty council to advise the administration. He was moving toward a more democratic administration. Bricker was concerned about the low number of registered students, the institute's fiscal problems, and its image. He attempted to increase enrollments by applying new strategies. He was concerned about low morale of faculty and staff because it weakened the institute's effectiveness. He soon became impatient and frustrated in attempting to reform the school so quickly. He realized the critical challenges that lay ahead and the dismal status at the institute. He suddenly resigned the directorship in late August. Dodge was reappointed until a permanent replacement could be found.[40]

Despite the controversy surrounding Johnson's resignation, he exerted a strong influence on the development of the farm school at Farmingdale. He set many precedents. His leadership helped to shape the character of the campus, especially in its design and physical development. He was committed to agricultural education and recognized its importance to the region. He believed the institute was unique when comparing it to other local and national educational systems. His policy of opening up the campus to the community was continued by his successors. The 1917 NYSSA *Bulletin* made the point, "The Trustees and Faculty desire to bring the school as close to the people as possible, and to have the State use the services of the school to the fullest extent." He had his supporters and detractors. Despite his shortcomings, Johnson nurtured the school's development. Ultimately, his leadership style and failure to modify his management style, led to his downfall. In time, institutional growth would develop gradually in overcoming the failures of the early years.

Johnson distinguished himself beyond his work at the Agricultural Institute on Long Island. Following World War I, in 1921, taking a leave of absence, he had visited devastated regions of France and reported on conditions in Turkey and other parts of the Near East. He witnessed the famine-devastated areas of the Soviet Union as chairman of the American Commission for Near East Relief. He urged Herbert Hoover, who led the relief effort, to send one million tons of seed to the effected areas. His firsthand experience in this communist country was unique. Working in the Soviet Union, he earned the respect of government officials who came to know him personally. Russian students were sent to study at Farmingdale. The leaders of the Soviet Union were so impressed with the school that seven similar institutions were built on the Farmingdale model.

Johnson returned to the Soviet Union later in 1923 as manager of another U.S. commission composed of U.S. senators and representatives. Foreign Minister Maxim Litvinoff greeted him on his arrival. Johnson's knowledge of the Soviet Union economy led to the publication of several books: *Russia at Work* (1928); *The Soviet Union at Work, Past, Present, Future* (1929); *Progress in the Soviet Union* (1931); and *Pocket Paragraphs on the Soviet Union* (1931). He became an authority on the Soviet Union, making a total of twelve trips there between 1921 and 1936. He was the commercial representative for a variety of American business and industrial concerns.[41]

FIGURE 3-8. The historical marker indicates the area at the campus Ornamental Gardens where Director Albert A. Johnson's ashes were buried. He was actually appointed to the directorship in 1913.

FIGURE 3-9. The World War I Memorial Oak Tree flourishes today on campus. It is a reminder of the dedicated service and sacrifices made by those who fought in the Great War, as it was then called.

During the 1930s and 1940s, Johnson patented improvements to railway cars, founded the Buy American Institute (1938), and advised the government on agriculture after World War II. He made his home in New York City and in Longmeadow, Massachusetts.[42]

Johnson was married to Ellen Glenn of Dahlonega, Georgia. They had two sons, Albert Richard, a set designer for theater, and William Glenn, a technical director for theater. When Ellen died in 1945, Johnson married Marie Stone Weston of Longmeadow. This marriage ended in divorce seven years later. He retired to Roslyn, South Dakota in the mid-1950s. He died May 31, 1963 at the age of eighty-three in Sioux Falls, South Dakota. College President Laffin received a request from the Johnson family to have his ashes and the ashes of his favorite cat buried in the Ornamental Gardens on the Farmingdale campus. The request was granted, and in a brief ceremony guided by Fred Harrison, plant manager of the college, Johnson's ashes were deposited in the soil, which is today marked by a plaque. Five years later, Dr. Laffin and Frank A. Cipriani, administration vice president, conducted a brief ceremony at the site in 1968 when the ashes of Johnson's first wife were also buried at the campus gardens. Thus, Johnson's only visit to the campus since his resignation in 1923 was a permanent one.[43]

FOUR

Halsey B. Knapp, 1923–1956

In education, pioneering should always be the order of the day.[1]

WITH THE RESIGNATION OF ALBERT A. JOHNSON, it did not take long for the Board of Trustees to fill the position of director at the State Institute of Applied Agriculture on Long Island. The record shows that no other individual was seriously considered. The board was impressed with the credentials of Garland H. Bricker, professor of agricultural education at Ohio State University, and appointed him as the next director. He resigned in late summer because of the many problems that lay ahead for the school. Bricker left no legacy. With a new appointee pending, the institute would have three directors during 1923.[2]

The Board of Trustees once again moved quickly to fill the position and unanimously appointed Halsey B. Knapp on September 26, 1923. Knapp's background was exemplary. Born in Port Byron, Cayuga County, New York, on September 1, 1888, he had an agrarian background, coming from a long line of farmers. He attended a country grade school and graduated from Port Byron High School in 1904, and four years later enrolled at the New York State College of Agriculture at Cornell University, working his way through college by serving as student assistant in several departments.

Following his graduation with a BS degree, he took a position, first as instructor and later as assistant professor, at Cornell's Department of Pomology (cultivation of fruit), assuming responsibility in extension work and fieldwork. He continued his studies at Cornell, earning a master's of science degree in agriculture in 1913. He remained at Cornell until 1916, and later served on the university's Board of Trustees. He married S. Gertrude Newkirk of Port Byron, New York in 1913, with whom he had four children. Knapp's ascendant career received a boost when he was appointed director of the New York State School Agriculture at Cobleskill in 1916. The school had just opened its doors, and his eight years there were successful. A new opportunity emerged when the directorship opened at Farmingdale.[3]

Under Knapp's administration, Cobleskill had grown from a handful of students to an enrollment of 149 young men and women who came from sixteen counties of New York State. While there, he had taken an active part in community service, charity, Sunday school, Chamber of Commerce, and local farm organizations. By 1923, he had placed the school on the eve of expansive growth, being in the midst of an extensive building program. But he believed that a great opportunity lay at Farmingdale. Knapp's leadership at Cobleskill received high praise and prepared him well for the challenges he would face in the new position on Long Island. Dr. Frank Pierrepont Graves, New York State commissioner of education, recommended him to the Farmingdale Board of Trustees: "Mr. Knapp has done a remarkable job at Cobleskill. He has been recognized as the ablest head of a secondary educational school in the country." Graves characterized Knapp as an "honest, well-trained, and pleasing man," and predicted Farmingdale would "become the foremost institution of its kind in the United States, and I personally believe that Director Knapp is the man [to lead the campus]."[4]

More praise for Knapp came forth. Berne A. Pyrke, New York State's commissioner of Farms and Markets Department, expressed warm approval of Knapp's relations with Cobleskill and the entire community. Schoharie County Judge Dow Beekman stated Knapp performed his work in outstanding fashion in his first directorship, and was a great stimulus to farmers, leaving a "first-class agricultural school." Albert R. Mann, dean and director of the New York State College at Cornell University, was "delighted" with Knapp's new appointment, urging the Farmingdale Board of Trustees to accept the conditions that Knapp had requested.[5]

On August 27, 1923, Knapp informed Farmingdale Board member Edmund R. Lupton of Mattituck, nephew of John M. Lupton, that he was ready to accept the directorship under terms and conditions he stipulated. Knapp had insisted on a unanimous vote from the Board of Trustees in his selection; absolute authority in administering the Institute; restoration of the director's salary to $5,000—he had been offered $4,000—and "that in addition to house, heat, light, and telephone the position carry the right to such maintenance as the farm afford;" that he be

FIGURE 4-1. Director Halsey B. Knapp sits at his desk in the Administration Building (Thompson Hall). His long tenure as Director, 1923–1956, earned him the respect of educators and community leaders.

allowed to complete his book on fruit growing that was under contract with publisher John Wiley & Sons; and that a truck and car be sent to Cobleskill to transport him, his family, and all his belongings to Long Island. At the end of August, Lupton and board president Baldwin notified Knapp that the board agreed to the terms, but wanted him to come down to New York City a second time for a final interview with the entire board. Knapp insisted he had met the search committee's conditions and was too busy with "Teacher Training and Home Making" curriculum matters at Cobleskill. The board did not pursue its request. On September 20, the Cobleskill Board of Trustees unanimously adopted a resolution affirming its appreciation and respect for Knapp and his work at the institution. Knapp then submitted his resignation, which was accepted amicably. On September 25 the Farmingdale Board of Trustees announced its unanimous appointment of Knapp as director of the State Institute of Applied Agriculture on Long Island. He assumed the position November 1, 1923. Thus began a new era for the institute.[6]

The institution that Knapp inherited would be vastly different thirty-three years later when he retired. An early 1924 description of the school indicated how much work lay ahead for him to alter its direction:

> The Institute is a finishing school in vocational agriculture, training specifically for country life and closely allied fields. It is unique among educational institutions in that an agricultural institution, it is located within twenty miles of the world's largest city, teaches by having its students perform the work on its farm and with the livestock, and operates on a twelve-month basis instead of the usual school year. Students come mostly from New York State, though other States and several foreign countries are represented in its enrollment. The courses vary in length from a regular course of three years down to one-day students for practicing farmers. The Institute also operates a Rural Teacher Training Department.[7]

The Long Island Agricultural and Technical Institute at Farmingdale, as it was known in 1956 when Knapp retired, had grown during his more than three-decade tenure from 66 full-time students to more than 1,436, and had added a technical component to its traditional agricultural program. A thriving adult education department also was in place. Nevertheless, at the outset in 1923, Knapp realized the problems facing the school by admitting, "It had gone through rough times. No one had a good word for it—strikes, dismissals, trials, investigations—one by the Deputy State Comptroller—just about all the things that should not happen to a school had been its lot."[8]

Knapp's first year as director was his most difficult. He "parted company" with the president of the senior class, as he put it. Within a few months he discovered a cell of the Ku Klux Klan (KKK) operating and espousing its beliefs on campus. The KKK, which at that time wielded great influence and power on Long Island, included members among the institute's ranks of faculty and staff. The Klan's prejudices extended not only to non-whites but also to recently arrived immigrants from central and southern Europe. KKK strongholds were located in Central Islip, Freeport, and Huntington during the 1920s. Knapp was told by a Klan member to fire his Irish Catholic bookkeeper. He promptly refused and ridded the campus of any Klan influence. The organization declined by 1930, but Knapp's problems continued. During his second month in office, just before Christmas, a state assemblyman visited him at his home to inform him that he was introducing a bill in the legislature to abolish the school. The governor, Alfred E. Smith, also recommended to the state legislature to have Creedmoor State Hospital take over the institute and establish a program in occupational therapy there.[9]

It was becoming evident that Farmingdale was experiencing a unique historical development. This is not hyperbole. Programs in the early years had attempted to meet the educational needs of students in the evolving Long Island region, yet challenges had arisen at critical points in its development, and the school was compelled to change course when failures emerged. As one studies the documents in the college archives, overwhelming evidence reveals the lack of guidance and understanding at the state level of the school's mission. Inadequate funding plagued the school for much of its existence, leaving inadequate support for its educational programs and the maintenance of its physical plant. For example, one frame building constructed immediately after World War I for the education of disabled veterans was still in use in 1956, even though it was intended as a temporary barracks for those veterans. The six schools of agriculture functioned at a disadvantage because of a constant lack of support from the educational and political establishments in Albany, according to Joseph Petrick in his study of the agricultural schools. Even a 1931 Special State Committee concluded that they were underfunded, but no concrete proposals were offered to deal with the issue. At Farmingdale, dedicated efforts were required of the staff and faculty to maintain the campus infrastructure and educational programs. The educational bureaucracy in Albany failed to comprehend the institution's proper place in the system. Knapp persevered through these challenges, as other leaders have.[10]

The most severe challenge to the actual survival of the Farmingdale agricultural school arose in 1926 when an attempt was made to close the school. The main attack came from an unlikely source, Gov. Alfred E. Smith, a man who rose from the streets of the lower east side of New York City to become a hero of the people. His success led to attaining the state's highest office and nearly to the American presidency in 1928. He won the gubernatorial elections of 1918, 1922, 1924, and 1926. (The term for governor then was two years.) What New York State had given in the 1912 law that created the school, the governor attempted to take away.

Smith dropped the bombshell March 22, 1926, when he urged in a special message to the legislature that the farm school be closed. He stated it "has not been a success" and demanded it suspend operations at the end of the semester. He charged that only a handful of students had enrolled there; few graduates entered agriculture; rising land values on Long Island led to a reduction of farm acreage; and the costs of educating students and keeping the campus in good repair were not cost efficient. The governor added, "If the State made a mistake in establishing the school, if it is not producing results in keeping with cost, good business requires that it be abandoned." Furthermore, in a letter to Abraham Erlanger of the National Farm School Conference in New York City, May 14, 1926, Smith reiterated a similar sentiment that the Farmingdale Institute "be abandoned as a school and that its pupils receive their education in agriculture at some other state institution."[11]

The governor wrote to Knapp in June stating he found no fault with his leadership and that Knapp had "rescued that institution from complete demoralization." However, it was poor business to have Farmingdale partially built and for the state to buy land for the construction of the Creedmoor State Hospital near the Nassau–Queens border. In fact, Smith recommended that the more than three-hundred acres at the school be turned over to Creedmoor, which was housed eighteen miles west of Farmingdale, to be used as a farm colony for patients for truck farming and occupational purposes. He categorically charged, "Farmingdale should never have been built, and if built should never have been planned on the elaborate scale originally designed for it. There is a grave question in my mind about all secondary schools of agriculture."

Smith pointed out that the commissioner of education "certified that the school at Delhi was useless" and thus questioned the value of all secondary schools of agriculture. He wanted to put them under the control of Cornell University, whose board of trustees could decide what to do with them. *The New York Times* agreed with the governor when it said, "the first step toward making our State institutions adequate is a reorganization of those now existing."[12]

Knapp responded to the governor with two letters. In office less than three years, Knapp indicated that the "groups now coming to Farmingdale represent young men of high standards, and with as great a promise of justifying the investment for them on the part of the State, as any with whom I have ever been associated." He cited the current National Farm School Conference being held in New York City that intended to recruit students from New York to attend the National Farm School in Doylestown, Pennsylvania. He asserted that "there is no real reason why young men and women, who are residents of New York State, need to go to Pennsylvania" to secure an agricultural education. Knapp stated that he was in office for only two and a half years and has tried to correct a difficult situation. He urged Smith not give up on Farmingdale.[13]

A year later, a nonpartisan group was formed in Nassau and Suffolk counties seeking legislation to close the Farmingdale school and convert it into a normal school. But Smith had already opposed this proposal because a normal school was already planned for White Plains in Westchester County. He also opposed another mental institution on Long Island.[14]

Knapp and his backers fought hard, committing themselves to what they considered to be a special quality education that Farmingdale offered. He challenged the figures used by the governor specifying that actual student costs were only $650 annually. Editor Mabel Witte Merritt of the *Farmingdale Post* declared the governor's figures were inaccurate, pointing out that the "State Education Department is pleased with the progress made in the past two years and figures now are much more optimistic than those used by the Governor, taken four years ago at the lowest ebb of the school's history." Hal B. Fullerton declared that one reason for putting the proposal of an "insane asylum in Farmingdale was to use the land at Creedmoor for developing private estates" and he urged support for the school. Elwood V. Titus, president of the Nassau County Farm Bureau, defended the school, as did E. W. Crawford, general superintendent of Pratt Institute. Knapp was committed to its mission, campaigning vigorously, talking to anyone who would listen, lobbying all groups—farm, religious, fraternal, civic, educational. He often stated, "I know that a public institution must have public support and understanding." Frank P. Graves, commissioner of education, stood by him, as did others who knew and understood the integrity and professionalism of the man.[15]

Political pressure contributed to the defeat of Gov. Smith's attempt to close the school. Petitions were circulated that overwhelmingly opposed the asylum, while few were opposed to the school. Leaders such as Col. Theodore Roosevelt Jr., son of the former president, and Henry L. Stimson, both Republicans and Nassau County residents, entered the battle in support of Knapp. Sen. George L. Thompson of Kings Park, said, "The proposition to scrap Farmingdale if put into the form of legislation, cannot get by the Senate. It never will pass if I can help it." Assemblyman John Broyle Jr. of Suffolk County said the Republicans opposed the closing of the Institute "because the Governor wanted to turn Farmingdale into a state insane asylum." Even Father Joseph Haldemaier, spiritual advisor at St. Rose's Industrial school at the Nazareth Trade Institution on Conklin Street, in Farmingdale Village, opposed closing the farm school and did not want an asylum in Farmingdale. He charged that the St. Rose students, all under sixteen years of age, would be put in danger, saying, "I fear for the safety of the girls and, in fact, for anybody who might be living in the vicinity of the asylum." The Republican legislative majority killed the bill, and in 1927 Gov. Smith abandoned his attempt to close the school.[16]

With the crisis behind him, Knapp concentrated on raising educational standards, making certain that the needs of both the young and the mature be met. He pressured the faculty to increase their commitment to enhance the sense of dedication that originally characterized the institution. A comprehensive flexible approach to the academic programs was implemented. Knapp built links with public and private groups, but it would take time before the most effective combination of courses and effective public relations could be developed. He was aware that the issue was essentially substantive rather than procedural.

FIGURE 4-2. Members of the 1928 "Girls Basketball Team" represented the Institute's policy of equal access and opportunity. Like the boys sports teams, games were played against local schools such as Hempstead High School and Farmingdale High School.

FIGURE 4-3. Students are learning and applying their knowledge at the Dairy Test Laboratory in the old heating plant, Conklin Hall, 1933. The Institute emphasized "hands on" education.

Campus life reflected a time when simpler virtues prevailed. Knapp, coming from a rural background and the upstate agricultural school at Cobleskill, recognized and appreciated the value of an agrarian society. Relocating to downstate Long Island, which was essentially less rural despite being adjacent to the nation's largest city, replicated a similar ecological setting. An examination of the *1925–1926 Freshman Manual* offers clear insight concerning student life at a public institution. Rules were published and were to be enforced by the Freshman Rules Committee. They were stated as follows.

Thou Shalt:

1. Show proper respect to all members of the faculty and upper classmen.
2. Respond willingly to all requests of upper classmen, managers, etc.
3. Learn all college songs and cheers and rules within two weeks.
4. Greet everyone with a cheery "hello."
5. Wear the required Freshman cap.
6. Wear coats and ties to all meals and ties to all classes.
7. Carry a box of matches at all times during the year and and respond willingly to all requests for their use.
8. Attend all athletic contests on campus and sit in the cheering section and CHEER.
9. Attend all student organizations, mass meetings and Freshman Labor Week.
10. Carry Freshman Rules at all times.

Thou Shalt not:

1. Crab
2. Smoke outside of the dormitory.
3. Speak to or escort a girl.

4. Take short cuts on the campus.

5. Wear bow ties.

6. Leave the campus after dark except Friday, Saturday, and Sunday nights.

Freshmen were instructed to dress "like a college man . . . and a neat appearance is one of the essentials of a college man." At a time when rules were clearly intended for men only and to be obeyed in a structured society, they played an important part in guiding student behavior on campus. Here was an attempt to copy the culture of private colleges and enhance the identity of the institute. Knapp himself was pleased with this system because he believed in a controlled environment that would lead to improved standards.

Students often spent some of their recreational time in town on Main Street. They would take their visiting parents there to attend a movie or for lunch or dinner. Businesses in Farmingdale Village placed advertisements in campus publications. For example, the *Freshman Manual* of 1932 contained an advertisement for the "Presto Restaurant and Lunch Room" located at 217 Main Street, Farmingdale. Diners were invited to stop at the restaurant for a Long Island Duck Dinner or a Chicken Dinner for a charge of $1 each. Regular dinners were priced at $.50 and reflected deflationary values during the Great Depression.[17]

The academic programs at the institute continued to expand and diversify. According to the 1927 *Bulletin*, in addition to the regular three-year program, the following six-month courses were offered: poultry husbandry; landscape gardening and floriculture; farm mechanics; unit courses in poultry husbandry and farm mechanics, summer farm camps; and teacher training. Two years later, the course in landscape gardening and floriculture was extended from six to nine months, and then to eighteen months. Such changes continued into the future as the school attempted to reach nontraditional students, young and old, male and female, thereby providing community service.

Knapp seized every opportunity to promote the Institute. In an article he wrote for an LIRR publication in 1931, he stated that Long Island was "not merely an overflow residential area for New York City, as some think. It possesses an extensive and a highly diversified agriculture. The special quality of the school emphasized the practical or applied phases of agriculture. The only way [to learn] to milk a cow was to milk her; the only way [to learn] to prune a tree was to prune it under the supervision of an expert. A blackboard demonstration will not do." Knapp also earned good will for the institute through his involvement in service organizations such as the Grange, Farm Bureau, and New York State Agricultural Society. He was a founding member of Farmingdale Rotary International in 1929, served there as its president. He was named a Paul Harris Fellow, a designation reserved for those individuals making significant contributions to Rotary. To this day, Farmingdale Rotary offers a scholarship in Knapp's name.[18]

Total enrollment, always a concern in the early years, had increased to 201 full-time students for the 1931–1932 academic year, not counting special programs. In 1935, the regular three-year program was reduced to two years for high school graduates, but applicants who had completed only two years of high school could take a year of preliminary training to enroll in the regular two-year program. Knapp was moving toward stabilizing the basic course of study, while at the same time attempting to craft special programs for unconventional students. In 1936, applicants had to be sixteen years of age and must have completed four years of high school to qualify for enrollment in the two-year program. Although horticultural courses always had been offered, the School of Horticulture was officially established in 1937 and received its first formal class for the fall term. A summer session was added. In 1939, total full-time enrollment increased to 359.[19]

New York State continued to reduce funding for all of its departments and agencies during the Great Depression. Of course, the economic crisis seriously impacted the Farmingdale Institute. An examination of the 1934–1935 personnel service salaries is revealing, because overall salaries had already been reduced by $3,600, a large sum in this period. Salary costs for all personnel came to $92,500. Director Knapp's annual salary for this academic year was listed at $4,500, but his actual salary had been lowered to $4,077. His original contract in 1923 had been established at $5,000 per year. The annual salary for each of the five department heads was listed at $3,600 but their actual take home pay had been reduced to $3,362. Nine instructors and three assistant instructors had contracted salaries ranging from $2,600 to $2,100 but their take-home pay ranged from $2,438 to $2,000, respectively. The campus librarian's salary was retained at $1,200 with no change. Knapp requested that all original salaries be restored or at least slight raises be given for 1935–1936. At a time of high unemployment and deflation during the Great Depression, individual pain was shared by all.[20]

Although these critical issues persisted, a bit of levity emerged. A long-held tradition was adopted when it was agreed to establish a mascot to increase the school's visibility and identity. Student Frank Mandato, Class of 1936, is credited with successfully urging the adoption of the "Ram" as the official mascot among the school's athletic teams. Mandato was a graduate of

Brooklyn High School, majored in agriculture, and starred on Farmingdale's football team. The Long Island sports pages repeatedly referred to him as "Ram" and rarely used his real name when reporting game results. The early reference to "Aggies" was eventually dropped as the school developed technical programs as its image changed. The Ram would become the mascot that symbolized campus athletic teams.[21]

In attempting to overcome depressed economic conditions, the New Deal under President Franklin D. Roosevelt initiated measures that benefited the State Institute of Applied Agriculture, its title 1924 to 1939. Knapp took advantage of all the aid that was available. Some examples follow. On July 1, 1937, President Roosevelt signed the George-Dean Act into law, which provided $14,000,000 for national expansion of vocational and career programs. Farmingdale received enough funds to hire nine new instructors to teach courses in vocational education programs. The National Youth Administration, another of the many New Deal innovations, sponsored an Agricultural Resident Training Center on campus in 1938. This training program enabled seventy youths to work their way through school for the next four years. These youths were unemployed, lacked marketable skills, were burdens on their families, and were on welfare. Also, an "Out-of-School" program was begun to train the unemployed in automotive repair, welding, blacksmithing, and general shop work for the years 1939 to 1941. The skills acquired in the program were used effectively when the students entered the armed services during World War II. The program helped in the development of technological training beyond agriculture.[22]

Numerous other New Deal projects were made possible by Works Progress Administration (WPA) allotments. Labor was provided by these government agencies to build a campus granary, fertilizer shed, sheep bar, a closed-implement shed and additional shed section, poultry houses, battery and incubator structure, tool house, vegetable shed, athletic stands and dressing rooms, wing of the Rural Engineering Building, packing house-cider mill, and calf barn. Various other structures were remodeled. Another WPA project enabled the institute to clear two parcels of land, one plot about fifteen acres and another thirty acres. Twenty additional acres were cleared for instructional purposes. The WPA built a new system of tunnels and pipes that carried steam, cold and hot water to all the buildings on campus. Such assistance allowed Knapp and his administration to maintain and even expand some programs.[23]

The New Deal federal art program Treasury Relief Art Project, along with the WPA, put many artists to work creating murals and sculptures in the United States. On Long Island, many of these works of art have survived. At the Farmingdale Institute, Frederick Marshall painted four oil-on-canvas murals on walls in Cutler Hall, depicting a redwood forest and a China rice harvest, and in Hicks Hall, scenes of wheat thrashing and cotton picking were depicted. These murals survive but are in poor condition. Today, Cutler and Hicks halls have been closed waiting for restoration. Also, designer and artist John L. Northam supplemented his income working for the WPA. He produced the original mosaic, "Home Sweet Home," in the vestibule of Thompson Hall. The mosaic remains there today in good condition.[24]

FIGURE 4-4. This rare group image of Director Knapp and the faculty was taken in Knapp Hall Lounge in the late 1940s. Front row, left to right, Professors Horton, Cutler, Roesch, Patterson, Hersman, Pyenson. Second row, Knapp, MacDougall, Foote, Musa, Wedell, Stephens. Rear row, Lewis, Stockbridge, Franke, Nevelle, Ingham, Rissmeyer, Wicks, Scarci, James, Fairbanks, Goetz, Gray.

FIGURE 4-5. Professor D. Hart Horton, Chairman of the Poultry Department, instructs a group of special students during World War II on raising poultry. Horton Hall is named in his honor and today serves as the administration building.

FIGURE 4-6. This in-depth view of Knapp Hall dining room reflects the organized pattern of campus life in 1950. Knapp Hall was theoretically named for Mrs. Knapp who died in 1930, but it was intended for Director Knapp. Public buildings could not be named for living persons.

Because of a dire need, two stately buildings were erected on campus during the 1930s. More than $250,000 was expended for the construction and equipping of Knapp Hall, indirectly named in honor of the director. State law did not permit buildings to be named for living individuals. The naming of Knapp Hall, therefore, nominally memorialized his deceased first wife, but the intention was to honor Knapp who had already established himself as a dominant educational leader. Gov. Herbert H. Lehman (1933–1942) dedicated the building October 30, 1937 in the presence of more than five-hundred invited guests, faculty, and students. Lehman identified Sen, George L. Thompson of Suffolk County as the "Father of the Institute" because he sponsored the enabling legislation that created the school. Actually, John M. Lupton and Franklin W. Hooper conceived the original legislation, but it had failed to be enacted when first proposed. Knapp Hall was modeled on the Georgian colonial architectural design. It housed the dining hall and lounge on the ground floor and a dormitory on the second floor. Faculty offices and dining hall are now housed there.[25]

The administration building, later named Thompson Hall, was completed in 1938 at a cost of $125,000, also in the Georgian Colonial style. The director's office, library, animal husbandry labs, Food Tech Department, dean's office, General Education Division, and classrooms have all been located there. The structure continues to function as faculty offices and classrooms. It was named for Sen. George Lincoln Thompson, whose roots were deeply imbedded in Long Island. Born in 1864 in Smithtown where he received a public school education, Thompson worked as a farm boy and sailed as a mate on his father's ship. During the 1890s, he began a successful general store enterprise, and established himself as a community leader in social and business matters. A committed Republican, he held many public offices, such as excise commissioner, postmaster, and board member of Kings Park State Hospital and Flatbush State Hospital. Thompson was first elected to the state assembly in 1909 and served there until 1914 when he was elected to the upper house of the legislature. He used his influence to support policies that advanced the interests of Long Island, especially the institute at Farmingdale. When he died at the age of 76 on September 2, 1941, he was the oldest member of the New York State Legislature in point of age and service. The institute lost a friend who advocated for its interests in the New York State legislative battles.[26]

Also, several other structures were erected during the 1930s. Mr. E. Hunt, campus carpenter, and his assistants helped in the construction of several buildings. One was the secondhand greenhouse, which was purchased in Glen Cove in 1923, moved, and assembled at the institute.

In 1938, the Bethpage State Park gave another greenhouse to the institute. The following year, E. W. C. Arnold, of Islip, donated a conservatory. M. Henry and P. DeForest of Cold Spring Harbor, donated two wings for the conservatory in 1939. These last two structures took shape during 1941 and 1942.[27]

Once again, the school experienced a name change; it became known as the State Institute of Agriculture and held this title from 1939 to 1946. However, the New York State Department of Education envisioned development of technical education and recommended the schools of agriculture at Alfred, Canton, Delhi, and Morrisville offer technical and industrial courses. Farmingdale assumed another name change in 1946, Long Island Agricultural and Technical Institute when its Industrial-Technical Division was begun. This name would last until 1953 when it became known as SUNY Long Island Agricultural and Technical Institute at Farmingdale. Despite the economic hard times, funds were made available from the state and federal governments to add personnel and erect new buildings to generate greater service to the public. As a result, the educational process at the institute stabilized preceding U.S. involvement in World War II. Amid all this change, the 1940 yearbook, *NYSSAN*, listed the following regular programs of study:

Agricultural Business
Agronomy and Farm Management
Animal Husbandry and Dairying
Health Education
Horticulture
Poultry Husbandry
Related Science (Social Science and Oral Expression)
Rural Engineering
Vegetable and Fruit Growing
Nursery Work
Floriculture
Landscape Construction

These diverse courses represented the expansion and growing relevance of the institute. Still committed to agricultural education, Knapp realized the need to add new programs, and he urged his faculty to remain current.

Instilling a sense of mutual trust among the faculty and staff was one of Knapp's priorities as he worked to achieve this goal throughout his long tenure. He also bound himself directly to the welfare of students when he assumed the position of advisor to the Student Council. He was a hands-on administrator who was involved in all phases of campus life. He promoted athletics to help students round out their education. Gerald D. Allard coached the football team. Merrill N. Knapp and Joseph Roesch were his assistant coaches. Allard also coached tennis and a winning baseball team. Student Michael Abbatiello, who eventually joined the faculty, played on the basketball team. The 1940 *Yearbook* included a senior class essay, part of which follows:

> Summer work began in April and it was a welcome change from the previous routine. Half the day was spent in the classroom and the other half on the Institute farm. At the end of June, class work ceased and the whole day was devoted to farm work.

Throughout the 1930s and 1940s, the Country Life Open House program, previously known as the Country Life Show or the Farm and Home Equipment Show, begun as early as 1920, demonstrated the school's educational programs while inviting the community to learn more about them. The 1940 Open House was extended to four days. Two years later, attendance exceeded ten thousand over the four-day period, with such featured exhibits as a victory garden, farm and equipment exhibit, Long Island Baby Chick and Egg Show, cattle show, farm machinery adjustment and repair, and household pest control, in addition to many other attractions. During the war years of 1943, 1944, and 1945, attendance was greatly reduced because of automobile tire and gas rationing and wartime restrictions. A full three-day Country Life Program was once again conducted in February 1946 with increased attendance. The Country Life Open House program had several main purposes: to promote the institute and enhance its image, to render a service to the public, to give the students experience in preparing and conducting exhibits, and to increase enrollments. Farmingdale's Country Life Program differed from other agricultural school programs because the exhibits and demonstrations were interactive. The entire faculty, staff, and student body were on hand to assist and answer questions. Knapp believed that this tradition earned respect and support for the institute.[28]

To accommodate further the educational needs of the public, the institute continued to create a variety of courses. The two-year agricultural and horticulture programs were well established by the 1940s; six-week, eight-week, and shorter courses were offered for teachers; evening classes were popular; older skills were upgraded; the unemployed learned new skills. Even though the institute was originally established for the young, a growing number of adult students took advantage of these educational opportunities. The large extension program also proved to be successful. During the 1939–1940 school year alone, faculty members traveled 7,105 miles by automobile and 4,752 miles by train to bring their knowledge to organizations and individuals throughout the state. Knapp assigned faculty members the task of keeping track of changes on campus, gathering data, recording department histories, and photographing campus events. For example, Professor C. Dick Thomson of the English Department was directed by Knapp to write a history of the campus. Vice President Locke James composed an essay on "War Time Services at the State Institute of Agriculture, Farmingdale" following World War II. Professor Frank Pyne produced a short narrative of "The New Log Cabin" that replaced the old one that was used by students and faculty. The extensive collection of original documents in the College Archives provides a clear picture of the history of the college. Knapp, and even Albert A. Johnson, was ever mindful of the importance of documenting the past, given the fact that the Institute was in a perpetual state of change. It left a legacy of primary source material allowing researchers to connect the past with the present.[29]

In 1942, the agricultural curriculum was expanded when the Institute received the Stony Kill farm in upstate New York as a gift from J. B. R. Verplanck and James Delancy Verplanck. The property was to be used as a teaching farm. The Verplanck family had acquired the land in 1683 from the Native Americans and had held it since then. The 750-acre farm lay between the Berkshires in the east and the Hudson River and the Catskill Mountains in the west, about ninety miles north of the Long Island campus. It contained good land for crop production, pasture and woodland, buildings equipped for instruction, farm machinery, a manor house, living quarters, and livestock. But it had lain idle since 1932, and much of the land had to be cleared and reclaimed. The gift specifically stated in the title transfer that the primary purpose of the farm was to serve as an outdoor laboratory to enable students to experience a broader range of learning. During World War II, a minimum amount of restoration was accomplished. After 1946, increased instruction by the institute was given at Stony Kill in soil conservation, pasture improvement, and care of woodlot. Dairy heifers, cows, turkeys, and capons were raised there. During the growing season Farmingdale's agricultural students were assigned there to work for brief periods under the supervision of instructors. Farming at Stony Kill effectively complemented operations at Farmingdale. In the late 1960s, Farmingdale decided it no longer needed the property and returned it to New York State. In 1973, the State Department of Environmental Conservation converted the acreage into a working farm and environmental education center. Today the property is used to teach visitors about ecological issues. Visitors have access to the hiking trails and the library at the Manor House. The Stony Kill Farm was added to the National Register of Historic Places in 1980.[30]

Two of the most beloved instructors passed from the scene during Knapp's tenure. Mary K. Peters died on January 3, 1943 at the age of seventy-nine, and her husband Clayton died on November 5, 1946, at the age of eighty-six. Knapp memorialized Mary in the 1943 *NYSSAN* Yearbook. This husband and wife team was closely associated with the formative years of the institute. Clayton was born in Bendersville, Pennsylvania in 1860, attended the University of Michigan where he received bachelor's and master's degrees in biology. He continued his studies at the laboratory of the Long Island Biological Association in Cold Spring Harbor conducting experiments related to inherited characteristics of one-celled animals. From 1902 to 1916 he chaired the Department of Science at Brooklyn Polytechnic Institute. While there, he organized science lecture series at the Brooklyn Institute of Arts and Sciences. He then joined the Farmingdale faculty as a science instructor, remaining until his retirement in 1933. He was a fellow of the American Association for the Advancement of Science. Mary also was born in Bendersville, Pennsylvania. She received a bachelor of arts degree from the University of Michigan in 1896 and subsequently taught at the Franklin and Marshall Preparatory School, Edinboro State Normal School, Brooklyn Polytechnic Preparatory School, and Bushwick High School. After arriving at Farmingdale in 1918, she spent twenty-one productive years there as instructor and librarian, retiring in 1939.[31]

The Peters devoted their lives to the institute. They were known as master teachers in the classroom and laboratory. Students were their primary concern as they extended themselves in helping them resolve personal and academic problems. Such commitment earned them the affectionate titles of "Ma and Pa Peters." They participated fully in campus life. Mary originated the idea of planting the Memorial Oak Tree in 1921 and having it dedicated to those individuals who fought on the Allied side during World War I. They served on numerous committees such as the Christmas Committee and the Discipline Committee. Their names were frequently mentioned in the minutes of faculty meetings. In 1922, the institute published their original collaborative work, *Plant Diseases*. A few years later their department title was broadened with the new name of "Academic and Sciences," which included English, citizenship, agricultural science, and agricultural chemistry. The Peters enjoyed conducting outdoor classes. They were considered master teachers, relaxed in the classroom, yet exacting in their standards.

Institute classes honored these two beloved mentors. The 1932 Yearbook was dedicated to "Pa Peters." The 1939 Yearbook was dedicated to "Ma Peters" in these words:

> Sentiment is an emotion scorned by most of us these days, yet even the most sophisticated cannot help but feel a pang of regret when we know that "Ma" Peters is leaving the immediate Institute family. We dedicate this book, the most prized possession of our campus, to Mary K. Peters in appreciation of her many years of devoted and loyal service to the Institute.

In October 1947, the Alumni Association placed a memorial plaque honoring the couple in the campus garden near Hicks Hall.[32]

Despite the institute's successful record of agricultural education, Knapp realized future growth lay in technical education. He acknowledged recent successes, but the curriculum had to expand to build on the changes resulting from World War II, while remaining committed to the traditional program. He thereby guided the establishment of a technical division in 1946 that put Farmingdale on the path of becoming a comprehensive two-year public educational institution. Long Island was being transformed by suburbanization, increased land values, new industries, and need for well-trained workers. The rise of the Levittown community in 1947, and other housing developments that followed, inevitably created a structurally altered region. Knapp turned to Horton Amidon, chairman of the General Education Division, to analyze the impact demographic growth was having on Long Island and how it affected the Institute.

Amidon's report was published February 1954. It revealed the population of Nassau and Suffolk counties had more than doubled in the previous thirteen years, from 604,103 in 1940 to 1,245,000 in 1953. More than 165,000 dwellings had been constructed since the end of World War II. Nassau and Suffolk counties had jumped ahead of all the counties in the northeast regarding economic growth. In terms of dollars, nearly 25 percent of New York's industrial plant expansion since 1945 had been on Long Island. In the two counties, industrial production workers increased from 8,000 before the war to 100,000 in 1953. Industrial payrolls went from $8,000,000 to more than $410,000,000 during the same period.

The Amidon Report indicated agricultural production continued to expand, even in this modern era. The housing developments that were beginning to emerge occurred on land unsuited for farming, and people gainfully employed in agriculture had increased slightly from 9,700 to 10,000 in 1950. Excluded from these figures were migrant laborers who numbered up to 5,000 in some years. Agricultural production in dollars had surpassed the 1945 figure. Acreage devoted solely to agriculture had decreased slightly during the twenty-year period from 1930 to 1950, from 151,000 acres to 150,000. Farming, according to the Amidon Report, was in no danger of disappearing at this time, actually having become intensified. Irrigation, fertilizers, and scientific techniques had essentially led to greater productivity.

Although the yearly number of high school graduates rose slightly at first in the post-World War II era, there was a dramatic increase in the number of students in the lower grades, which would eventually result in greater demand for postsecondary education. The report noted that this trend was already being felt in the number of Nassau–Suffolk high school graduates entering the Institute. The overall population growth, as shown in official census data, reflected the obvious impact on the Long Island region (Table 4.1):

The Amidon Report projected greater postsecondary student demand for agricultural and technical education. Based on the study of the institute's graduates of the classes of 1951 and 1952, it was shown that nearly 46 percent came from beyond Long Island. Additionally, about two-hundred students came from New York City to study agriculture and ornamental horticulture. Despite New York City's excellent educational system, it lacked the facilities for which Farmingdale was becoming famous. About 25 percent of the agriculture and ornamental horticulture students took positions on Long Island, whereas nearly 50 percent worked in upstate New York, and the remainder went to other states. Knapp was impressed with the findings. These trends influenced and confirmed the overall expansion of SUNY, which had been officially chartered 1948.[33]

Knapp was a hands-on administrator-educator. His leadership placed him at the center of campus life as he monitored students' progress, guided his faculty, maintained ties with community

Table 4.1. Overall Population Growth in Nassau–Suffolk Counties, 1920–1950

YEAR	POPULATION
1920	236,366
1930	464,108
1940	604,103
1950	948,894

organizations, participated in professional associations, and lobbied officials to support the Institute. He demanded complete dedication from those who served under him. He promoted agricultural education, but also encouraged curriculum innovation, realizing new programs were necessary to accommodate the changing needs of a just society. The critical situation he inherited in 1923 was a constant motivating factor for him to work that much harder for the welfare of the Institute. His reputation grew as he nurtured educational growth.

Yet Knapp was in reality a more complex person. Noted for directing a rigidly disciplined campus and himself setting the example for hard work, his expectations for achieving the highest standards seemed limitless. From the beginning of his directorship emerged a supreme leader, who cajoled, suggested, and coerced to attain cooperation and dedication from faculty and staff. He made similar demands on himself. Throughout the Farmingdale State College Archives can be found memo after memo from Knapp suggesting that certain events be organized in a particular fashion, allowing recipients of such memos little room to maneuver or make counter proposals. Concerned with campus details, there were reports written with care and forwarded to him from key assistants and faculty: Locke James, Horton Amidon, Robert McLaughlin, David Allee, A. J. Holub, C. Dick Thomson, A. M. Halleck, Robert Davidson, and Raynor Wallace, Anne Synek, among others. Whether dealing with a holiday faculty meeting, maintenance of the Campus Village, a new program, curriculum changes, or personnel problems, his strength of personality usually prevailed.

It must be remembered that the period of Knapp's long tenure as director preceded the inception of democratic administration and unionized faculty and staff at Farmingdale. It also must be emphasized that Knapp had naturally assumed many prerogatives and considerable power over the years. He was influential in community and statewide affairs. He believed that a democratic society rested on educational opportunities for all its citizens. Having achieved a positive statewide and national reputation, he effectively had become somewhat of a legend. Toward the end of his tenure as director, however, personnel issues surfaced that increased campus tensions and public scrutiny.

Regarding an understanding of such a perspective was Knapp's memo of June 9, 1947, to "Mssrs. Amidon, Foote, Lincoln, Raymaley, and Stockbridge," comprising a "Committee to Examine the Possibility of Creating a More Favorable Status and Environment for Members of the Faculty in the Discharge of Their Duties." Knapp specifically excluded salaries and the forty-hour week from being examined because the "nature of the calling does not permit it. The State itself

FIGURE 4-7. Director Knapp addresses the incoming 1950 class in front of the Administration Building, now Thompson Hall. It was an annual tradition. In his address, Knapp greeted the students, related the history of the Institute, and emphasized what was expected of them.

does not contemplate it." He recommended the committee should consider how much discretion faculty should have in using their out-of-class time during the workday and how instructors should be compensated for teaching evening classes and working on legal holidays. He instructed that he be kept informed of the committee's progress and that he was available to give assistance. "As a corollary it follows that you will issue no opinions, hints or prophesies in the meantime."

It was evident that such pressure from on high greatly influenced the direction the committee would take. The committee released its report November 10, 1947, and it did not cover salary, promotions, or the forty-hour week. It included general duties of the faculty, vacation time, sabbaticals, office hours, and goals, all amounting to a restatement of earlier policies.[34]

Two years later, *Newsday* published a front-page headline in its July 1, 1949 edition, "PROBE 'COERCION' AT STATE AG SCHOOL." The story revealed that state university officials had launched an investigation into charges that institute authorities had declared war on any form of faculty union. Two professors, Gordon E. Clifford and Harry M. Daniel, alleged that pressure had been regularly placed on them to resign, but they refused. A third professor, Elmer Schwertman, had resigned June 22 because "I couldn't take it any more." The three claimed they were in this predicament because they had expressed their "opinions on such matters as a teacher organization, teacher contracts, sick leave, and vacations." At the time, civil service regulations identified personnel as "classified," meaning there were no specifications regarding contracts, sick leave, tenure, and vacations. Clifford, Daniel, and Schwertman asserted that Knapp totally opposed their activities, especially their efforts to establish a union. They did belong to the Civil Service Employees Association (CSEA), but the organization lacked strength. Other allegations were presented: They were hired without contracts, were given no written curriculum, were stalled by a lack of supplies, and, in Schwertman's case, had to reside in the Village of Farmingdale. For their outspokenness, they alleged the Knapp administration applied pressure on them to resign. Without important guarantees of its faculty in terms of salaries and working conditions, apparently Farmingdale was facing a personnel crisis as it was moving to a full-fledged institution of higher learning.

Knapp defended himself by stating the dispute was an internal affair. Although Frank L. Tolman, president of the CSEA, insisted, "Morale was so bad that something should be done immediately," no strong action was taken against Knapp. SUNY President Alvin C. Eurich agreed to the demand of a grievance hearing and that all persons concerned would be heard. At the conclusion of the grievance hearing, Eurich ruled on August 23, 1949, in favor of Knapp and against the professors. Eurich said he had "examined the case from many angles" before arriving at his decision. The SUNY Central Office, however, usually supported the administration in then current labor–management relations, a time well before unionization. The professors disagreed but had no other course of action but to resign.

The following month, on September 15, a confident Halsey B. Knapp addressed the faculty at a meeting of the Industrial Technical Division:

> Your jobs are important. You are here because each of you has some definite contribution to make. Before others will regard highly what you seek to do, you must think highly of it yourselves. Then we must accord each other an equal rating. It is my desire that all things that enter into policy and courses of action both at department and Institute levels shall come just as far as possible out of free discussion—before decisions are made. We cannot hold a Town Meeting on every item and subject. That is not to be expected. We do operate on a representative or delegate basis in our society. In our case, that would mean committees, special assignments to smaller and particularly qualified groups, etc.,—but we are not going to gain a quick and mechanical efficiency at the expense of expression and discussion and participation and sharing. That would be gaining the form and losing the substance. Our biggest job is not finding equipment and money and people with technical competence. It is rather to create an environment, an atmosphere and a state of unity in essentials but with many individual differences freely expressed, of interdependence and mutual need and appreciation and participation in which technical competence may flower and in which people may be happy. Our primary resources are not physical and material. They are points of view, attitudes of mind, how men approach things—from an affirmative base or negative one. They are mental and spiritual. It is not easy to describe them but when we have them we know it and when we lack them we suffer.[35]

As time went on, Knapp found himself justifying his role as leader and decision maker. He became sensitive to criticism, whether expressed or implied. He would not yield his traditional role, even though he set up a Committee on Personnel Policies, on October 17, 1950, modeled on a similar state university-wide committee. He appointed to that committee consisting of Professor Davidson, chairman, Professors Rakowski, Cook, Franke, Hraba, Levey, Stockbridge, Bowman, Amidon, and Schweizer. Knapp expected a "free exchange of views," but he warned, "Let us be clear at the outset that this is not a grievance committee." Furthermore, the plight of the faculty became even more evident when a campus revision of "A Report on Personnel Policies" was announced on December 1, 1952. The section on tenure indicated there was "no statutory provision for a tenure system." Professionals held their positions on a "merit basis" so long as "relationships are mutually satisfactory."[36]

At the request of the SUNY Central Office, Knapp informed Albany on the progress of personnel policies. He said he cooperated with his colleagues in achieving harmonious relations.

He defended himself as a faculty member pointing out that nearly all decisions went through appropriate faculty committees in adhering to procedures. He forwarded relevant personnel policy reports to Albany.

Betty Mountain, who was associated with Farmingdale as a student majoring in agriculture and an active member of the Alumni Association, presented a positive view of Knapp. The 1939 New York City World's Fair, held in what is today's Corona-Flushing Park, had invited the institute to participate. A campus exhibit was proposed, titled "Milk Maids on Parade." When it became known that Mountain was black and the institute refused to replace her, the World's Fair withdrew its invitation. Although Knapp, his administration, and students stood by her, the exhibit was not presented. In contrast to Betty Mountain's experience, Dr. Michael Abbatiello, an ornamental horticulture student and later professor, stated to the author that he had participated in an institute-sponsored exhibit, "Gardens On Parade," at the 1939 World's Fair. Apparently, Knapp managed to distinguish between the two Farmingdale exhibits, withdrawing from one and participating in another. Despite this setback, Betty Mountain excelled in her work as a student leader in interschool debating contests, and when she graduated in the agricultural curriculum in 1940, she presented a graduation address in which she challenged racial discrimination, "An American Problem—An Opportunity." She maintained a long friendship with Knapp and characterized him as "fair and conservative."[37]

Abbatiello, who graduated from the ornamental horticulture program and was hired by Knapp as a technical assistant, described Knapp as dogmatic, strong, and fair, an administrator who never fired anyone because he expected them to resign. Abbatiello had a distinguished career as professor and coordinator of veterinary science technology at the college. He recalled the reprimand he received for walking on the campus grass with his students following a woody plants lesson. Knapp had seen them from his office in Thompson Hall, which then served as the administration building. Abbatiello remembered Knapp's colored memos. If an instructor received a "pink" memo it meant he had done something wrong; a "blue" note signified the instructor was in good standing.[38]

Abbatiello recalled the situation when instructors took advance study. In his case, he had to use vacation days for the time he attended summer school at the University of Maryland. When he attended the doctoral program at St. John's University, he was required to have Knapp's permission. It was especially difficult to take postgraduate courses because the campus work schedule was so long. Monday through Friday the faculty had to be on campus from 8 a.m. to 5 p.m., and on Saturday from 8:30 a.m. to noon.

Based on Knapp's long history as director, one can conclude that he was a benevolent leader guiding a paternalistic administration. His long service caused him to assume ultimate power to the extent that he would not tolerate opposing views. He was unable to separate his personal–professional identities with that of the welfare of the institute. Knapp maintained control of campus affairs as a condition he insisted on when he was first hired in 1923. It was not an idle request, especially when the future of the school was then in doubt. According to Abbatiello, he had his "favorites" whom he could rely on. Knapp protected faculty jobs in depressed economic times. Abbatiello stated Knapp was the "captain of the ship," an apt description from one who worked for him. Other faculty and staff members confirmed this view.

Overshadowing all the exhibits of the 1956 Open House program was Knapp's retirement statement on February 23. Since he placed so much importance on the event, it was appropriate that he would make the announcement on this occasion. The event had become an integral part of the annual rhythm of campus life since 1920. He was directly involved in the planning of the program, which he believed displayed the positive side of the Institute. On the other hand, he insisted that Open House was a student and faculty affair.

Knapp was conscious of the fact that he had saved the institute and had shaped its educational future. Others agreed. His sense of historical posterity motivated him to assign faculty members to write "histories" of the institute, which chronicled events. These "histories," often unsigned and at times lacking detail, nevertheless provide vital information of campus life. Knapp realized the historical record would bolster his and the Institute's achievements. His initial announcement of his intention to retire officially on June 30, 1956 was sudden and dramatic. His statement was embellished with much nostalgia covering the highlights of his thirty-three years as director. Excerpts follow:

> Thirty-three years ago Farmingdale was a quiet village in a countryside of villages. Its name was appropriate. The Institute has changed. First, it was a school of agriculture—vocational in nature. It possessed 68 students. . . . In the past ten years, 11,000 full-time students have come to Farmingdale. . . . In the past ten years we have an enrollment in courses of 36,000. We are now enrolling 8,000 in such courses. . . . We are in the very heart center and nerve center of the most sensitive and productive areas of education in the United States at the present time. . . . Of over 1,412 full-time students this year, 436 are in Agriculture and Horticulture. . . . We have developed at Farmingdale a special know-how

> in providing education. No other institution possesses it to a like degree because it is the result of an experience and an environment, which no other institution has had.[39]

Following his retirement from Farmingdale, Knapp went on to pursue a remarkable career as a consultant in agricultural and educational matters. He served for more than three years as project leader for the International Cooperation Administration of the U.S. State Department, administered by Cornell University, to aid in rebuilding the Agricultural College of the University of the Philippines. In 1961, he returned to the Philippines as consultant for the United Nations. He served as past vice president and chairman of the planning and policy committee of the Near East Foundation, and traveled to Lebanon, Syria, and Greece in connection with agricultural development programs.

Knapp was a member of the Farmingdale Rotary from 1927 to 1957. His contacts and work in this influential service organization helped advance the position of the school. After his retirement, he remained active in Rotary International. He was a Paul Harris Fellow. A Rotary scholarship is presented in his name annually.

He died on September 7, 1976, at his home in Stony Brook. Survivors included his second wife, the former Grace Van Nostrand, two daughters, a son, and seven grandchildren. His first wife, Gertrude Newkirk, had died in 1930. His life's work has been associated with the institute at Farmingdale, which he molded to the needs of the twentieth century. More than fifty-thousand alumni have taken up leadership positions throughout the world, and many were influenced by his example. At the time of his death, Farmingdale symbolized the model two-year agricultural and technical college. The term, "The Farmingdale Way," has come to represent Knapp's philosophy of education, what he achieved during a productive career, and the special mission of the college in a free society that offers equal opportunity to all.[40]

A testament to Knapp's leadership and dedication of the faculty can be appreciated in the story of Peter Tesdesco, Class of 1930 of the State Institute of Applied Agriculture at Farmingdale. After graduating from Farmingdale High School he was accepted at the New York University (NYU) Law School. Tedesco expressed his gratitude for the guidance at Farmingdale High School given to him by Weldon E. Howitt for the opportunity to attend NYU. However, he could not afford the $375 and other expenses for even one semester's tuition. Therefore, he applied to and was accepted at the Training Class for Teachers at the institute. Tuition was free and he was able to work part time to meet expenses. He also learned that he could qualify for

FIGURE 4-8. Coach Tom Watt prepares his team for competition. Football was one of the most successful sports on campus, but was dropped in 1963. Watt also served as Athletic Director.

a temporary teaching license after only one year of study. His achievements at Farmingdale were outstanding: 1927, 1928, 1929 member of the Athletic Association; baseball, 1927, 1928, 1929; basketball, 1928, 1929; cheerleader, 1927; athletic editor, 1929; winner of the local speaking contest, 1927; winner of the international speaking contest, 1927; and winner of the National Oratorical Contest of the U.S. Constitution in Farmingdale, 1928. He acknowledged benefiting from the encouragement provided by Professor Edith Lange, Knapp, and others at the institute.

Tedesco remembered the death of the first Mrs. Knapp in 1930. All the institute divisions sent representatives to pay respects to Mrs. Knapp during the services on campus. Professor Lange chose Tedesco to represent the teacher's division. Following a period of teaching, he became principal of the Woodward Parkway Elementary School, principal of East Memorial Junior High School, and principal of Weldon E. Howitt Junior School. Tedesco's career, motivated by dedicated professionals, typified the many successes of the Knapp era. The legacy of Halsey B. Knapp will be forever associated with Farmingdale State College, a Campus of the State University of New York.[41]

FIVE

The World War II Era

> The Country Life is to be preferred; for there we see the works of God; but in cities little else but the works of Men; and the one makes a better Subject of our Contemplation than the other.[1]

World War II (1939–1945) altered the direction of the State Institute of Agriculture on Long Island at a time when Director Halsey B. Knapp and his faculty were battling to overcome the effects of the Great Depression, which although not ended appeared to be under control. The United States entered the war in December 1941; events before and after this date reshaped the Institute. The Campus Village would be built to accommodate some of the more than one million veterans who entered college under the benefits of the GI Bill of Rights—the Servicemen's Readjustment Act of 1944. New educational programs and courses were introduced to accommodate the public and contribute to the war effort. An Industrial-Technical Division was established to supplement the agricultural and ornamental horticulture programs. In 1948, SUNY was founded, and Farmingdale became an important part of this statewide system of higher education under the State Board of Trustees. The local College Council would remain in an important advisory capacity. In the 1950s the institute entered a new stage of its development as new faculty with advanced technical skills and advanced degrees were hired.

In the meantime, Knapp prepared his faculty and student body to adjust to the emerging national and international wartime emergency. The institute clung to its traditional agricultural education mission. The editor of the 1942 Yearbook, *NYSSAN*, conscious of the nation's needs, the institute's mission, and World War I contributions of a previous era, stated:

> At the beginning of this second quarter of a century, in the history of the State Institute of Agriculture, the Class of 1942 is departing into a world torn with strife and anguish. . . . It must be decided whether they will serve in the armed forces of the United States or engage in the field of agriculture for which they are trained. This education will enable them to become successful farmers. The armies of the United State depend on food to carry out a victorious campaign against the totalitarian governments and the farmer must furnish the food supplies. There must be an equilibrium between agricultural workers, the men engaged in industry and the men actually behind the guns. If this balance is upset, none of these units can function with any degree of success. It is the agricultural worker who . . . holds the key to victory. The balance is upset because men have left the farm in order to engage in industrial work or the armed services. Young men, whose primary interest is in agriculture, are needed to replace those who have left. Without them, the balance cannot be righted.

The campus community responded in many ways, but the most important was answering the call to arms. A total of 658 former students and graduates served in the armed forces, and 23 made the ultimate sacrifice.[2]

The institute joined in nationwide wartime preparedness activities. Several months after the European phase of the war began in September 1939 it cooperated with the Civil Aeronautics Administration (CAA) in sponsoring Civil Pilot Training classes to teach full-time students theory and operation of light aircraft. Upon completion of the program students were able to secure a private pilot license, and pave the way to more advanced wartime training. Capt. Moore of the CAA and U.S. Army Air Force explained the program during a special student assembly on campus. Beginning December 1, 1939 Professors Norman H. Foote and Ira L. Williams provided seventeen hours of instruction covering the history of aviation, theory of flight, parachuting, meteorology, air regulations, and aircraft power plants. The following February, students received seventeen hours of dual flying and seventeen hours of solo flying under the supervision of Capts. Ashley C. McKinley and Samuel T. Moore at the Babylon seaplane base. The airplane used in the program was a two-seater Piper Cub with a fifty-horse power Continental motor, equipped with dual controls and pneumatic floats. In the next half century, the program would become one of the most advanced in the nation.

In January 1942, after the attack on Pearl Harbor the previous month, an official American Red Cross First Aid course got underway on campus. The five-week course, designed to prepare civil defense work, was offered to students and faculty. At the same time, the Women's Land Army of northeastern states was trained on campus. It functioned under the auspices of the Farm Security Administration, United States Employment Service, War Manpower Commission, and New York Education Department. Another full-time work and training program was initiated at the institute to prepare high school students studying farming to increase food production. There were 261 boys who participated. Similarly, a Crop Corps Camp was established on campus for college women to engage in food production.

These specialized short-term innovative programs developed because of the exigencies of the wartime military draft and need for industrial workers. Knapp insisted on the institute's total commitment during the emergency. The war stimulated an active interest in vegetable gardening, poultry production, fruit growing, dairy management, and general farming during evening and afternoon sessions covering periods of ten weeks throughout the war emergency. Enrollments in these programs and other specialized courses varied. With the rationing of sugar, training in beekeeping was offered on campus. However, contributions to the wartime effort were not limited to agriculture. The Rural Engineering Department trained workers for jobs in the booming defense plants on Long Island, leading to cooperation with the Grumman, Liberty, Ranger, and Republic Aircraft manufacturing companies. Defense courses were offered in metal and machinery repair, machine tool operation, aviation sheet metal work, and blue print reading. A course for bus drivers was given to help maintain motor vehicles for wartime use. The Ornamental Horticulture Department, in cooperation with Capt. Peter Rodyenko of the Army Reserve Corps, offered courses in protective concealment and camouflage that included aerial photographs and obscuring of war materials. The program was limited to horticulture seniors and graduates or others having relevant experience in the field. More than eighty-eight individuals signed up to prepare for an emergency or who might enter military service.

The institute continued its extension services to individuals and organizations. In the first year alone of America's entrance into the war, 2,213 individuals visited the campus for conferences seeking information with faculty to solve special problems; 119 presentations on agriculture were given to organizations on Long Island with nearly 10,000 individuals in attendance; 3,086 letters were mailed in response to farming questions; and 1,388 soil samples were received and tested on campus. Such detailed recording of activities reflected the numerous demands Knapp made on faculty and staff. The Animal Husbandry Department, Poultry Department, Horticulture Department, and Crops Department recorded similar detailed accomplishments. Every campus resource was put to use in the effort to win the war.[3]

FIGURE 5-1. Professor George L. Franke, Chairman of the Department of Animal Husbandry and Dairy Industry, presents the first place award to student John Gibbons of Rockville Center with his entry in the class for Guernsey cows and championship for the breed, 1950.

FIGURE 5-2. During World War II women participated in special courses to help the war effort. This student is applying her technical skill in an advanced course at the campus radio lab in the basement of Knapp Hall.

World War II affirmed Knapp's dedication to "his" students and the importance of a Farmingdale education. Locke James, vice president and executive assistant to the director, related to recently hired administrator Frank A. Cipriani in 1964 about an ongoing correspondence between Knapp and Farmingdale students who had entered military service. Throughout the war, Knapp kept handwritten carbon copies of his letters and filed them with the students' original letters. This experience revealed a compassionate side of Knapp of which few were aware. Students regarded Knapp, who always considered himself part of the faculty, as an "understanding loyal friend." The graduating class of 1949 dedicated its yearbook to Knapp for his accomplishments, loyalty, and leadership. Knapp also was completely committed to the war effort, using the campus to join in the World War II Civil Defense program. District Principal Weldon E. Howitt of the Farmingdale Public Schools was a leader in this work, and he had a hotline to the regional headquarters in White Plains. Knapp allowed him to serve as an airplane spotter in Thompson Hall cupola. Howitt's shift was 5 to 7 a.m. Other local citizens participated in this endeavor on a scheduled basis.[4]

It became evident the school that was established in 1912 to train teenagers in the New York City metropolitan area had experienced numerous changes during its first four decades. Not only was Long Island evolving from its roots as a rural-agricultural region, events were already accelerating institutional growth. Two world wars, a devastating economic depression, an emerging technological revolution, and educational reforms were altering its original mission, making increasing demands on its resources and human capital. New courses and programs were developed, formal and informal, to meet current needs. The Farmingdale agricultural school that had overcome challenges to its survival was a constant reminder to its leaders that compelled them to work much harder to excel. As a public institution, it had no choice but to prove itself on a continuous basis. Few educational systems were so adaptable in so brief a period of existence.

Ever since 1916, women have been part of the Institute, although few in number in the early years. It was during and after World War II that their enrollments increased and activities were recorded in its publications. The 1950–1951 student handbook described the "Liatins" (Long Island Agricultural and Technical Institute) as an association consisting of institute women who met weekly to build ties between the Agricultural and the new Industrial-Technical divisions. They sponsored social events and served as a medium to express their concerns. There was also a local chapter of the Young Women's Christian Association that conducted social activities and assisted children at the Nassau County Tuberculosis Sanitarium. They participated in sports and clubs. When the Industrial-Technical Division was established in temporary quarters on Conklin Street in the Village of Farmingdale, a special Women's Lounge was located at the rear of the Recreation Hall. Resident women of both campuses were allowed to be out one late night until 11 p.m. during the week. Saturday curfew was listed at 12:30 a.m. and Sunday night at 10 p.m. Female students were permitted to receive guests in the lounge in early evening.[5]

As expected, student enrollments declined in the regular two-year programs during World War II as students responded to the call to serve in the armed forces. But as explained previously, wartime demands required the institute to reach out to a varied student body, especially from the adult ranks. This enrollment trend can be seen in the number of regular graduates:

1941: 123
1942: 113
1943: 59
1944: 38
1945: 24
1946: 16

These figures do not include students in eight-week agriculture programs, six-month poultry students, the Women's Land Army, prevocational and high school farm cadets, evening students, other short courses, and extension services.[6]

On the brink of World War II, the institute staff had been stabilized with a committed group of experienced educators. By this time, Knapp had hired eminent leaders in their respected fields. Core faculty remained with greater responsibilities, conducting increased extension services and food production work, preparing to teach veterans returning from World War II. Formal educational activities, however, continued during the war under dire circumstances. The 1942 *Yearbook* included the following clubs and sports: Student Council, *Aggazette*, Fire Squad, Sunrise Grange, Glee Club, Phi Sigma Chi, Dairy Club, Poultry Club, Horse Club, Sing Quartette, Camera Club, Civilian Pilots Club, football, baseball, basketball, and Varsity Club. Athletic competition, however, was discontinued from 1943 to 1945 for these war years.

Regardless of the impending world war in 1939, the educational process had to be maintained. The established tradition of the Annual Country Life and Home Show, as it was labeled then, took place from February 28 to March 2, 1940, according to the programs in the college archives. This twenty-first annual event opened with a featured Hobbyist Exhibit that was limited to student exhibits and demonstrations. A wide variety of exceptional educational craftsmanship was put on display as examples of original diversions of the creator's leisure time. The Hobbyist Exhibit provided an entertaining experience to campus visitors. Invitations had been extended to high schools in the New York City metropolitan area to attend the Country Life program. Those who visited the campus were divided into groups, and knowledgeable guides accompanied them to the various departments explaining the functions of each. The general public was also invited to visit the campus to witness educational demonstrations. The Animal Husbandry Department exhibited products obtained from sheep, milk production, and butchering hogs. The Agronomy Department provided information regarding pasture improvement, cost accounting of silage, potato seed treatment, and new potato varieties. The Poultry Department featured the Long Island Baby Chick Show whose entries were limited to Long Island poultry men and women and separated into three varieties. Exhibits included the importance of cross breeding for broiler production, disease, and diagnosis of poultry. The Ornamental Horticulture Department presented a garden clinic that proved invaluable to those who tended lawns and gardens. The clinic covered insect control, rectifying adverse soil conditions, and proper fruit pollination. The Chemistry Department combined science, agriculture, and industry to illustrate how and what products could be created from raw materials. Families also were pleased with campus events, the children especially enjoyed playing with the farm animals. It was clear that that these exhibits and demonstrations reflected a traditional educational experience.[7]

Continuing its community service during the war, the institute released a "News Item" on March 8, 1945 announcing the fourth annual spring series of evening courses for the "production of food by victory gardeners and backyard poultry keepers." More than 240 students had already enrolled to "supplement resources at a critical time, and strengthen the bill-of-fare at home." Many more would sign up. Scheduled for two hours, the following courses were included: Fruit Growing, The Home Grounds, Soil and Crop Management, Garden Pests, Farm Management, Swine Management, Family Garden, Dairy Cattle Management, Poultry Keeping, Electricity and Its Use in the Home, and Soil Testing. Such a comprehensive list of courses highlighted the agricultural basis of the institute and allowed civilians to participate in the war effort.[8]

Beginning in 1940, and continuing throughout the war, students created and maintained a weather station on campus to assist the U.S. Weather Bureau forecasting meteorological conditions. The Weather Bureau believed its existing facilities in the Long Island area were inadequate and that this station would link up with others to complement a series of other regional stations. Data from Farmingdale contributed to accurate forecasting of weather conditions, benefiting aircraft safety. Daily reports were collected by students who forwarded these reports from the campus to the Weather Bureau office at Battery Place in New York City. These reports contained temperature, humidity, precipitation, and wind. Weekly reports were also dispatched.

C. Dick Thomson, a widely respected professor in the English Department, composed several informal histories of the Institute. Writing at the time of World War II, he pointed out that the applied education of students was of paramount importance to the institute. Their training there was "unusually effective in preparing students to earn a living in their chosen field." It was practical. He referred to a study covering a period from 1919 to 1942 that showed more than 75 percent of the graduates were engaged in productive agricultural work or related fields for which they were trained. Information was obtained from 722 of the 889 students who had studied in programs for six months or longer. This survey did not include the larger number of students who took shorter courses. Thomson concluded, "To the best of our knowledge none of our graduates has ever gone to jail or to an insane asylum. This is one indication that the Institute program makes for well rounded development in the broader sense of living."[9]

Closer examination of the curriculum during the war is instructive to understanding the educational requirements at the Institute. At this time, the two primary fields of study were agriculture and ornamental horticulture. The 1942 Catalog of the School of Ornamental Horticulture specified a student applicant had to have (a) sixteen units of high school study consisting of four in English, two in mathematics, one in chemistry or physics, one in biology or general science; the remaining units to be made up of natural sciences, history, mathematics, social sciences, languages or vocational subjects; or (b) have a New York State academic diploma in agriculture; or (c) may be considered for entrance on the merits of an individual's life experience. In all cases, good health and character were required. The average freshman age was eighteen at this time. The same catalogue stated that in order to graduate from the School of Ornamental Horticulture a student had to complete sixty hours of credit; have a satisfactory record during the summer semester; have a satisfactory settlement of all bills and accounts; and have six months of approved employment in the field of ornamental horticulture. During the second year, the course was divided into three areas from which students had to choose: floriculture, landscape planning and construction, or nursery. The catalogue stated that nearly all graduates of the last three classes found employment. However, the institute's philosophy concerning employment opportunities was reflected in the following statement, "It must be remembered that young graduates were usually not expected to enter managerial jobs, but are encouraged to start from the bottom. After a good apprenticeship, the graduate, depending upon his abilities and personality, progresses rapidly," according to the 1942 catalogue.

Student expenses were slight during this period, especially compared with contemporary standards. As with other public institutions of higher learning, tuition remained free at Farmingdale; non-residents paid $100 per year. There was a standard semester maintenance charge of $125, which covered room, board, and limited laundry service. The summer session amounted to $230. Books cost up to $30 per year. Other minor annual expenses included a student fee of

$10 and a student-medical fee of $16. The institute strongly recommended that students reside on campus. Three dormitories accommodated 155 male students. Mott House, the original farmhouse on the property, accommodated an additional 20 students. Off-campus housing was available in private homes for those unable to secure campus dormitory facilities. Women lived off campus during this period. The catalogue indicated dormitory students achieved higher grades because of curriculum demands and greater availability of their instructors. The Farmingdale educational system approximated a total living and learning experience that contributed to the close association and mutual trust among students and faculty.[10]

FIGURE 5-3. This class of women listens attentively to a lecture in the early 1950s. Women were always well represented in the school's educational programs.

The School of Ornamental Horticulture encouraged women to enroll to take advantage of increasing employment opportunities during the war. The policy was continued after the war and predated equal opportunity programs a generation later as part of the feminist movement. This 1942 catalogue listed eighteen faculty and staff in the horticultural program, including Knapp, two women, librarian Ruth Hitchman, and assistant instructor of flower design Emily Steffans. Louis J. Pyenson, professor of plant pathology and entomology, was the only individual holding a PhD.

The institute library contained more than six thousand volumes in 1942, chiefly technical in nature. Daily and weekly newspapers, periodicals, journals, specialized bulletins, and reports of experimental stations also were available for study. The institute had recently acquired the collection of more than one thousand rare items from Leonard Barron, noted horticultural editor, author, and member of the institute's Advisory Council. The library was located at various campus sites over the years: at the present Book Store (which had also served as a gymnasium), on the second floor of Thompson Hall, in Whitman Hall, and finally to its current one in Greenley Hall.

Americans have experienced greater social and economic mobility because of increasing educational opportunities. World War II accelerated this process as a result of the passage of the GI Bill of Rights that provided subsidized educational benefits to honorably discharged veterans. The benefits dramatically effected life on the Farmingdale campus during the transition period from war to peace. Responding to the post-war housing and educational crisis, a mini-community emerged on campus in the summer of 1946 with the construction of a veterans' housing complex. Army barracks were moved from Republic Field, about a mile away, to the campus for this purpose. These barracks were converted into spare, efficient, but comfortable apartments for returning veterans and their families who assumed residency in these buildings that fall. The institute willingly extended itself to house and educate veterans for a decade in this way.

The mini-community, called the Campus Village, was located between Knapp Hall and Thompson Hall, where Whitman Hall now stands. It offered thirty-five apartments for student-veterans and their families. Each apartment was fully equipped with hot and cold water, steam heat, refrigerator, stove, modern sink and cabinets, fixtures, and a bathroom. Contained in the housing complex were four one-room apartments, twenty-three two-room apartments, eight three-room apartments, a storage building, and a community laundry with two electric washers and clotheslines. As the families settled in, new sights and sounds graced the campus where now children played, dogs romped about, and mothers could be seen pushing baby carriages while their husbands attended classes and performed laboratory and fieldwork.[11]

Most of the Campus Village was torn down in 1956 when new housing became available throughout Long Island. Population growth shifted from the city to suburb. Numerous Levittown-type housing subdivisions were being constructed. The expansion of suburbanization altered the face of the region, which, in turn, reshaped the character of education at the institute. The Campus Village laundry building was not razed until 1981 because of the need for new classroom space. For a while, after 1956, the laundry facility served as a classroom, and afterward students knew it as the Dew Drop Inn where light snacks and drinks could be purchased. The Dew Drop Inn was the final reminder of the Campus Village.

FIGURE 5-4. The Campus Village provided temporary housing near the Administration Building (Thompson Hall) for World War II student-veterans and their families from 1946 to 1956. New York State Governor Thomas E. Dewey, front center, is seen inspecting the 35 apartments. Director Knapp is second from left.

FIGURE 5-5. The 1949 graduates proceed to the area between Cutler Hall and the Gardens for commencement. This is the first class to wear caps and gowns. The Campus Village Veterans Housing can be seen at left.

Walter G. Becker lived at the Campus Village from 1951 to 1955. He had enrolled as a student in 1947. Several years later he was hired as a technical assistant by Professor Daniel Hart Horton, for whom Horton Hall is named. (Horton Hall now serves as the Administration Building.) Becker lived at the Campus Village with his wife during this period, and two of their children were born there. For $37 per month they had a two-room apartment with bath, including all utilities. The rent for an apartment with an extra room was $43. Becker remembered that laundry room assignments were rotated on a monthly basis among the families at the Campus Village. He completed his career at Farmingdale where he eventually achieved the rank of professor of agriculture.

The 1948 student yearbook, which was then known as the *Islander*, presented a student's view of Campus Village life by describing its residents as representing "a wide range of family life, from newly-weds to old married folk of ten years. The present population is 35 families, which includes 20 children. The birth rate is undoubtedly among the highest in the country."

Generally, a spirit of friendliness and cooperation prevailed at the Campus Village. The families joined together to form a Campus Village Association, which worked to improve community life. The association organized parties and other social gatherings, making special requests for assistance from the administration whenever the need arose. Knapp made sure the buildings and grounds were well maintained and that the student-veterans and their families blended in with campus life.

A year after the Campus Village was erected New York State Gov. Thomas E. Dewey (1943–1954) visited Nassau County on June 12, 1947, to inspect housing and educational facilities being used by veterans. He first arrived at Jones Beach for a luncheon at the Boardwalk Café. Powerful political leader J. Russell Sprague, Nassau County executive and Republican Party county chairman and national committeeman, introduced Dewey as "the next president of the United States." (President Franklin D. Roosevelt was elected to a fourth term when he defeated Dewey in the 1944 election. Dewey again received the presidential nomination in 1948, became the odds-on favorite to win, but lost to Democrat Harry S. Truman in one of the greatest political upsets in American history.) Dewey made his Long Island trip to Lido Beach to inspect the veterans' emergency housing. He also visited the housing facilities at the Long Island Agricultural and Technical Institute, Hofstra College, Mitchel Field, and Adelphi College.

Dewey's tour of the institute was both an official and political event. He arrived mid-afternoon at the campus in a convoy of five state automobiles, four Nassau County motorcycle policemen and two New York State troopers. State Housing Commissioner Herman T. Stichman accompanied him. Knapp and Congressman W. Kingsland Macy, Suffolk County Republican leader, met the governor on the steps of Thompson Hall, which was then the Administration Building. The group retired to the boardroom for refreshments.

Since the governor's visit was primarily to inspect veteran-student housing, he visited the Campus Village where he was warmly welcomed. He strolled through the village, stopping to inspect two apartments. He called upon the apartment of Mr. and Mrs. Ted and Hazel Wheeler, complimenting them on their neat apartment and their collection of fish. A photographer took pictures of him and the Wheelers on the front porch. The official entourage continued down the path to the next apartment of Mr. and Mrs. Rounds. Dewey paused to look at the Rounds' baby and commented how attractive the living facilities were. More pictures were snapped. He chatted with more veterans, wishing them luck in their studies. Before leaving, he expressed complete satisfaction with the Campus Village facilities.[12]

Knapp continued his deep involvement in campus affairs. He was a scrupulous administrator in striving to maintain the cleanliness of the institute. His memos found in the college archives document communications with his staff when the physical condition of the campus did not meet his high standards. He relied especially on Professor Horton Amidon, chairman of the General Education Division, to correct any problem that arose. In a memo addressed to Amidon, for example, he expressed dissatisfaction with the appearance of the Campus Village, pointing out that he discovered "dried reeds or grasses, which certainly constitute a fire hazard . . . every time I go by the building in which the baby carriages and other items are stored, I take one quick look and look away."

Knapp was concerned that visitors and "our Council" might see this "general state of leaves, wreckage, disorder and confusion." He expected the people who use the area to carry out their housekeeping responsibilities.[13]

World War II was one of the great watershed events of the twentieth century. Minorities, women, and second- and third-generation children of immigrants seized those opportunities for advancement that were essentially closed to their ancestors. The post-World War II period witnessed less racial, gender, and ethnic discrimination in higher education. Government programs and judicial decisions generated possibilities for equal treatment in realizing the American dream of success. An increased public awareness allowed the less fortunate to develop their abilities to achieve social and economic mobility, and New York State would attempt to remove barriers to higher education. The Institute of Agriculture at Farmingdale had already established a long tradition of equal access to all, but policies resulting from the war accelerated the process. It was inevitable, then, that events in New York State would lead to progress in providing higher educational opportunities to its citizens.

Before 1948, New York was the only state not to have a state university. It was remarkable that of the nation's forty-eight states, the Empire State lacked a university structure and had to rely essentially on arrangements made with private institutions. Within New York City, however, such public institutions as City College, Brooklyn College, Hunter College, and Queens College offered an excellent liberal arts and sciences education. Nevertheless, there existed in the state 138 private institutions and 32 public colleges, each acting somewhat independently without any coordination, under the general control of the Board of Regents. This public collection was made up of eleven teachers colleges, five institutes of applied arts and sciences, six agricultural and technical institutes (a category to which Farmingdale belonged), a maritime academy, and nine other campuses operated for the state under contract with private institutions. The reality was that citizens of the state were unable to avail themselves of a public liberal arts and sciences college or a research university because none existed. As a result, each year thousands of students left the state to attend other colleges and universities. Upon completing their out-of-state education, many of those students did not return home, causing the loss of an elite leadership group. In contrast, by 1948, many of the great state universities across the country had achieved a distinguished record in public higher education. This unique situation for such a progressive state as New York can be traced back to 1784 when the State Board of Regents was established to supervise all educational programs, including private colleges and universities. Over time, the private institutions successfully maintained a monopoly, blocking reform attempts to establish a public university. The private colleges argued that they saved taxpayers money by preventing a duplication of educational services. By 1942, New York State's total budget expenditures for higher education ranked second to last among the states.[14]

World War II changed all this when congress in 1944 passed the GI Bill of Rights providing educational benefits to all qualified veterans. Millions of honorably discharged veterans demanded to enter college. In New York State pressure mounted to meet that need, which could not be satisfied by the limited resources of the private institutions. Dewey and the legislature thereupon created the "Temporary Commission on the Need for a State University" in 1946. Owen D. Young, past chairman of General Electric, headed this twenty-one-person blue-ribbon panel.

The Commission's eighteen-month study called for the establishment of a state university. Enabling legislation signed by Dewey April 4, 1948, became effective July 1. It called for the appointment of a fifteen-person Board of Trustees to govern the new public system of higher education, replacing the Board of Regents, whose opposition was overcome. SUNY initially included a structure consisting state-operated units of higher education: eleven teachers colleges, six agricultural and technical institutes (including Farmingdale), six two-year institutes of applied arts and sciences, six public colleges operated by private institutions, and the New York State Maritime Academy at Fort Schuyler. The agricultural and technical schools, for example, were somewhat autonomous operations until they had been placed under direct supervision of the State Education Department in 1927. The new 1948 law streamlined the higher educational system. It also called for the acquisition of two medical centers, one in Brooklyn and the other in Syracuse, and twenty-two community colleges. Eventually, SUNY would include four university centers, thirteen university colleges, four health science centers, six colleges of technology (the title of agriculture would be dropped), four specialized colleges, five statutory colleges, and thirty community colleges. Farmingdale and the other agricultural-technical institutes could now be granted accreditation by the Middle States Association of Colleges and Secondary Schools and were further certified to grant associate degrees. The university was further strengthened in 1960 to allow for more independent SUNY control on the recommendations of the Henry T. Heald Commission on Higher Education and the passionate leadership of Gov. Nelson A. Rockefeller (1958–1973) who was committed to building a quality state university system.[15]

The new State University of New York's rapid growth caused the private colleges to worry about their survival. Rockefeller responded by getting the state legislature to enact the "Bundy Aid Law" of 1968. Named for former Ford Foundation President McGeorge Bundy who chaired the committee that devised the plan, financial assistance was given to private colleges for each student receiving a degree.[16]

The new system of public higher education that was created in 1948, and expanded during the next two decades, failed to take into account its impact on the agricultural and technical institutes. The final report of the Temporary Commission on the Need for a State University did not deal with the agricultural and technical institutes, except a brief mention by the president of Cornell University, Dr. Edmund E. Day, who was concerned about retaining its arrangement with the state system of maintaining control of Cornell's College of Agriculture and other specialized colleges. The commission did resolve the conflict of educational philosophy over whether the liberal arts and sciences should prevail over technical education for grades 13 and 14. Out of this compromise came the recommendation that the technical-terminal (vocational) program was to be offered to the majority of students, while the intellectually gifted students would be selected for the traditional liberal arts and sciences program. Additionally, the commission recommended that community colleges be established to solve the residential "going away problem"—allowing for local control—while the SUNY Board of Trustees was charged with "the supervision of general programs." [17]

Caught up in all of these major changes in higher education was Knapp, who expressed concern about the gap in education at Farmingdale because of the continuous lack of adequate funding. In April 1948 he said there were 405 students enrolled in the Farmingdale Agriculture and Ornamental Horticulture two-year programs. "We could have many more if we possessed facilities and personnel adequate to care for them," he stated. He acknowledged that more than 65 percent of the total population of New York State resided within a radius of one-hundred miles of the Institute, and that lack of adequate state support hampered Farmingdale's mission to meet increased enrollment demands. Budgetary issues were not new for the school, but they became magnified in this period of rapid growth. The Temporary Commission did not address this issue, nor was it able to grasp Farmingdale's unique role within the SUNY system.[18]

A similar criticism arose by some leaders that New York State was creating a huge financial commitment to higher education when it was charged that the state already failed to pay its fair share of elementary and secondary education. E. R. Eastman, a member of the Board of Regents and editor of the *American Agriculturist*, led the way when he wrote a series of editorials from January to March 1949 charging that Dewey now refused to pay for the state's share of higher education's expenses. Others echoed these concerns. Sen. Francis J. Mahoney, Democrat from Manhattan, asserted the community college system, in which local governments pay a percentage of the costs, is being promoted "at a time when local officials are crying that they do not now get enough state aid to maintain present services." The institute at Farmingdale throughout its history had become accustomed to fiscal disadvantage. The creation of SUNY did not immediately resolve Farmingdale's problem of inadequate funding. Knapp, nevertheless, continued to urge his faculty and staff to accomplish more with less at a critical time when the Institute was embarking upon establishing the Industrial–Technical Division in 1946 and providing for returning war veterans.[19]

Those leaders who had envisioned SUNY gave little attention to the mission of the agricultural and technical institutes at Alfred, Canton, Cobleskill, Delhi, Farmingdale, and

Morrisville and their role in the system. What made matters worse was the fact that Farmingdale was different from the other five Institutes because it was located close to New York City in a densely populated area known for its high cost of living. Local appeals failed to resolve the needs of Farmingdale as it continued to expand. Huge sums of tax dollars were allocated to other SUNY campuses. Funding for community college physical plants was on a fifty/fifty basis, and about two-thirds of their ongoing expenses came from student tuition and county revenues. In contrast, Farmingdale received little money for faculty and staff, and not enough for maintaining its aging physical plant. Indeed, Farmingdale was required to send all tuition and most fees to the State Treasury and had to plead for its fair share of funding through the governor's budget. As indicated previously, New York State provided tax dollars directly to private colleges, including religious institutions of higher learning, through the Bundy Aid Law (1968); this hurt the institutes because it drained the State Treasury. Also, the agricultural and technical institutes were not permitted to seek private money.[20]_

Despite the growing prosperity following World War II, lack of fiscal support placed the campus and its faculty and staff at a disadvantage. In January 1950, for example, Knapp was forced to notify twenty-two instructors of the need to limit their expenses concerning attendance at an important Buffalo Symposium so that more persons could attend. He suggested expenditures for meals be moderate, that "we cannot patronize the Hotel Statler Dining Room" because excellent meals can be secured elsewhere, and that each person subtract $5 from his expense account and "make this his personal contribution." He requested travel be by train to Buffalo in order to same time and money. Although seemingly trivial, such a restrictive financial situation prevailed at a time when the institute at Farmingdale was facing additional expenses on its way to becoming a full-fledged institution of higher learning.[21]

During the 1970s, the post-Rockefeller years witnessed an economic recession that forced budget cuts in education that would continue for many years. Throughout the nation, student campus demonstrations, reflective of the counter Cultural Revolution and the anti-war movement, weakened overall support for higher education. Uncontrolled SUNY expansion was brought under control, but community colleges grew virtually unchecked because of their beneficial funding system and proximity to the student population. The four university centers had to be maintained at a high cost. Farmingdale's problems became more critical as it struggled to meet growing demands on its faculty, staff, and maintenance of its physical plant. Dr. Charles W. Laffin, president from 1961 to 1976, understood the obstacles Knapp experienced. Farmingdale faced challenges to expand its horizons. On numerous occasions Laffin expressed his frustration

FIGURE 5-6. These smiling freshmen are proudly sporting their "beanies." No longer in style today on college campuses, the beanie was acceptable headdress in the 1950s.

at Albany's failure to address Farmingdale's limited funding. His successor, Dr. Frank A. Cipriani, arrived on campus in 1964 and assumed several key administrative positions before he became president from 1978 to 2000. He also experienced firsthand the Farmingdale dilemma and believed that only through redirecting and re-engineering the campus mission would New York State recognize Farmingdale's rightful place in the SUNY system. Of course, creative leadership and political support were necessary. The challenge appeared extremely critical, and Cipriani

FIGURE 5-7. Students can be seen in various scenes demonstrating the many activities they performed, from gathering hay to outdoor class instruction to shoveling snow during the school year of 1949–1950.

later stated, "No President alone can create a plan and implement it without the strong support and participation of dedicated and talented people who view the institution as a vital and living organism." How the transition and transformation of the college was achieved under Cipriani will be chronicled.[22]

In February 1979, in an attempt to seek economic parity within the SUNY system, fifteen Farmingdale faculty and nonteaching professional employees filed a class action suit against the SUNY Board of Trustees, the state budget director, and the state attorney general. The suit, filed on behalf of the 1,500 employees of SUNY's six two-year agricultural and technical colleges, charged discrimination in pay, job tittles, and funding. The United University Professions (UUP), the statewide collective bargaining unit, financed all legal expenses up to $25,000, of which $15,000 was eventually spent for lawyers and court fees. In September 1982, New York State Supreme Court Judge John Burke handed down a decision ruling against the fifteen plaintiffs. The UUP filed an appeal. In January 1986, the State Supreme Court Appellate Division supported the lower court's decision by again ruling against the plaintiffs. The UUP decided not to appeal further and acknowledged that some positive points had been achieved: the UUP had the right to sue for its members; that there were inequities in SUNY; that these inequities were brought forward and publicized; that a disparity fund in the most recent contract was evidence of a minor correction to those inequities, as was the issue of classification for non-teaching professionals; and that the UUP leadership had addressed unique problems pertinent to the agricultural and technical colleges. Furthermore, in its decision, the Appellate Division Court also warned that more suits could arise to correct future discriminatory practices within SUNY.[23]

As this case was winding down, the Farmingdale Faculty Executive Committee (FEC), governing body of the college, passed a resolution stating its opposition to the new schedule of campus presidents' salaries in SUNY, because it was especially discriminatory to the two-year colleges. The resolution, adopted October 16, 1987, stated the new schedule "was predicated on inappropriate and unrealistic criteria, [and] dramatically perpetuates the discrimination that has long permeated the University since its inception." The FEC requested that the SUNY Board of Trustees establish "a plan to remove the existing unethical unit-based discrimination, disparities, and inequities." Traditionally, all Farmingdale's chief executives have been the lowest paid. With the class action suit and this resolution, SUNY was alerted to some of the most glaring issues that needed to be resolved. As Farmingdale was progressing to four-year institutional status, demanding fair treatment, and shedding its "vocational" image, New York State was put on notice to improve the professional status of its faculty and staff.[24]

FIGURE 5-8. This 1967 aerial view of the campus shows Roosevelt Hall (circular building) at top, with Laffin Hall at left, and Knapp Hall below. Nold Hall, Gleeson Hall, and Greenley Hall are not yet built. Thompson Hall (with cupola) is to the right of the Circle, and below it, slightly to left, are Hicks Hall and Cutler Hall. Whitman Hall is above Thompson Hall, with the Greenhouse below. Melville Road can be seen at left.

FIGURE 5-9. Students enjoy a game of ride the pony as springtime sets in, 1960. They are proudly wearing beanies. Hicks Hall is in background.

FIGURE 5-10. Two students chat on the steps of Thompson Hall as they wait to go to class. Students dressed more formally during the early 1960s.

SIX

The Industrial–Technical Division

> In the heart of the Village, directly across the street from St. Killian's Parochial School, was located the aged and weathered group of buildings which served the Institute as the first home for technical curriculum.[1]

Despite the agricultural foundation of the State Institute of Agriculture at Farmingdale dating back to its formal opening in 1916, it was clear that in the mid-twentieth century, future growth lay in industrial and technical education. The effects of World War II had a major impact throughout American society. The war left an altered economy that demanded a workforce whose education and training needed to be more technical in nature. As this trend influenced Farmingdale, the agriculture program slowly declined and was finally ended in 1987, while the scientific technologies assumed an ever-growing role. Once again, the school found itself having to adapt to changing conditions as part of an evolving economy. It was comforting to look back nostalgically to past achievements on which the agricultural school was founded, but educational offerings had to be broadened to succeed in a more complex and competitive economy. Thus, the institute embarked on an innovative program that produced one of the most comprehensive two-year colleges in the nation, eventually becoming a four-year institution that offered baccalaureate degrees in applied sciences and technologies.

An early definition of technical education referred to those educational and training programs relating to industry or applied science that prepared individuals for jobs and occupations requiring specific skills. The emergence of technical institutions in industrialized European nations during the nineteenth century greatly influenced the growth of such schools in the United States.

Originally, this type of education was not considered to be equivalent to college-level study, and was therefore offered in vocational or trade schools. The evolution of two-year technical institutes or colleges arose to offer short sequences of courses in preparing individuals for hands-on positions such as crafts, data processing, managerial, electronics, mechanical technologies, and instrumentation. In 1944, the Board of Regents announced its *Regents Plan for Postwar Education in the State of New York* in which vocational training would be assessed. The report concluded that the original school of agricultural education either be closed for lack of funding or be properly funded to accomplish an enlarged mission in technology. Moreover, as interest in technical education increased, a Division of Technical Education was added to the New York State Education Department in 1948. These developments encouraged the original six agricultural institutes officially to serve the needs of students in what was then considered vocational education. In this capacity, Farmingdale, which had already established an Industrial-Technical Division in 1946, served as a prime example in the transition of its original agricultural secondary school mission to become a two-year institute and eventually a four-year college of applied technology.[2]

The concept of technical education, as it was understood and implemented at Farmingdale during the 1940s, is described in an unsigned document in the College Archives. Initial models were established at Rensselaer Polytechnic Institute (1824), Massachusetts Institute of Technology (1865), and Pratt Institute (1887) in Brooklyn, all recognizing the growing need for trained industrial workers, and which guided leaders at Farmingdale and others in Albany who were responsible for public education. The curriculum pattern was based on an integrated sequence of courses of technological subject matter that included shop and laboratory experimental work. It differed from vocational trade education by its advanced level and nature of subject matter content and instruction, providing for specialization in occupations that required skills more demanding than purely manual labor. The curriculum continuity distinguished itself from the lecture-series and self-study pattern of the "Mechanics Institute" or the "Athenaeum" from which prominent technical institutes had evolved. Curriculum development focused on practical application of the then emerging engineering sciences and technologies. A vocational high school degree was no longer adequate. A two-year technical education, based on evolving technologies, was now essential to meet the growing needs of a booming post-World War II economy. Knapp, with support from his faculty and the College Council, spurred on by the New York State Board of Regents and Department of Education, seized every opportunity to have the institute advance itself into a more modern educational system.[3]

There were legislative attempts to establish technical institutes in New York State during the early part of the twentieth century. The agricultural schools had already assumed the name of "institutes" in the 1920s and 1930s as they began to add courses in technology. Canton adopted chemistry and electrical courses, as did Alfred in ceramics, Delhi in building construction, and Morrisville in horology and instrument repair. Farmingdale expanded its program in rural engineering and the agricultural sciences. Some of these were primarily trade school courses and not equal to standards of postsecondary education. But Farmingdale shared in this advanced trend when it became known as the State Institute of Applied Agriculture on Long Island (1920), State Institute of Applied Agriculture (1924), and State Institute of Agriculture (1939). In 1946, following World War II, Farmingdale took the title of Long Island Agricultural and Technical Institute when it added the Industrial-Technical Division.

Knapp endorsed these campus innovations because he was aware of the many changes brought on by World War II. He presented an important speech to the New York State Conference of Farm Organizations, a group that included representatives of nine statewide agencies concerned with the welfare of farming and country life, at Syracuse, on October 27, 1948. The speech demonstrated his commitment to the relatively new type of technical education, which Farmingdale now practiced. He distinguished technical education from vocational training and expressed his philosophy of education.

> Technical training includes not only a knowledge of current practices, but a sufficient understanding of the scientific principles underlying them so that the individual is not bound to a rule or a routine. Understanding the principles of plant and animal nutrition, of science and mechanics, as far as we know them at the present time, the individual is able to change and still hold his place as a useful member of society. Technical education gets away from the classroom, factory, assembly-line type of effort to learning through participation and application with personal attention, supervision and guidance at least three years beyond graduation. . . . Included also in a technical type of training, and I deem this more important with anything else, is an awareness of what is going on in the world at large, an acceptance of the democratic idea of responsibility and accountability.[4]

Nevertheless, Knapp repeatedly stated that agricultural education must remain an important part of Farmingdale's mission. As late as February 1956, he reported that of the 1,412 full-time students attending during the 1955–1956 school year, 436 students were enrolled in agriculture and horticulture. He commented, "There seems to be a curious notion in some quarters that because farms go out of commission in Nassau County, interest in and need for such training diminishes. On the contrary, they increase. Our applications at this date are ahead of any previous comparable period." He firmly believed that as the population increased, the percentage of high school students interested in agriculture, horticulture, and country living would also increase. Contributing to this belief was his proud conviction that "we have developed at Farmingdale a special know-how" in providing such education.[5]

Many studies report that conditions at mid-century pointed to the need for technical education because of the increasing growth of knowledge and importance of science and technology. For example, at the inception of the American economy, human physical force cleared the land and plowed the farms, but efficiency demanded that use of skilled workers with advanced training was necessary to achieve greater productivity. The wartime revolutionary effects accelerated this trend. One typical summary study concluded that technology must "maintain its contact with basic scientific and mathematical theory." Such thinking helped to influence the expansion of the institute's mission.[6]

Progress continued during the 1940s in the movement to establish technical educational institutions. A publication, *Bulletin 228*, of the U.S. Office of Education recommended the establishment of technical institutes throughout the nation. New York State confirmed this position in its 1944 *Regents Plan*. The New York State plan recommended the establishment of sixteen new institutes of applied arts and sciences, which, combined with the original six existing institutes, would total twenty-two. If the plan were put in place, two-year technical education would be within reach of 90 percent of New York State's population. Although not all the recommendations were adopted, mainly because of the establishment of the regular two-year community college system, the principle of expanding the higher educational system was accepted.

Following the release of the Regents' report, the Bureau of Industrial Technical-Education conducted a survey to determine technical occupations of New York State industries that would be served. The results of the survey, conducted by Dr. C. K. Beach, demonstrated the close relationship between technical education and economic growth. The state legislature appropriated money for another study to identify which specific curriculum programs were relevant to be funded. Recommendations followed. Dr. J. Cayce Morrison, assistant commissioner for research, directed the latter project. The bureau's report was again accepted and submitted to the legislature. Legislation subsequently emerged providing for the establishment of five experimental institutes of applied arts and sciences to be built in geographically accessible locations. Simultaneously, in March 1945, the Bureau of Industrial-Technical Education recommended, accompanied with appropriate plans, the construction of new buildings for technical education at the Farmingdale Institute. The program itself was to be implemented after World War II, and the legislature appropriated money the following month to start the program in temporary quarters. The State Budget Office delayed funds until March of 1946, when the school's mission would be officially altered to include the expanded program, along with another campus name change: Long Island Agricultural and Technical Institute.[7]

FIGURE 6-1. The old Nazareth Trade School in the Village of Farmingdale served as the main building for the new Industrial-Technical Division of the Agricultural Institute. It was known as the Conklin Street School. The main campus lacked facilities for the new program.

FIGURE 6-2. David Allee was appointed June 1, 1946 to head the Industrial-Technical Division. He hired faculty and guided the installation of equipment and renovation of the Nazareth Trade School building, which was a Catholic orphanage. He then moved the Division to Lupton Hall to its permanent home ten years later.

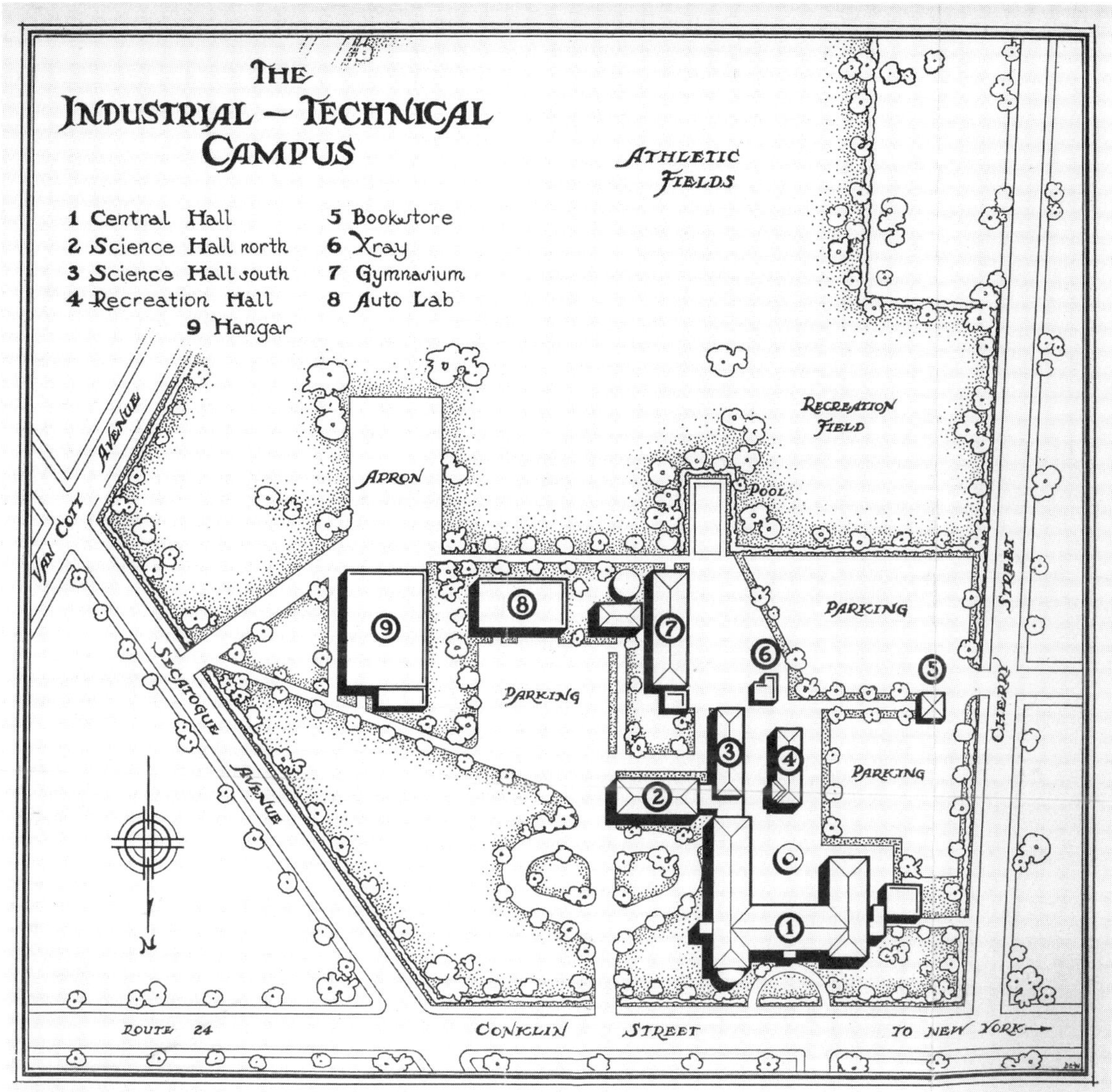

FIGURE 6-3. The Industrial-Technical Division was surrounded by Van Cott Avenue, Secatogue Avenue, Conklin Street, and Cherry Street, which also borders St. Killian's Catholic Church. Today the Weldon E. Howitt Junior High School occupies the location.

Much credit for the successful establishment of the new program goes to the pioneering efforts of David W. Allee, first director of industrial and technical education at Farmingdale. Knapp had put on a search for the most qualified individual for the new position. After a careful investigation, he notified Dr. Louis Wilson, state commissioner of education, that Allee be requested to go to Farmingdale for an interview concerning implementation of the proposed program. In his thorough and efficient manner, Knapp interviewed Allee and was so impressed that he immediately appointed him to guide the program. Allee accepted the appointment and assumed the position on June 1, 1946. He set about working to get the program off the ground. Allee's commitment in this endeavor soon inspired his new hires to devote their energies to such an innovative educational system. Through trial and error, and especially hard work, a successful program emerged.

Facilities on the main campus were inadequate for starting the Industrial-Technical Division. Following careful study, Knapp selected the buildings housed at the Nazareth Trade School in Farmingdale Village to serve as temporary quarters. The Catholic Dominican Sisters had opened the Nazareth Trade School in 1900 for underprivileged children, orphans, and wayward boys. The facility accommodated five-hundred needy boys who received instruction in baking, shoemaking, painting, printing, and other trades. Later, girls were added. In 1940, the Nazareth Trade School closed because attendance declined. During World War II, the United States took over the buildings and grounds for use as a training center for the Army Air Force. On June 18, 1946, the Farmingdale Union Free School District No. 22 purchased the property for $100,000. It was here, at the old Nazareth Trade School, 520 Conklin Street, Farmingdale that the Industrial-Technical Division opened in fall 1946.The institute paid a rental fee of $10,000 per year to the Farmingdale school district.[8]

Allee was a strong, knowledgeable administrator; the type of leader Knapp appreciated. He dedicated himself to establishing a successful program. The faculty Allee hired was also a motivated group of proud professionals who developed among themselves a close personal relationship. This faculty understood that they were embarking on an important mission and bound themselves to succeed. Allee reminisced briefly about those early years when he addressed a 1974 Rotary meeting in Farmingdale. "When I came to Farmingdale (checking road maps), there were 70–80 students in Agriculture and Horticulture. . . . The war years had placed the School of Agriculture in a difficult position for training in agriculture, and it had taken on many 'defense' training activities."[9] He quickly adapted himself to the challenges ahead, and he developed a rapport with his faculty who were expected to contribute extra time in making industrial and technical education successful. Farmingdale's new educational enterprise proved to be a pivotal event in its storied history.

David W. Allee was born in Minneapolis, Minnesota in 1909. He attended Union College, received a Civil Engineering Bachelor of Science degree and continued his education at New York University, Cornell, and Paul Smith's College. He gained engineering experience at General Electric, New York State Department of Public Works, American Locomotive Works, and City of Schenectady Engineering Department, engaging in surveying, engineering, and construction work in private practice. He served as acting director of Industrial Arts and Vocational Education for the Elmira Board of Education from January 1943 to October 1945. His next work experience as research associate in the State Education Department in Albany contributed to his preparation in advancing the technical education movement. While serving in this capacity, he assisted from October 1945 to May 1946 in setting standards for the institutes of applied arts and sciences. His specific responsibility was aimed at overseeing curriculum development in the major technical areas. He played a central role in the planning of state institutes, and he wrote a report to the governor's commission justifying funding for the program. Working under Dr. Lynn A. Emerson, Allee coordinated technical education programs and cooperated with Dr. Francis Schoemaker, who had created the general education curriculum. Allee described his early involvement in two-year technical education:

> In the fall of 1944 the New York State Educational Department started a study of the State's needs for post-secondary industrial-technical education. As the survey was being compiled, I was given a leave of absence from Elmira to work in Albany on the project of planning new schools. The plan had two objectives: 1. Expand the six State Institutes of Agriculture to include industrial or other technologies as needed. These schools had many unused facilities and could be adapted and expanded with a minimum time and money. 2. A system of two-year community colleges (Associate Degree) throughout the State to provide instruction as needed in the region. These could be financed one-third by New York State, one-third by local government (city, town, or county), and one-third by student tuition.[10]

Of immediate concern to campus officials was publicizing the new industrial-technical program. Notification was sent to all Long Island high schools from the middle of May to June 1946 to inform them of the new division, in addition to the regular agriculture and horticulture curricula. On July 1, the institute announced that new technical courses and curricula were available to high school graduates and veterans. The courses offered for the fall semester were: Building Construction; Highway and Bridge Construction; Aircraft Manufacture; Aircraft Maintenance and Operation; Electrical Equipment with Industrial Electronics; Industrial Chemistry; Refrigeration, Heating, and Air Conditioning; Industrial Instrumentation; Metal Products Designs, Production, and Inspection; Technical Dental Service; Food Administration; Power Laundry and Dry Cleaning; Advertising Art and Design; and Radio and Communications.[11]

When Allee assumed the position of director of Industrial-Technical Division on June 1, 1946, he surveyed the facilities of the institute and, with the aid of his just-hired faculty, began renovating the campus. He was aware of the problems that lay ahead, knowing that he had to create a completely new model institution. Theoretical plans had to be created, modified, and applied. Over the summer, the Nazareth Trade School was brought up to date with new classrooms, laboratories, offices, library, heating, lighting, plumbing, and all instructional equipment. Simultaneously, the Campus Village on the institute's grounds was being erected for war veteran students and their families. There was a flurry of activity on the main campus and the Conklin Street campus.

The Conklin Street campus consisted of nine buildings: Central Hall, Science Hall North, Science Hall South, a recreation hall, the bookstore, X-Ray, the gymnasium, the auto lab, and the hanger. There was also a recreation field. The gymnasium accommodated physical education classes, but was inadequate for major sporting events. The science buildings were situated at the far end of the courtyard and could be reached by passing through a tunnel. The rhythm of lectures and lab work pulsed through these buildings. The "hanger" served many functions, as an aircraft laboratory, auditorium, gymnasium, assembly hall, and was used by the Construction Technology Department. This structure was later transferred to the main campus when it became Allard Field House, and was used as a bookstore, gymnasium, and assembly hall.[12]

In the meantime, prospective students were contacted, interviewed, and accepted for enrollment. The curriculum that was adopted originated from research completed earlier in Albany. September 30, 1946 was identified as the target date for registration with classes to begin October 1. However, World War II had caused shortages of materials, forcing officials to delay the actual opening date to November 4. The program became operative with twenty-one full-time instructors, seven adjunct instructors, one counselor, two technical assistants, and an office staff of four.

The student body numbered 344, of which 100 were veterans. Allee commented, "Almost nothing was really finished when school started . . . I remember [staff members] Dave, Judy, and Janet the day before (Sunday) sweeping and mopping the dining hall, washing down tables, filling sugar bowls . . . getting ready for the first meal Monday morning."[13]

Knapp and Allee inaugurated the new division with a group of professionals who were willing and able to assume responsibilities beyond the classroom. The hours would be long and the work difficult. Referring to the first person he hired, Allee said, one of the "smartest things Halsey ever did was to call me to his office . . . and offer me the services of Alphonse Perry" as a technical assistant. Perry had graduated from the agricultural engineering program before the war. He moved up from technical assistant to professor over the next three decades and continued to participate in institute affairs after retiring. Another outstanding individual recommended by Knapp and who was hired as a technical assistant at the same time was Viggo Hansen. Two other instructors to arrive were Donald Waite of the Building and Construction Department and Sherman Mears of the Mechanical Department. These four men joined Allee in carrying out the plan for the new division. Waite led in the rehabilitation of the Nazareth Trade School buildings and rooms while Mears secured the necessary equipment. More instructors were hired by mid-summer and they quickly immersed themselves in the work to establish the Industrial-Technical Division.[14]

The State Education Department had recommended the original curriculum that was to be adopted. Allee was familiar with the course content because of his work in Albany. Most of the basic instructional and related equipment originated from war surplus material. Numerous trips were made to the Government Surplus Office on Park Avenue in New York City to examine the latest listings of available surplus equipment. Viggo Hansen took the lead to visit the Maspeth Navy Warehouse and the Brooklyn Navy Yard to search and secure equipment. Grumman Aircraft, Republic Aviation, and Liberty Aircraft also donated similar excess material. The Conklin Street School curricula reflected the imagination of those pioneer educators. Their experience matched the challenges in the early years of the establishment of the agriculture school that was chartered three decades earlier. Faculty could be seen providing individual attention to students.

The new Physics Department, chaired by Professor Carl Judd, conducted classes on the second floor of the main building. Most of the shops and laboratories were located in the basement. Army and Navy surplus equipment could be seen throughout. Van Cott Avenue, Secatogue Avenue, Conklin Street, and Cherry Street bound the downtown Industrial-Technical Division.

FIGURE 6-4. Director Knapp, not seen, is addressing an assembly at the Conklin Street School, 1948. Immediately following World War II the majority of students were veterans pursuing an education under the G.I. Bill of Rights.

FIGURE 6-5. The original faculty of the Conklin Street School gathered for a group picture in 1947. Known as the 520 Club, named for the School's address, they are from top row left: Raynor Wallace, C. Dick Thomson, Al Perry, Viggo Hansen; second row: James Irwin, George Drennan, David Allee, Carl Judd, William Haydu, Bert Willenbrock, Ray Bowman; front row: Don Waite, Jack Cogan, Al Hraba, Walter Truex, Ed Roberts.

As a young man from Huntington, Anthony Mastroianni began a lifelong association with Farmingdale when he enrolled at the new campus in September 1948, the same year SUNY was chartered. Mastroianni graduated two years later from the building construction program, which was renamed civil engineering technology. The class comprised a combination of returning World War II veterans and recent high school graduates. He had little contact with the main campus and Knapp because his education was centered at the Conklin Street Industrial-Technical Division under the leadership of Allee. He applied his skills in the U.S. Navy's Construction Battalion, better known as the SeaBees. After his 1950 graduation from Farmingdale, Mastroianni was employed as a civil engineer and superintendent of all types of construction. He received a master's degree from C.W. Post University, and later retired as the Suffolk County public administrator.[15]

Mastroianni joined the Alumni Association and became an active lifelong member. In July 1967, Gov. Nelson A. Rockefeller appointed him to the Farmingdale College Council. He was reappointed by Gov. Malcolm Wilson in 1984, and by Gov. Mario Cuomo in 1992. He served as council chairman and vice chairman. He retired from the council in 2000 after thirty-three years of continuous service, believed to be the longest tenure of any SUNY College Council member. He has received many awards for his contributions to the college, including:

1974 SUNY Farmingdale Alumnus of the Year
1979 SUNY Council Members Founders Award
1980 SUNY Farmingdale Evening College Recognition Award
1996 SUNY Farmingdale Rams Horn Award
1999 SUNY President's Award for More Than Fifty Years of Continuous Service to SUNY

Mastroianni played an important leadership role as a member of the College Council during the transformative presidential administrations of Charles W. Laffin Jr. and Frank A. Cipriani.

The Farmingdale electrical technology (ET) curriculum typified the development of practical educational innovation. The 1945 State Education Department Survey of Industrial and Technical Education emphasized the need for trained workers in specific geographical locations. The ET program met that need on Long Island. Critical employment opportunities grew in the field of electrical equipment, radio communication, and precision instrument manufacturing. The two options in electrical equipment and radio communications were included in the initial offerings. Robert T. Lincoln and Frank Evans were the first two instructors in this department. An industrial instrumentation program, originally planned for the Mechanical Department under Sherman Mears, began in 1947. Instructor James Irwin headed the Industrial Instrumentation Department in March 1948. The change established the concentration of options within the ET Department. Lincoln chaired the department and provided the necessary guidance. Other faculty members who brought expertise and varied backgrounds were Everett Bach, Gordon Gifford, Alex Levey, Norman Lurch, and Everett Rowley. An advisory council of community leaders was selected from industry and labor to assist the faculty to maintain high standards in the program.

The institute's radio station, WATI, began as an extracurricular activity, a result of the initiative of freshman student Richard Lorenz in ET who, with the help of communications instructor Alex Levey, requested a modest sum of $100 for the purchase of equipment to start the project. The request was granted in September 1953. Other students and faculty donated more equipment. Lorenz, Levey, Joseph Glaab, and several more students, put together the basic transmitter necessary to broadcast over the main campus. Tests were successful. Additional contributions of material, money, and labor made it possible to set up a radio station in the basement of Knapp Hall. Under faculty supervision, students organized the entire project. WATI began operations in February 1954, and live coverage of the Country Life Open House took place. The station broadcast the schedule of events with remote amplifiers.

Casimir Rakowki, Society of Mechanical Engineers, joined the faculty in 1947 as an instructor in machine shop and mechanical design. His considerable expertise contributed to the technical division's high standards. His career at Farmingdale was so outstanding that he was awarded titles of Excellence in Teaching and Distinguished Service Professor by SUNY. Admired by students and faculty, he served as a consultant at national and international levels. He was self-taught, an innovator in the field of automated machine technology, and a consultant to corporations in providing the skills needed to be competitive. He considered Allee "a pioneer who had to put together a unique group of faculty who could do what they said they could do." It was a "hands-on" faculty. Their knowledge was applied in creating laboratories, putting together machinery, and modifying courses to meet curriculum needs. They established rapport with their students, working closely with them and mentoring them. In the early stages of the technical division, Rakowski remembered that it "was difficult to get industry to accept our students because we were known as a trade school." He remembered when Farmingdale was finally recognized as a

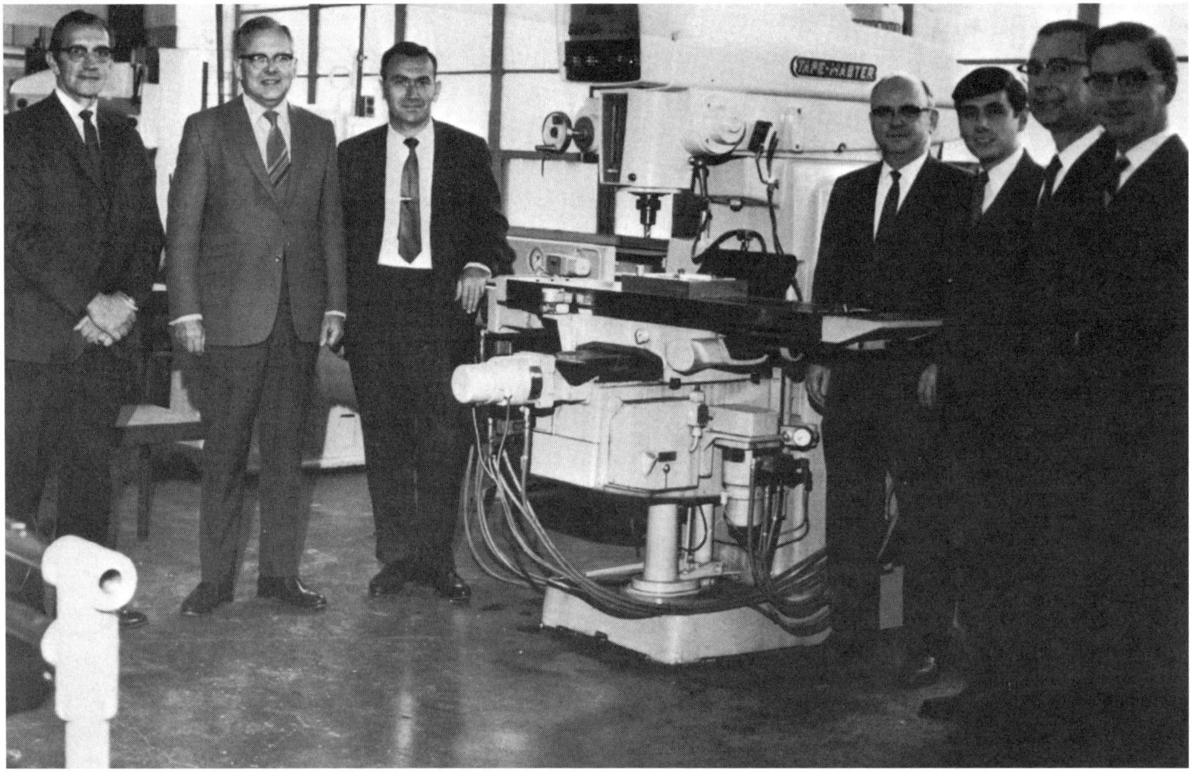

FIGURE 6-6. A 1960s photo of pioneering professors who taught in the Technical Division when it moved from the Conklin Street School to Lupton Hall on the main campus. Left to right: Casimir Rakowski, Frank Pyne, Ed Mayer, Bob Keegan, Tom Campbell, William Tobin, Robert Williams.

quality technical institute in the past decade because "there [were] over 20 jobs available for every Farmingdale graduate in Electrical Technology and Mechanical Technology, and 75 percent of our graduates are supervisors in the field. One of our graduates directs a 70 million dollar plant on Long Island."[16]

In the early 1960s, Rakowski combined his creative efforts with Professor Thomas Campbell of the Mechanical Technology Department to launch a pioneering program by installing comput-

FIGURE 6-7. Faculty and friends leave Lupton Hall after the dedication ceremony naming the "David W. Allee Wing" of the Technical Center in Lupton Hall, June 1994. Lupton Hall was named after former College Council member John M. Lupton of Mattituck.

ers to instruct students in designing and manufacturing techniques specifically for industrial use. Computer-aided design and computer-assisted manufacturing (CAD/CAM) systems applied small and large computers that advanced the engineering and manufacturing world with the means of communicating with mathematics, graphics, science, and other engineering concepts. The new model, labeled *Unigraphics* and implemented at Farmingdale under Project Directors Campbell and Rakowski, was actually three systems in one. Campbell explained:

It is a Computer-Aided Design tool for designers, engineers, draftsmen, detailers, or others interested in a cost effective transition from beginning through to finished product. It is an Automatic Drafting system for anyone producing high-quality finished engineering drawings, and it is a Computer-Aided Manufacturing system for manufacturing managers looking for the most advanced methods of producing punch paper tape for automotive machine tool application.

The Unigraphics system accommodated four design stations, each operating independently of each other and run with "its companion product, Uniapt, which means utility language for a numerical control part programming." Interactive computer graphics lessened production time and increased productivity at lower cost throughout the design-manufacturing cycle. Professor Rakowski later wrote to Gov. Hugh Carey (1975–1982) explaining the Farmingdale program that stressed the interrelation of economic growth and educational development. Carey responded:

The programs at the State University Agricultural and Technical College have played a significant role in preparing Long Island firms to keep pace with rapidly changing requirements in their fields of specialization. I am taking the liberty of sharing your letter with State University Chancellor Ernest L. Boyer, and Commerce Commissioner John Dyson, so they will be aware of your thoughts on this important subject.

Today, the Mechanical Engineering Department offers a bachelor of science degree, an associates in applied science, and a certificate in manufacturing methods and numerical controls.[17]

Having two campuses, one in downtown Farmingdale and the original site at Melville and Broad Hollow Roads, posed logistical problems for some faculty. Professor Anne Senyk, who was hired in 1947, related how she and professors Ronald Dougher and Raynor Wallace of the General Education Division had to meet their classes on time. After teaching classes on the main campus from 8:00 to 8:50 a. m. they had to "fly" to the Conklin Street campus to meet their 9:00 a. m. classes. Of course, traffic in those years was much lighter than it is today, making it possible for them to meet their teaching commitment without a minute to spare.[18]

Raynor Wallace (1917–2008) joined the Farmingdale faculty in 1946 as an instructor of English and humanities, advancing to the rank of professor. During his forty-two-year tenure at Farmingdale he was English Department chairman, faculty senator, and served on numerous committees. He remembered his early teaching experience at the new Industrial-Technical Division. "Until 1952, I used to ride my bicycle back and forth from the main campus to Conklin Street. . . . When I first arrived on campus, the college was undergoing a major transition." He recalled new programs such as "dental hygiene, the technologies, and English" being added. The college honored him with the initiation of the Raynor Wallace Poetry Award. Wallace was a graduate of Dickinson College (BA) and Columbia University (MA).[19]

One program housed at the Conklin Street School was the Dental Hygiene Department. The College Archives contain an unsigned chronicle describing the Dental Hygiene Department, one of the most successful programs of the new technical division. At the time when legislation was passed to establish institutes, the New York State Dental Society urged the State Education Department to inaugurate a dental hygiene curriculum. The Dental Society had recommended the program be for one year because of the immediate need for trained personnel in the field. Director Allee insisted on a more comprehensive program to be extended for a two-year duration, and his recommendation was implemented. The program was started in November 1946; its purpose was to train individuals as dental hygienists, chair assistants, and radiographers to serve in dentists' offices, school clinics, and other institutions. Open to high school graduates, the curriculum included gross anatomy, elementary physiology, histology, biochemistry, pathology, bacteriology, pharmacology, community dentistry, child psychology, chair and laboratory assisting, and dental anatomy, radiology, hygiene, and prophylaxis. This rigorous course of study was enriched with courses in general education to prepare students for informed citizenship.

The first dental hygiene class was inaugurated under the supervision of Dr. John Oppil McCall, former director of the School of Dental Hygiene at the Guggenheim Clinic, New York City. Dr. Vernon Bodecker, a leader in dental hygiene education and a medical writer, helped organize the program and remained on staff until his retirement in 1949. The first instructor to serve on the staff was Evelyn Shay, a graduate of the Columbia University School of Dental Hygiene. Upon the resignation of Dr. McCall, Dr. Josephine Luhan became head of the department. The institute secured war surplus dental chairs and other equipment from the U.S. War Assets Administration. The first class was restricted to eight women because of the lack of dormitory space. Clinic space was also limited at the Conklin Street campus, and Hicksville High School allowed the Farmingdale students to do oral hygiene work there. Similar arrangements were made with Grumman Aircraft employees to provide adult clinical practice for the students.

Dental health teacher training also was offered as an elective, and students who completed the course received a provisional teaching certificate. In the beginning, a darkroom, x-ray machine, and laboratory comprised the department's facilities. By 1952, a fully equipped clinic was in place. Special graduation ceremonies for seven students were held in June 1948 because of a conflict with the State Board examinations. Five graduates secured positions in private practices and two in public school systems. The second group of graduates held capping exercises in Knapp Hall in June 1949. Two days later, regular commencement exercises were held combining agriculture, horticulture, and Industrial-Technical Division students. The New York State Dental Society established a Memorial Medal in 1949.

In 1954, the Council on Education of the American Dental Association presented full accreditation of the program at Farmingdale, with special commendation for its unique clinic achievements. Such recognition extended job opportunities to the graduates and made them eligible for licensing examinations in all states. A special feature of the dental hygiene program since its inception has been the regularly scheduled clinical practice. These clinics offered free full prophylaxis for faculty, staff, and students, and to the community for a nominal fee. Clinical work afforded dental hygienists practical experience in chair assisting, sterilization, and x-ray. The pioneering achievements of the program contributed to the success of the Industrial-Technical Division. Today, the Dental Hygiene Department is one of the strongest at Farmingdale and offers an associates of science and a bachelor's of science. It is "tailored to provide comprehensive upper-level studies that will prepare dental hygienists to adapt to the emerging new roles of oral healthcare."[20]

The 1946 *Bulletin* listed programs in aircraft manufacture and aircraft maintenance. Five years later, aircraft operations was added to supply trained personnel in an industry experiencing constant changes in commercial air transportation, airport operations, and military aviation. The Civil Aeronautics Administration certified this new aircraft operations program for preparing private and commercial pilots. Professors William J. George and Albert Hraba guided the program. Today the college's Aviation Department offers bachelors degrees in both aeronautical science/professional pilot and aviation administration. It is a leading aviation program in the Long Island region and the only professional pilot program in the SUNY system.

The Industrial-Technical Division of the Long Island Agricultural and Technical Institute graduated its first formal class on a Monday morning on June 28, 1948. Among the eleven major curricula, 212 young men and women received diplomas from Knapp. (With the addition of 157 students graduating from the main campus in traditional programs, the total number in the Class of 1948 came to 369.) Allee introduced the seventeen students who graduated with honors. Of these honor students, ten came from Nassau County, four from Suffolk County, and three from

Brooklyn: Two were women. Edmund R. Lupton, chairman of the institute's council, presided at the ceremonies and the Rev. W. R. Hampshire of Farmingdale's St. Thomas' Episcopal Church gave the invocation. Dr. Lawrence L. Jarvie, head of the Agricultural and Technical Institutes, New York State Education Department, presented the keynote address, emphasizing the pioneering work of the Institute. Dr. Jarvie pointed out students' obligation to use the free education they received because "ultimately the investment must pay off in the form of active and good citizens." The formal ceremonies ended with selections from the institute's band and chorus under the direction of George Hutchison. A reception, hosted by the ladies of the faculty and staff, was held in Knapp Hall for graduates and guests.[21]

In researching the documents in the Farmingdale State College Archives, the following essay was found that depicts the deep sentimental attachment its author, English Professor Bernard Palmer, expressed toward the downtown campus. It is titled, "The Conklin Street Story."

> In the heart of the village, directly across the street from St. Killian's Parochial School, was located the aged and weathered group of buildings, which served the Institute as the first home for technical curriculums. Time and weather had not succeeded in bestowing the respectful patina of age upon these plain, red-brick buildings. The installation in 1953 of parking meters out front on Conklin Street emphasized the urban nature of this temporary college campus. The modest main entrance never did properly announce the complex of buildings and activities, which lay beyond the door. The squared-off courtyard, replete with fire escapes protruding from the building's sides, was a popular student meeting place, particularly during Spring and Fall quarters. The student lounge building and student parking area, the latter dubbed "Anzio Beachhead" by GI students, completed the main group picture.

Palmer continued with this image of the original Industrial-Technical Division campus's physical setting:

> The four-storied main building was an impressive sight, extending over eleven acres in downtown Farmingdale. Both the design and construction of the building reflected the virtues, attitudes and short-comings of the turn of the 20th century. So many modifications had been visited upon this one-time Catholic orphanage that it was difficult to visualize

> the original interior design of the structure. Quite properly, the first floor was given over to Administrative offices for the Technical Division and the Evening School, a Cafeteria, and faculty offices and classrooms. The sparseness of the office furnishings and the lack of decoration in the classrooms attested to the temporary feeling which was characteristic of our ten-year tenure in the building.

The heart-warming description of the main building continued:

> When the Institute expanded its facilities in 1946, the building was an obvious and necessary makeshift home for the new curriculums. The story of the conversion of this building is a tale of near-heroic proportions. The classrooms bear mute, scarred witness to the passage of many more students than it was ever dreamed would be accommodated in those temporary quarters. The high ceilings of two generations ago, dark paneled walls—and patched, post-war wallboard were a common mixture in the offices and classrooms. The second floor repeated this pattern—offices, classrooms, and a Library, Auditorium and men's dormitory section. Again the same basic pattern on the third floor. Time was when the fourth floor was a beehive of student activity, for our utilization of the old building would have been an efficiency expert's delight.[22]

The thirty-second annual Country Life Open House Program was held on both campuses February 22–24, 1951, and more than one-hundred demonstrations and exhibits were presented. The exhibits at the Conklin Street School included student projects, illustrating various fields of industrial-technical progress. The Building Construction Exhibit, designed and built by students, featured drafting techniques, blueprint processing, and designs and drawings of a colorful scheme of model homes. Other successful exhibits included advertising art displays; mechanical technology and industrial chemistry laboratories and shops in operation; ET transformer and generator operations; student-built radio and television transmitters and receivers. Students displayed a number of industrial measuring and controlling instruments used for automatic controls on industrial machinery. Faculty joined students to demonstrate and illustrate the educational benefits of this popular program. Knapp and Allee continued to believe that opening the institute to the public gained much public support for a taxpayer institution. Also, the visits by thousands of children, parents, and teachers enhanced its image. As a part of the newly formed SUNY system in 1948, Farmingdale was striving to achieve its own identity and establish a viable role in higher education.[23]

FIGURE 6-8. Members of the Aircraft Operations Department gather for a meeting in 1970. Their education and experience combined to produce students who served as dispatchers, airport managers, and related positions in the growing aerospace industry. Chairman Lou Howard is at center, fourth from left.

On the original main campus, the new home for the Industrial-Technical Division was named for John M. Lupton of Mattituck, a member of the New York State Assembly (1906–1910). His nephew was Edmund R. Lupton of Riverhead, a member of the New York State Assembly (1937–1956). Both Luptons served on the College Council. After consulting with his staff, Knapp agreed to hold the dedication ceremonies on February 21, 1953. Lupton Hall opened later in the fall term. Knapp identified the new building as the most expensive and advanced on campus.

The Conklin Street School closed gradually. Allee moved his office to the main campus in 1953. The Advertising Art and Design, Dental Hygiene, and Business departments remained downtown, while the other departments began to relocate. The institute had originally leased the Conklin Street School land and buildings for $10,000 per year from the Farmingdale Union Free School District No. 22 for ten years, with an option for another year, which it took to 1957.[24]

FIGURE 6-9. A 1950s Homecoming exhibit highlights this event. Clabisforum was an underground "mod secret society" according to the description found on the back of this archival photograph.

Allee held the position of acting director of the institute from 1960 to 1961. Upon his retirement, he helped develop several schools in Africa and the Far East. He was chief of technical training for the United Nations. He was president of the Farmingdale Rotary Club and was named a Paul Harris Fellow from this service organization. He died in 1985. Two years later, eleven members of the Class of 1948 participated in a special program focusing on his career and the birth of technical education at Farmingdale. Former dean, Bert Willenbrock and President Frank Cipriani guided alumni, faculty, administrators, and former professors in reviewing the historic period of 1946 to 1961. In attendance were Allee's wife and son. In June 1994, the College Council and faculty further recognized Allee's contributions by naming a wing in the Lupton Hall

Figure 6-10. Students are participating in a tug of war during a campus competition. Streamers decorate the ceiling and hay can be seen on the floor.

Technology Center after him. During the first ten years of his leadership at the Conklin Street School, 2,136 students graduated from the Industrial-Technical Division.[25]

Today, as one passes along Van Cott Avenue, Secotogue Avenue, Conklin Street, and Cherry Street, a grove of trees, a parking lot, and the Weldon E. Howitt Junior High School can be seen. The original Industrial-Technical facility no longer stands, but it represented an important part of the history of Farmingdale State College. A new dawn lay ahead.

SEVEN

The Charles W. Laffin Jr. Years, 1961–1976

> Charles W. Laffin Jr. was caught between the history and traditions of the institution and the changing laws and culture in Higher Education. Laffin worked hard to make clear to everyone that Farmingdale's tradition was not something locked in the past but that the institution's history was one of anticipated change.[1]

The retirement of Director Halsey B. Knapp on June 30, 1956 was a significant event in the history of Farmingdale State College because of the dominant role he played in saving and guiding the institution during his long tenure. For thirty-three years his steadfast leadership overcame seemingly impossible obstacles, especially following the controversial resignation of Director Albert A. Johnson, and when Gov. Alfred E. Smith attempted to close the school. The Great Depression forced Knapp to implement an educational system with limited resources, a situation that coincided with the general economic situation. The World War II era saw low enrollments, forcing him to use campus facilities efficiently for hosting special programs and for making extraordinary appeals to aid the war effort. He recognized the need for innovation by establishing an Industrial-Technical division that set the institute on a new path of educational growth. His faculty demonstrated an unequalled work ethic in the face of his strong control of campus affairs. Knapp established a warm relationship with students and reassured them of a bright future because, as he often asserted, they were privileged to receive a tax-supported Farmingdale education. He extended the campus to the community. Yet an underlying current of discontent and frustration existed among the faculty who lacked a professional schedule, earned low pay, and lacked job security. His administrative assistants conformed to his policies, fearing to challenge him despite the eruption of a serious labor dispute that arose.

Few educational leaders were more closely associated with an institution of higher learning than Knapp was with Farmingdale. In his farewell address at the Country Life Open House Program, on February 23, 1956, he recognized and accepted the dramatic changes that had occurred during his years as director. He remembered when "violets grew in profusion on Hempstead Plains." He combined realism with nostalgia when he quoted Daniel Webster, "The same sky indeed lies above our heads. The same ocean rolls beneath your feet but all else, how changed!" He realized that it was time for him to move on. Laying aside these sentiments, who would follow in Knapp's footsteps to guide the Institute in the future?

The institute conducted a nationwide search for a new director. The most impressive candidate for the position was William A. Medesy (1909–2000), former dean of the University of New Hampshire. Born in Cleveland, Ohio, he graduated with a bachelor of science degree from Purdue University (1931); received master's of forestry degree from Yale University (1933); and a master's and an EdD degree from Columbia University in 1950 and 1952, respectively. He worked in the United Forestry Service from 1933 to 1940 and was appointed to the faculty of the College of Forestry at the University of New Hampshire in 1940. During World War II, he earned the rank of captain in the army and served as a field artillery officer in the campaigns of North Africa and Europe. He was awarded the Bronze Star and Purple Heart.[2]

Medesy's impeccable credentials earned him the Farmingdale directorship. He was respected for his handling of an incident at the University of New Hampshire when he was assistant dean of students. In 1946, a local campus fraternity refused to pledge a Jewish student. Medesy took immediate action by advising the Greek letter fraternity to comply with the decision of the fraternity's national office to accept the Jewish student. In addressing the issue ten years later, in April 1956, Medesy pointed out that progress had been made at the University of New Hampshire in eliminating discriminatory practices, and the fight for equality of opportunity for all would continue. Throughout his career, he insisted that students and colleagues pursue ethical behavior in their personal and professional relations, a tolerant attitude that endeared him to Farmingdale. Medesy earned a distinguished record as an educator and was promoted to the positions of dean of men and administrative assistant for the graduate school at the University of New Hampshire.[3]

Medesy assumed the directorship at the institute in July 1956, the month following Knapp's retirement. He was officially installed as director on May 10, 1957 at the campus auditorium-gymnasium. John Cranford Adams, president of Hofstra College, gave the major address. Medesy's tenure as director (1956–1960) saw the continuation of the programs created by Knapp and Allee;

he served as a caretaker of the institute, which was on the brink of another major transformation. He presided over the important May 30, 1959 dedication ceremony of Hicks Hall, in memory of Henry Hicks (1870–1954), who was a "Humanitarian, Horticulturist, Friend and Benefactor of the Institute." On the same day, Horton Hall was dedicated in memory of Daniel Hart Horton, head of the Department of Poultry Husbandry from 1924 to 1956, "who will long be remembered by his students and his fellows as Teacher, Counselor and Friend."[4]

Although Medesy continued the policies of the previous administration, and as the Farmingdale Institute and SUNY expanded, there were stirrings among the faculty of a desire to advance their professional status. Apparently, with Knapp gone, faculty members felt less restrained to articulate their demands. Thus, they presented an eight-page petition to Medesy, Dr. Lawrence L. Jarvie, executive dean for the institutes and the community colleges, and the SUNY Board of Trustees. The petition was titled, "To Approve A Ten-Month Year for the Academic Faculty at the Farmingdale Institute and to Take Whatever Action May Be Necessary to Obtain Approval from Other Governmental Authorities as May Be Necessary." A summary of reasons was provided to support the request:

1. An eleven-month work year for the faculty is not necessary for carrying out the institute's program and accomplishing its objectives.
2. The eleven-month year makes it difficult to recruit and retain good faculty.
3. The positions of many career public school teachers on Long Island have certain advantages over the median position at the Farmingdale institute.
4. The eleven-month arrangement contains inherent injustices that result in low faculty morale.
5. Most units of SUNY are officially on a ten-month year.
6. The subjecting of a professional group to a nonprofessional work schedule both impedes the work progress and results in lower faculty morale.

Supporting evidence was spelled out in detail in the petition. For example, during two consecutive years under Medesy's leadership, the institute witnessed the resignation of twenty-one faculty members. Six resigned to teach high school, three to teach grade schoolt, three to teach college, seven to work in industry, one to work in extension services, and one to join the military. Specific summary reasons were given:

- Low salaries with no incremental schedule.
- The liberal arts colleges were on a ten-month schedule
- Professional growth was hindered.
- The schedule inhibited recruiting quality faculty and students.

The petition contained no signatures, nor were specific names ever revealed. No date was listed, but it occurred within Medesy's four-year tenure. The recipients of the petition took no action—no response was made. Professional scheduling remained the same. However, as the campus situation worsened and conditions in society changed, it was a factor in influencing the policies of Laffin when he assumed the presidency in 1961.[5]

Medesy resigned as director at Farmingdale in 1960 to pursue his career in the western part of the United States. He was appointed president of Mesa College, in Colorado, where he served from 1963 to1971. He retired from college administration in 1971 and died in 2000. His career was well respected in Colorado that he was honored posthumously with a citation read into the Congressional Record.[6]

With the resignation of Medesy, Allee, head of the Industrial-Technical Division, filled in as acting director from 1960 to 1961 until a permanent replacement could be appointed. Another search ensued, leading to the selection of Laffin, who would serve as president from 1961 to 1976. Laffin's presidency presaged a new era for the institute. Up to this time, every previous campus chief had held the title of "director," but Laffin set a precedent by assuming the new title of "president." Use of this title became permanent for all who followed. Other significant precedents emerged under his leadership.

Laffin was born in Jamaica, New York. During World War II he served in the military in North Africa and Sicily, and was discharged in 1945 with the title of captain. He first served in the Cavalry and his unit was transferred to the Army Air Corps' Provost Marshal Unit in Europe. He received the Silver Star. During the Korean War (1950–1953) he was called back to active duty. Upon returning to civilian life he received a bachelor's degree from Colgate College, a master's degree from Syracuse University, and a doctorate in education from New York University in 1959. He was a pioneer in the community college movement. Laffin began his professional career in higher education in 1946 at New York City Community College where he served as executive dean and vice president. From 1954 to 1964 he was visiting professor at New York University School of Education conducting courses related to community college and technical institute subjects. He established a reputation as an expert at the two-year college level, serving as a consultant to newly planned community colleges in Pennsylvania, New Jersey, and New York. This experience earned him a 1959 appointment to organize the newly created Nassau Community College in Garden City as a part of SUNY, to become its first vice president before moving to the nearby Farmingdale campus as president two years later in April 1961.[7]

FIGURE 7-1. Former Director Halsey B. Knapp, right, returned to the campus in 1970 to visit with President Charles W. Laffin, Jr. They are examining the new SUNY Master Plan proposals that would affect the College.

Laffin's immediate assessment of the institute recognized the need to highlight the profile of the institute within the Long Island region and the SUNY system. Through internal reforms, he guided the school to a higher collegiate standard. The name he had inherited, SUNY Long Island Agricultural and Technical Institute at Farmingdale, was replaced in 1966 with the new title of Agricultural and Technical College at Farmingdale. Under his leadership Farmingdale advanced from an agricultural-technical institute with programs that emphasized hands-on education to a higher status career-oriented institution of higher learning, boasting a tradition of small classes conducted by a caring faculty. Laffin helped to introduce distinct curricula that included every facet of modern technology. He helped to establish the Educational Opportunity Center for disadvantaged, minority, and nontraditional students. By 1975, the college offered full- and part-time programs in agricultural and engineering technologies, human services, business, arts, and sciences. He hired a distinguished faculty with advanced degrees, publications, and teaching experience, putting them on a professional schedule that replaced the Monday to Friday, 8 a. m. to 5 p. m. and Saturday morning schedule. He presided over a period of enormous growth. The 1961 total enrollment of 1,676 students increased a decade later to 6,800 full-time students and 7,700 evening and part-time students. This increase was part of a larger collegiate trend across the nation. Under Laffin's leadership, Farmingdale organized the college into thirty-four two-year programs leading to associates degrees in applied science, science, and arts. The campus boasted gardens, cultivated farmland, and a farm animal complex with cows, chickens, and pigs; more than thirty thousand school children and others visited these facilities each year. A newspaper article, "The Farm Is A Classroom," highlighted the unique work–study program of the three-hundred agricultural students whose farm bounty, produced on 150 acres, was sold. But the college also had computers, general aviation training (GAT) link simulators to prepare students in the operation of aircraft and flight procedures, a fleet of airplanes at Republic Airport for training pilots, and other sophisticated programs. The aerospace technology curriculum was praised by *The New York Sunday News* as the only program of its kind in the northeast. The campus possessed the first Urban Center as a part of the equal access program, administered by an integral unit of SUNY, providing resident facilities for 1,200 full-time students and an additional 1,500 part-time students. It was the only institution of its kind in the metropolitan area to offer such an educational program.[8]

Laffin recognized the changing demographics on Long Island. Electronics, aerospace, and health care industries were growing and jobs needed to be filled. Farmingdale had achieved success in broadening its original mission of training modern scientific farmers. But it now was assuming a leadership position in preparing young men and women for positions in complex, technically oriented industries. "The legislature never heard of a community college back in 1912 when they first established this campus, but they had the concept," said Laffin.[9]

Laffin's official presidential installation took place May 11, 1962. Locke James, campus vice president, had sent a letter to Albert A. Johnson, the first director of the school, inviting him to attend the ceremony. Johnson sent regrets, April 6, 1962 and reminisced about his organizing efforts in establishing the agricultural school five decades previously. He said most people were no longer interested in the type of education that Farmingdale originally offered, and he had heard little about its growth, despite the fact that the college had increased enrollment and was evolving to a new level. Johnson stated that his post-Farmingdale career involved considerable travel, especially to foreign countries, citing more than thirteen trips to countries in Asia, Europe, and North Africa. He visited cities in the Near East to make economic surveys, traveling alone by air. "I wish it were possible for me to attend the inauguration of your new President, Charles W. Laffin, Jr. but my present duties make it impossible at this time of year." He appreciated the invitation. The two-page letter was on official stationery of his consulting company with the heading, "The A. A. Johnson Syndicate (Home Office, Boston, Massachusetts), A. A. Johnson, Managing Director."[10]

In this period of transition, Laffin put together a group of talented individuals to help him guide the institution. He accomplished this with fifteen administrators who were committed to implementing newly established programs. They were John M. Purcell, vice president; Frank A. Cipriani, vice president of administration; Noel Palmer, vice president of the Urban Center; B. D. Willenbrock, vice president of student affairs; James F. Nihan, vice president of continuing education; Pearl Brod, dean of students; Eugene O'Neill, dean of instruction; Joseph Monaco, associate vice president of administration; Arthur H. Maybin, director of campus planning; George Roukis, assistant to the president; Frank Elkins, director of public relations; Michael Murray, director of personnel services; Frederick J. Walsh, associate dean of instruction; William Byrne, director of the Computer Center; and Raymond Rodriguez, assistant dean of special services. The president insisted that his administrative team work together in realizing the promises of the civil rights and feminist movements.[11]

The United States' escalation of the war in Vietnam made it even more difficult to administer campus affairs because of student demonstrations and strikes caused by the antiwar movement in the late 1960s into the 1970s. Student activists throughout the nation challenged traditional authority and established institutions. Drug use compounded social problems. Farmingdale was not entirely immune to these events. Laffin became increasingly sensitive to the hostility of young people to the Vietnam War and the established social order. His military service made him even more aware of the reality of war at a time when his oldest son was serving in Vietnam. With little guidance from Albany, he had to balance freedom of expression with the need to maintain campus security. He managed the campus student protests with a firm but compassionate policy that permitted the college to continue its educational mandate. His administration and faculty supported his leadership. Cipriani believed some logistical changes could limit chaos by shifting events from the central part of the campus to the periphery. He was instrumental in moving the administration office from Thompson to Whitman Hall and then to the newly constructed administration building, eventually named Laffin Hall, to counter student vandalism, student protests, and civil disobedience. Such action led to improvements of campus security.[12]

Laffin closely monitored civil rights events at the national level to gauge the impact on the Farmingdale campus. When James H. Meredith, a black air force veteran, was refused admission to the University of Mississippi, the U.S. Supreme Court sustained a lower court order to have the university accept him for the 1962 fall term. Gov, Ross Barnett defied the court order, whereupon President John F. Kennedy sent federal troops, marshals, and federalized national guardsmen to enforce Meredith's enrollment at the Oxford campus. The rioting that developed was suppressed by President Kennedy's action, but two people were killed and seventy wounded. Laffin expressed his concerns in an October 1962 message to graduates of the 1963 class.

> It is difficult to imagine tear gas, shotguns and steel helmets ever casting their shadows here, . . . That this has happened on any American university is a sorry affair. But our nation, to remain free and strong, must be under a government of laws, not men. May you help make our world of the future a place like your College—peaceful in the sunlight without walls or barriers for those who seek education here.[13]

Farmingdale experienced less unrest than did other campuses across the country. The students came mostly from working-class families who appreciated a public education. The faculty was also more moderate and much less elitist. When Columbia University student militant leader Mark Rudd, of the Students for a Democratic Society (SDS), called for closing down college campuses throughout New York State in May 1971, Farmingdale sought help from the Nassau and Suffolk County police departments whose well-trained officers, many of whom were students and graduates of Farmingdale, brought their presence to maintain order. The college administration appealed to Mel Jackson, local leader of the Congress of Racial Equality, to assist in keeping the campus functioning. Jackson also appreciated the school's special educational programs offered to minority students, and he addressed the Farmingdale black and Hispanic students on campus saying, "This is not our fight. If you join the off-campus [SDS] students you will be hurting yourselves and your families and you will be followers and not leaders." The Farmingdale students heckled the outsiders, numbering about twenty, who had come to close down the campus. Cipriani, meeting with colleagues of a Middle States Accreditation visit at this time, learned of the difficulties student protests were having on other campuses, but he indicated that Farmingdale fared much better with fewer demonstrations and protests. It was a difficult time for the American nation as the exuberance of youthful idealism, and sometimes arrogance and intolerance, clashed with the nation's institutional leaders' failure to end an unpopular war, sometimes weakening efforts to achieve equal opportunity for all.[14]

As a chief administrator, Laffin was aware of the changing relations between employer and employee. Under the provisions of the New York State Public Employment Act (1967), also known as the Taylor Law, public employees now had the right to organize and bargain collectively concerning the terms and conditions of their employment. The law prohibited strikes. To put the program into effect, the SUNY Policies of the Board of Trustees required all non-teaching professionals to be evaluated annually. With this new system to guide him, Laffin addressed the issue by presenting a comprehensive paper, "Evaluating the Performance of Non-Teaching Professionals," at the American Society for Engineering Education Annual Conference at Colorado State University, on June 16–19, 1975. His presentation reflected the complexity of modern labor relations and his sense of fairness in achieving harmonious relations and increased productivity with his non-teaching professional employees. His belief in democratic administration was extended to his faculty. He applied these principles when the university faculty and staff organized in 1973 into a statewide union, the United University Professions (UUP). The UUP affiliated with the New York State United Teachers. Earlier, on February 18, 1969 the American Federation of Teachers granted a charter to Farmingdale to constitute the local union chapter under the title, "State University Federation of Teachers at Farmingdale, 1905." Seventy signatories were listed on this original charter located in the College Archives.[15]

Laffin confronted the ongoing problem of inadequate funding for faculty and staff salaries, as well as critical maintenance of the physical plant. He knew, as did his successor Cipriani, that Farmingdale was very different from the other agricultural and technical colleges, which

FIGURE 7-2. The Drama Cub placed second with this float display. It was one of the many competitive exhibits during the 1967 Homecoming event. Lupton Hall can be seen at left, rear.

were in rural areas with lower cost of living expenses. In the middle of 1972, budget cuts were particularly severe at Farmingdale. Its fleet of six airplanes, used in its aircraft operations curriculum, lay idle at nearby Republic Field for lack of money to pay for fuel. Students and faculty complained that custodial services were virtually nonexistent, and that programs needed to be expanded. Professional salaries remained low. Only $30,000 was appropriated to purchase new books for the $8 million college library, which was nearing completion. Laffin experienced long

FIGURE 7-3. The interior of the new student-activities and physical education building, Roosevelt Hall, highlights the unique construction that employed a pre-stressed, post-tension roof/ceiling. There are no internal buttresses or cantilevers. A game with Webb Institute is taking place, 1967.

battles with the SUNY central administration in seeking funding adjustments based on fairness and equity. He met with limited success. He altered his strategy and decided to move toward establishing an upper division to offer bachelor's degrees, but the endeavor was cut short by his sudden death in 1976. This strategy was not lost on Cipriani, who assumed the presidency two years later.[16]

Despite attempts to resolve these fiscal problems, Farmingdale continued its policy of offering small classes taught by faculty who extended support to students, some of whom were experiencing problems in their academic and personal lives. Although most students came from the Long Island region, there were others who enrolled from distant areas. One student who applied seeking the Farmingdale educational experience was William Fichtner, graduate of the 1976 Class of Criminal Justice. How did this young man arrive at Farmingdale from Cheektowaga, near Buffalo, New York, during the period of social upheaval? Don Harvey, a member of Farmingdale's admission staff, successfully recruited him by pointing out the school's special advantages. Fichtner was uncertain of a career direction, but a trip to a Broadway show with Harvey awakened his interest in theater. Following graduation, he went on to become an actor in screen, theater, and television, performing alongside the world's leading actors and directors. For his ongoing support of the college, he earned a place on the 1995–1996 Alumni Honor Roll, and Alumni President Richard Papp presented him with the 1999 Alumnus of the Year Award. Feeling he owed a debt to his mentor for bringing him to Farmingdale, Fichtner and others created the Don Harvey Memorial Scholarship and has returned to the campus to present the award. At the eighty-ninth Commencement Exercises on May 18, 2008, Fichtner received the Honorary Doctor of Humane Letters. He credited Farmingdale for his discovery of the performing arts.[17]

A campus schedule change occurred when Gov. Rockefeller announced that Farmingdale and two other SUNY units, Harpur College at Binghamton and the College at New Paltz, would experiment with a trimester system, which was implemented in June 1963. It was short-lived, however. The plan called for the academic year to be divided into three equal terms with students attending two semesters, and having one off. The purpose of the new flexible trimester schedule was to use the campus more efficiently in order to increase enrollments and enable qualified students to accelerate their education. It was conceived to accommodate the rising number of applicants until the physical plant could be enlarged. On February 18, 1965, the first diplomas given to graduates of a trimester program in the SUNY system were presented to 109 seniors in the Allard Field House. The graduates had enrolled as freshmen in June 1963. However, after three years, the college faculty and administration evaluated the program and concluded that the trimester system be discontinued, stating, "The College at Farmingdale can operate year-round with excellent campus utilization without benefit of Trimester." Thus, the trimester schedule ended in 1966. Nevertheless, by October 1965, full-time enrollment had reached 2,633 students, the highest ever and with a 19 percent increase over 1964. Of the total, 1,868 (71 percent) were men and 765 (29 percent) were women. For the same period, the Evening College counted 1,489 students in the 1965 summer term, 5,533 in the 1965 fall term, and 5,089 in the 1965 spring term for a total enrollment of 12,111, an increase of 22.2 percent over the previous year. Classrooms had to be rented at a local high school to accommodate the extra students. As indicated earlier, by 1972 full-time student enrollments had reached 6,800 and evening/part-time enrollment numbered 7,700.[18]

Laffin acknowledged the challenges of growth. As part of the 1960 SUNY Master Plan and the revised Master Plan of 1964, which provided for the addition of new roads, parking facilities, and new buildings, he worried about the effect of the state's proposal to demolish the existing Barnyard Complex. This instructional area housed livestock, a dairy barn unit, poultry facilities, pens, silos, paddocks, and shelters for swine and sheep, all needed for the animal science curriculum. Would leaders in Albany phase out agricultural education completely or replace the Barnyard Complex with a new infrastructure and still retain the animal science program? Laffin turned to the community for its support of the program for maintaining its traditional agricultural mission. He composed a letter, dated April 6, 1966, that was addressed to Martin Buskin, education editor of *Newsday*, seeking his assistance, but after consultation with his staff decided not to send it. In the original draft he crossed out Buskin's name and had the revised letter sent to local leaders who were friends of the college.

> Over the past 50 years, Farmingdale has developed an international reputation of excellence in the field of agricultural education. It has brought into agriculture, because of its proximity to the greater metropolitan area, young men and women raised in an urban community. Over 90 percent of our agricultural students come from the Tri-county Long Island region. Within the various agricultural and related programs of study there are presently 454 students, making this the largest program of its kind in New York State. Our graduates, who are the major products of this educational program, have proved vital to the agricultural industry of Long Island and New York State.

Laffin noted that more than thirty thousand school children made annual visits to the campus animal farm complex as part of a broad educational experience. Referring to its past achievements, he insisted that the agricultural program being offered so close to New York City still provided great value to the downstate region and SUNY. In the original draft of his letter, there was a section that Laffin eliminated; it requested that friends of Farmingdale send a letter to Dr. Samuel B. Gould, president of SUNY, 8 Thurlow Terrace, Albany, New York "for the continuation of the agricultural program at this college." Laffin, always conscious of doing the right thing, believed that it was more discrete to omit this section because it might be perceived as too confrontational. He was, however, following a practice that Knapp had used in making public appeals. Nevertheless, the hope of continued agricultural education eventually weakened, and the College pursued a new mission.[19]

Distinctions were made between the community colleges and agricultural-technical colleges in the revised 1964 SUNY Master Plan. Community colleges were encouraged to expand to serve local needs, but they were not to become four-year institutions. More than 95 percent of the state's population resided within commuting distance of a community college. Their funding would be different. A new college of liberal arts and sciences was planned for Nassau County (at Old Westbury). The agricultural and technical colleges were designed to meet statewide needs, and would be permitted to establish new technical programs if they attracted students from all areas of the state. Aside from these brief references, little attention was given in the thirty-two-page Master Plan document to the unique role Farmingdale played as an agricultural and technical college, as well as its sister institutions. Despite increasing technical programs, Farmingdale's agricultural program and its geographical position close to New York City continued to be little understood and appreciated.[20]

As the college grew, Laffin embarked on his own expansion plan. He had announced a building program in his first year as president calling for an $8 million expansion for the construction of a student union building, library, gymnasium, classroom-laboratory facility, and more dormitories. Theodore Roosevelt Hall was completed in October 1965 at a cost of $1.67 million as a student activities facility. It was a circular structure and the first to be designed employing a prestressed, post-tension annular roof. There were no internal buttresses or cantilevers. Its roof is essentially flat, rising a scant three inches from circumference to center. The real estate section of *The New York Times* on March 6, 1966, featured the building's unique round catenary roof in a front-page photograph. Roosevelt Hall has provided many useful campus services as a College

Union building with club meeting rooms, gymnasium, bowling alley, student lounge, recreation center, commuter lounge, and a four-hundred-seat theater/auditorium (Little Theater). The New York Knickerbockers of the National Basketball Association used the Roosevelt Hall gymnasium as a training and practice camp prior to the official opening of the 1969–1970 basketball season.

Another building, Walt Whitman Hall, was officially dedicated on June 12, 1964, during a cornerstone-laying ceremony. The ceremony was conducted before commencement exercises; attending were New York State Assembly Speaker Joseph F. Carlino, Laffin, College Council Chairman Mortimer J. Gleeson, faculty, and students. Since the building was named for the poet who was born three miles north of the college, trustees for the Walt Whitman Birthplace Society participated. The following year, on June 14, 1965, Long Island Congressman John W. Wydler addressed Farmingdale's 630 graduates as commencement speaker. He remarked on "how impressed" he was "with the kindness, competency and dedication" of the faculty and administration. He praised Laffin's leadership and acknowledged the $8 million campus expansion program. In fact, he participated earlier that same day in the dedication ceremony of Roosevelt Hall. Wydler's speech was entitled, "Is Academic Freedom Worth Saving?" He defended the free speech rights of students to demonstrate and protest the escalation of the war in Vietnam. But he criticized "those demonstrations by intellectual beatniks who seek license and notoriety." He called on all college administrators to maintain the integrity and security of the educational process. This view coincided with Laffin's sentiments during the period of campus upheavals. Closely related to the campus physical development was the dedication of the Ralph Bunche Plaza in 1973. Laffin Hall (the former administration building), Roosevelt Hall, Greenley Library, and Knapp Hall surround the Plaza. On this site stands a plaque honoring Ralph Bunche (1904–1971) for his achievements as a civil rights leader, scholar, and teacher. He was the first person of color to receive the Nobel Peace Prize (1950).[21]

In 1972, a state-of-the-art athletic facility was built on campus and was named George E. Nold Hall. Nold was a retired assistant professor of physics and mathematics at Farmingdale, He died in 1971 at the age of seventy-two. A graduate of the U.S. Naval Academy with a bachelor's degree and from New York University with a master's degree, he taught at Setauket High School and West Islip High School before joining the Farmingdale faculty (1950–1968). The college honored him for his naval career, for winning gymnastic championships at Annapolis, and for his teaching career. Before the construction of Nold Hall, athletic teams used the bookstore as a gymnasium and a facility in downtown Farmingdale. In the 1940s, a converted barn was used for athletics. Allard Field House was built in 1953 with a seating capacity of one-thousand for basketball games. After 1965, Roosevelt Hall gymnasium replaced Allard Field House as the new site for athletic competition. Nold Hall was a completely new facility, but it was also the first centrally located indoor–outdoor complex that the Farmingdale athletic program could call home. It had a seating capacity of more than four-thousand. The complex featured a deck indoor swimming pool with a one-meter diving board. The main gymnasium contained three regulation basketball courts, eight badminton courts, four volleyball courts, four tennis courts, and a ten-lap-to-the-mile track. The facility also included four racquetball courts, four indoor squash courts, a large weight-training complex, a wrestling room, and one of the most modern training rooms in the country. Modern equipment and a laundry room supported the overall athletic program. Finally, the outdoor amenities included twelve all-weather tennis courts, a quarter-mile all-weather track, and a twenty-station golf driving range, lacrosse/soccer fields, three softball fields, and a baseball field.[22]

The athletic program grew as the college joined various conferences. By the 1940s, the school's teams no longer competed against clubs, faculty, and high schools. Farmingdale's teams played in the New York Institute Athletic Association and the Metropolitan Junior College Association, and the Knickerbocker Conference in the 1950s. The athletic program advanced following World War II—no teams competed from 1943 to 1945—but the popular sport of football was dropped in 1963. Athletes were turning to other sports and it was difficult to secure players to field football teams. Another obstacle to maintaining a football program was budgetary priorities, as money was used to fund other sports and educational programs. Many area schools did not have football programs, thereby making it difficult to find competition. In the late 1960s the college joined the National Junior College Athletic Association, allowing it to compete under a structured system with teams in the same association, and it gave the Athletic Department a national affiliation. Gerald Allard, who was appointed athletic director in 1929, retired in 1964. He was both founder and first president of the New York State Institute Athletic Association and the Metropolitan Junior College Association (1949). Allard was one of the most influential athletic administrators in the region and helped to make Farmingdale a competing power. Since the college is today a four-year institution, it is a current member of the National Collegiate Athletic Association Division III, offering eighteen men and women's intercollegiate sports. It also holds membership in the Skyline Conference, Eastern College Athletic Conference, and the Collegiate Track Conference. Students not wishing to participate in intercollegiate sports may choose to participate in the college's intramural program.[23]

FIGURE 7-4. Left to right, Professors Ronald Dougher, Ann Senyk, and Horton Amidon of the Social Science Department, which was in the General Education Division, are preparing a three-credit course to be presented on New York City television station Chanel 11, WPIX, 1968.

Laffin encouraged the faculty to raise the standards of the college's educational programs in their academic and professional work. In1968, Farmingdale became the first two-year college in New York State to offer a three-credit course delivered over New York City's Channel 11, WPIX. The course, "Living Today," was produced by Ronald Dougher, Ann Senyk, and Horton Amidon, professors in the General Education Division, who together taught thirty-two one-half hour programs that consisted of lectures, interviews, audiovisual materials, and panel discussions. Using practical life situations, topics featured post-college problems. More than three hundred students were enrolled in the TV course, consisting of nearly 50 percent of the senior class; the other half took the course the following semester in the traditional classroom manner.[24]

"Living Today" was not the college's only foray into educational televised courses. In the fall semester, 1976, during the celebration of the Bicentennial of the Declaration of Independence, Professor Frank J. Cavaioli taught the three-credit, thirteen-week series educational television course, "The Adams Chronicles." Based on 300,000 pages of documents known as the "Adams Papers," this course covered four generations of the John Adams family, and was presented via public television on channels 13, 21, and 31. Farmingdale, with 207 students enrolled, was one of 305 institutions around the country formally taking the course. Experts considered the nationally syndicated home-study program, funded by the National Endowment for the Humanities, "a major breakthrough in the growing effort to make colleges adapt to the technological revolution." Ann Diehl, a student who later went on to become a dean at Farmingdale, was one of the students who enrolled in the course, paying $67 in tuition. The television format was ideal for such a student as Diehl, who had young children at home who watched the prime-time history program with her. Students also met monthly for a seminar with their professor, and had weekly discussions with him on campus or via telephone. In 1977, Cavaioli taught the black history three-credit home-study television course, "Roots." Following the same television historical dramatization format, seventy-seven students enrolled to earn college credit at Farmingdale.[25]

As the academic profile of the college continued on its upward trajectory under Laffin, Professor Raynor Wallace of the English Department brought Phi Theta Kappa (PTK), the National Junior College Honorary Scholastic Society, to Farmingdale in 1963. Mu Omega was the name given to the local chapter. Professor Robert C. Blank of the History Department assumed the role of campus advisor in fall 1966, and continued in this capacity until his retirement in 1991. This honor society had its roots at Stephens College, Missouri, 1910. The American Association of Junior Colleges recognized PTK as the official honor society for two-year colleges

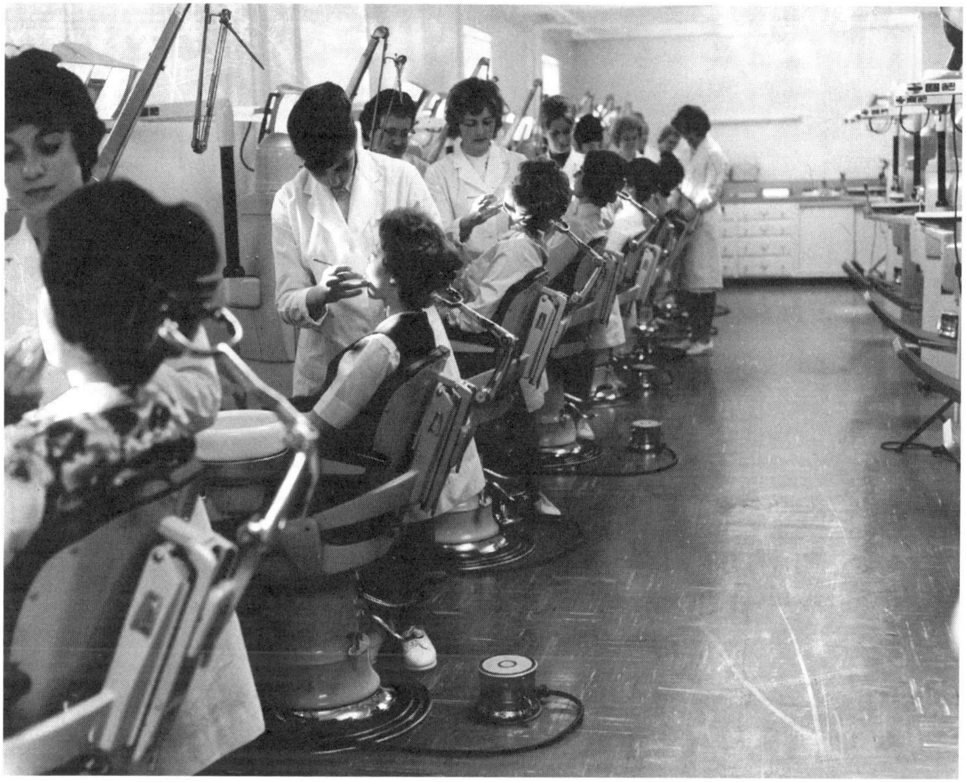

FIGURE 7-5. Dental Hygiene students gain practical experience as they treat voluntary patients in Ward Hall, 1970. The treatment is free to students, faculty, and staff. The first Dental Hygiene class graduated in 1948.

in 1919. Today, PTK is the largest honor society in American higher education with more than 2.5 million members and 1,270 national and worldwide chapters.

The Farmingdale Mu Omega Chapter has distinguished itself over the years through campus and community service, but one achievement that stands out is the tutorial program established with Wyandanch High School in Suffolk County. Chapter members volunteered their time, often up to four hours per week, assisting educationally challenged students with their schoolwork. Local newspapers, the SUNY newsletter, and SUNY Central Office praised the project. Laffin

FIGURE 7-6. Pictured are graduating nursing students of the Class of 1972 in front of Knapp Hall. The curriculum included a balance of courses in the humanities and social sciences. The students' educational experience took place in the classroom, laboratory, and in a variety of clinical settings.

personally commended all the honor students for their work, which continued for more than two years in the 1970s. PTK membership was extended to eligible students in the College of Continuing Education in 1970. Professor Blank assumed an important leadership role in the national organization by becoming its regional coordinator and chairman of its Board of Directors. He developed the prestigious Summer Honors Institute program. Rod A. Risley, national executive

FIGURE 7-7. The members of the Agricultural Department shown here in 1970 are: front row, left to right: R. Reutlinger, E. Buck, G. Mowry, R. Stockbridge, E. Wallkam, and V. Bellard. Back row: W. Becker, S. Carubba, C. Struck, T. Bruetsch, D. Barney, J. Visco, K. Hilbert, E. Patterson, and J. Lawrence.

director, commented, "We commend the college leadership for their support of the Mu Omega Chapter of Phi Theta Kappa throughout it long and rich history. We especially salute the leadership of Robert Blank." The chapter continued to expand its tutoring and outreach programs, conducting local and national conferences, as well as providing college service.[26]

Other honor societies have been established at Farmingdale. Epsilon Pi Tau is an international society that recognizes student excellence in fields devoted to the study of technology and for those persons preparing for practice in the technology professions. Sigma Phi Alpha is the National Dental Hygiene Honor Society that recognizes scholarship, service, and leadership among students and graduates of dental hygiene educational programs. Alpha Mu is the name of its local chapter at Farmingdale. Sigma Beta Delta acknowledges scholarship and achievement of students of business, management, and administration. Chi Alpha Epsilon is the national honor society that recognizes academic achievement of students attending institutions of higher learning through nontraditional criteria. The local chapter is Gamma Eta, chartered at Farmingdale in December 2001. Proficient students were also recognized by being selected for the dean's list, president's list, Hilda Ward Valedictorian Award, receiving awards for academic excellence, and participating in honors courses.[27]

This pivotal era of the 1960s and 1970s in the history of Farmingdale State College came to an end when Laffin died suddenly at Mid Island Hospital of bilateral pneumonia and heart failure on December 25, 1976. Laffin's impact on the college was similar to previous long-serving campus leaders. College Council member Anthony Mastroianni said Laffin "was caught between the history and traditions of the institution and the changing laws and culture" of higher education. Laffin believed his position as president was not permanently bound to the past and that change must be anticipated and assessed. He sought to maintain the agricultural curriculum, which nevertheless was in decline; at the same time he was extending academic programs. He witnessed a temporary resurgence of student enrollments in the agriculture curriculum, which he attributed to "a great thirst among young people to go back to the soil." He added, "The lawn is now the status symbol in suburbia." Mastroianni, who worked closely with Laffin, observed that Laffin made the College Council more understanding of his goals, which were to honor the traditions of the college, protect the academic freedom and safety of the faculty and students, and to open opportunities to women and minorities. Mastroianni and other council members were "greatly impressed" with his "leadership abilities and his dedication to Farmingdale." Laffin helped to expand Farmingdale into a comprehensive two-year institution of higher learning that focused on career-oriented education enriched with social science and humanities courses. His leadership produced greater educational opportunities for all. He was sensitive to the material and professional needs of the faculty and was their advocate in dealing with the SUNY bureaucracy in Albany.[28]

Off campus, Laffin assumed leadership roles in many civic organizations. His dedication to public service was marked by his position as president of the Long Island Regional Association Council of Higher Education; member of the SUNY Council of Presidents; member of the Board of Directors of the Long Island Association of Commerce and Industry; member of the Nassau and Suffolk Economic Developmental Council; Chairman of the Industry Committee of Wage and Labor Laws, appointed by the U.S. secretary of labor. He distinguished himself in other ways: as president of the New York State Junior College Association; chairman of the Nassau County Auxiliary Manpower Planning Board; member of the Society for the Advancement of Manpower Association. He applied his expertise and knowledge when he traveled throughout Asia and Europe to assist in advancing the development of two-year technical educational institutions. As a result of this experience, he authored several professional studies based on his foreign consulting work.

Laffin was further recognized for his many other community achievements. He received the Distinguished Service Cross from the Bishop of the Long Island Episcopal Diocese. He was renowned for his leadership in the National Conference of Christians and Jews, was chairman of the 1972–1976 Long Island Collegiate Olympic Fund, and was involved in the United Way and Episcopal Charities. Dr Ernest L. Boyer, chancellor of SUNY, described Laffin as a "man of great commitment, unusual vision, and a strong supporter of all phases of higher education." Laffin's dedication to public service, religious groups, higher education, and especially to Farmingdale College and its students was exemplary. He was proud of the Distinguished Alumni Achievement Award bestowed on him by the New York University School of Education Alumni Association. Farmingdale established the Charles W. Laffin Jr. Memorial Scholarship Fund in his memory. Also, Excelsior College, originally founded as Regents College in 1971 to assist busy adults to earn college degrees with flexible distance education, established the Charles W. Laffin Jr. Memorial Award in recognition of his leadership that gave momentum to the fledgling community college movement and for his service to Excelsior College, America's first virtual university. Upon his death, Farmingdale librarian Parker Van Hoogenstyn organized a special memorial display in the college library to honor him.[29]

Laffin's passing created a vacancy in the presidential office. Vice President John Purcell temporarily assumed the position. The SUNY Board of Trustees selected campus Academic Vice President Mauro S. Zulli to serve as acting president until a new president was appointed. Zulli had served the college since 1956 as professor, Mathematics Department chairman, Mathematics and Sciences Division chairman, faculty senator, fiscal officer, and member of the Curriculum and Budget committees. He earned a bachelor's degree in mathematics from Adelphi College (1953) and a master's from Columbia University (1957). He held memberships in many professional and academic organizations. This set of credentials earned him the title of acting president of the Agricultural and Technical College at Farmingdale from 1977 to 1978.[30]

FIGURE 7-8. A Food Tech student is processing milk in Thompson Hall in the 1970s. Faculty and staff availed themselves of the benefit of discounted milk purchases, as well as fruit and vegetables, all produced on campus.

FIGURE 7-9. Noel Palmer, Assistant to the President for Special Programs, left center, leads a student group to register for a summer program in Farmingdale's Educational Opportunity Center, 1973. President Charles W. Laffin, Jr. is at right.

The stage was set for the selection of a strong leader with superior credentials who would prepare the college for the future, a future that would be decidedly different from the past. Up to this time, three individuals had shaped the college: Albert A. Johnson (1913–1923), Halsey B. Knapp (1923–1956), and Charles W. Laffin Jr. (1961–1976.) But the new leader would be confronted with the challenge of building on the past and having a clear vision for the future. Past leadership had appreciated the unique educational institution that Farmingdale was, and also

FIGURE 7-10. Students are welcome to enjoy a campus chicken barbeque in 1962. First year students are wearing beanies, or dinks, with "SUATI 64"embroidered on them for their graduating class.

recognized how unfavorable its position had been in its relations with New York State and its educational bureaucracy. As events unfolded, the new president had to produce a realistic plan that would succeed in overcoming obstacles to preserve the very existence of the college.

In a postscript to the career of Charles W. Laffin Jr., a special ceremony honoring his memory was held on campus on May 19, 1977, dedicating the administration building in his name. Walter Lynch Jr., chairman of the College Council presided, assisted by Zulli. Mortimer J. Gleeson, chair-

FIGURE 7-11. Student antics on the steps of Lupton Hall, including two students wearing freshman beanies embroidered with "SUATI 64." SUATI stands for State University Agricultural and Technical Institute.

man emeritus of the College Council, conducted the actual dedication of the Dr. Charles W. Laffin, Jr. Administration Building. SUNY Deputy Chancellor Murray Block, close friend and colleague of Laffin, presented a laudatory address reflecting on his career and their thirty-year association, "A Remembrance of Dr. Charles W. Laffin, Jr., Praising What Is Lost Makes the Remembrance Dear," borrowing from William Shakespeare. Block focused on Laffin's "great and comforting legacy" in creating a comprehensive institution of higher education with a "big Heart."[31]

EIGHT

Dr. Frank A. Cipriani Heralds the Future, 1978–2000

> Today the College is perfectly poised to evolve its traditional programs into the new multi-disciplinary professions, which have developed from the great scientific activities of the past 50 years.[1]

In the last quarter of the twentieth century, the college faced another of its many challenges, perhaps more critical than before. The landscape was changing as a result of society's rapid advancements in science, computers, electronics, transportation, international business, agricultural economics, health sciences, space, and more. Would it continue on the path that had been established under the leadership of Dr. Charles W. Laffin Jr. by offering only two-year degrees in agriculture and technology? Laffin had successfully led the college in many of these areas. An aviation program was initiated with a fleet of airplanes at nearby Republic Field. The first SUNY-based Urban Center to help the academically and economically disadvantaged population had been established on campus. A highly qualified faculty and staff were hired to implement new programs. The faculty benefited from a new professional academic schedule. But was it enough? The strong agricultural tradition was deeply imbedded in the very fabric of the college. The successful establishment of technical education beginning in 1946, however, had laid the basis for a more comprehensive institution of learning at Farmingdale, and the evolving trend in increased enrollments moved toward satisfying the needs of a society in flux. It has been pointed out how Knapp and Laffin praised the agricultural curriculum and sought community support to continue it. But changing demographics resulted in a more modern Long Island, one quite different from its agrarian-rural roots. Increased land values, the housing boom, high taxes, the end of a defense economy, and the emergence of a service economy forced leaders at the college to re-examine its mission. As Long Island was being transformed into a suburban postindustrial society with a growing population, it was imperative Farmingdale recognize and accept fundamental transformation in its attempt to create high-tech curricula with a strong foundation in the humanities and social sciences. As enrollments in the agricultural curriculum were declining, it became clear that it was no longer fiscally and educationally viable.

At Farmingdale, becoming an important institution of higher learning meant adapting to the new statewide system. Events surrounding the establishment of the State University of New York in 1948 at first produced enthusiastic praise, but soon leaders began to realize it was overbuilt and too expensive to manage. Gov. W. Averell Harriman (1955–1958), who followed SUNY founder Gov. Thomas E. Dewey (1943–1954), generally ignored requests for its expansion. Gov. Nelson A. Rockefeller (1959–1973), an advocate of establishing a great state university, expanded SUNY during the 1960s. The mood was soon reversed by events, which led to severe budget cuts in the SUNY system. Even Rockefeller in his last year as governor instituted a series of funding reductions. Retrenchment and consolidation continued under the gubernatorial administrations of Malcolm Wilson (1973–1974), Hugh Carey (1975–1982), and Mario M. Cuomo (1983–1994).[2]

The financial situation worsened for Farmingdale. As the oldest public college on Long Island, Farmingdale faced increased competition for student enrollment and funding when new public institutions of higher learning were chartered during this period: SUNY Stony Brook (1957), Nassau County Community College (1959), Suffolk County Community College (1960), and SUNY Old Westbury (1965). Expansion of private colleges on Long Island and in New York City, as well as the City University of New York (CUNY) campuses, further complicated matters for the Farmingdale Agricultural and Technical College whose mission would soon be re-evaluated. The traditional agricultural program was experiencing a decline at the same time that more students were enrolling in the technical and liberal arts programs.

This was the setting under which Frank A. Cipriani was hired in 1964 as assistant dean in the School of Continuing Education. For the next thirty-five years he would take the lead in overcoming the challenges that lay ahead in attempting to reshape the college. He rose rapidly through the ranks, becoming president from 1978 to 2000. Even during his tenure as president, he remained grounded in academic work, assuming the title of professor of history and political science, often returning to the classroom when his administrative duties permitted. He worked closely under President Laffin and learned firsthand the unique problems Farmingdale faced within

FIGURE 8-1. Dr. Frank A. Cipriani served in various administrative positions from 1974 to 1978, and as president from 1978 to 2000. He guided SUNY Farmingdale from a two-year agricultural sand technical college to a four-year baccalaureate degree institution. He is pictured here with his academic gown and presidential medal.

the SUNY system. He soon learned that in the competition for public money, there were upstate and New York City politicians who regarded Farmingdale as primarily an agricultural college that was no longer relevant. Moreover, the college sat on 380 acres, valued as high as $1 million an acre, and if sold could help the state during this period of financial crisis. The mere suggestion of closing the college elicited comparisons of Gov. Alfred E. Smith's attempt in 1926 to convert it into a state hospital to be used as a farm colony.

Before joining Farmingdale, Cipriani served in the U.S. Air Force, where he was honorably discharged with the rank of captain and the rating of navigator-flight instructor. He was a member of the American Society of Safety Engineers and worked at an international insurance company while engaged in graduate studies. He advocated for international education and supported a core of humanities and social sciences courses as a sound foundation for technical education.

Cipriani was a full-time member of the administrative staff at New York University's (NYU) business office and was working on his doctorate when Dr. James Nihan, dean of the School of Continuing Education at Farmingdale, invited him to fill the position of assistant dean. A lifelong resident of New York, Cipriani was born in the Italian American community of Corona, Queens County. A graduate of Brooklyn Technical High School (1951), who was inducted into its Hall of Fame (1998), and a Queens College alumnus, Cipriani knew little about Farmingdale. He had completed all his course work at NYU, except for his doctoral dissertation. He was interviewed at Nihan's home on Melville Road, across the street from the campus, and then was taken to see Laffin, whose goal was to upgrade the profile of the faculty and administration. Laffin was impressed with Cipriani's background and hired him immediately, granting him time to complete his doctoral dissertation. Cipriani assumed the new position on August 8, 1964, beginning what he considered to be an exciting and fulfilling career.

Vice President Robert McLaughlin, who would become president of Herkimer Community College in 1968, welcomed Cipriani to the college. Carl Schilling, former assistant dean, advised Cipriani to "let Eileen Deger, Senior Stenographer, do all the scheduling and don't get in the way of the clerical staff who had been doing all that was needed for many years." Although he had ideas of his own, much of it based on his leadership position in the service and his work at NYU, he followed their advice during the first trimester. The clerical staff consisted of nearly all women, all of whom were competent, did not have college degrees, and genuinely wished him to succeed. He established a working rapport with them and the curriculum department chairpersons. His first responsibility was to solve scheduling problems. Under the old system that he inherited, the Evening College enrollment rarely exceeded 1,500 per trimester. He believed that the number could easily be doubled or tripled. In fact, the new class format he soon set up actually achieved an enrollment of more than 2,000 students, and a record total of more than 5,500 registrations, most of who registered in two or three classes. He concluded from this experience that personnel time and campus resources were wasteful and inefficient. The information he gathered from student questionnaires and faculty consultation allowed him to reform the scheduling process to one that became beneficial for students and faculty. Cipriani presented to Nihan a new classroom and laboratory schedule matrix that allowed for four classes in the evening, effectively quadrupling student enrollment. Nihan was reluctant to accept such a radical change, but after consulting with Laffin accepted the new system. The president made it clear that growth was on the horizon and had to be met with new ideas. This policy was in line with Gov. Rockefeller's statements to streamline the university. On the second night, the new registration system was put into practice, Laffin and McLaughlin, who had previously served as dean of continuing education, came to witness the process, and they were impressed. Cipriani's first test as an administrator met with success, and it influenced the president to promote him to the position of assistant to the president. He was now allowed greater freedom in making decisions relative to student counseling, enrollment, curriculum, credit transfer issues, non-credit courses, workshops, symposia, security, and staffing matters. While all this was taking place, SUNY decided to end the trimester experiment and Farmingdale reverted to the traditional academic semester system in 1966.[3]

In the early years as assistant dean, Cipriani was responsible for creating new courses and symposia, which accounted for nearly 1,500 non-credit students annually. During one of the public seminars dealing with retraining individuals with advanced skills for employment, an older woman, Sylvia Kaplan, asked her instructor why institutions of higher learning were not offering courses specially designed to educate mature women and the "disadvantaged" for the workplace. She said that as children had grown up and left home, mature women could now be trained for productive employment. The instructor answered that this was not the mission of higher education, and she was cut off. After class, she reported this to Cipriani who challenged her to write an outline of what could be done. She composed an essay complete with recommendations and presented it to him, whereby a course was devised and offered at Farmingdale to prepare women and minorities for re-entry employment skills. The course was advertised, offered for a $20 registration fee, and immediately filled to capacity. The program was such a success that the college was awarded the Freedoms Foundation Award for inspirational service to the nation. Laffin received the award in the form of a mounted medallion and miniature American flag, which he proudly displayed on his desk. Laffin credited Kaplan for this successful initiative.[4]

It must be emphasized that in its early years, the school had established a policy of equal opportunity, although limited, and experienced steady enrollment increases of women and minorities. New specialized courses such as math anxiety workshops and technical training eventually expanded to what became the Long Island Educational Opportunity Center, a New York State program that offered tuition-free, non-degree education for disadvantaged individuals and minorities who were not attending secondary school and who were not eligible for college admission. Physical facilities also were modified to accommodate students with disabilities. Equal educational opportunity for all has been a proud tradition at Farmingdale since the school's beginning.[5]

Cipriani was assisted by Dr. Joseph Monaco, who arrived on campus in 1966 as a paid intern as part of a New York State Civil Service initiative for professionals training to work in public service. Monaco's work experience included time with the IRS and the Federal Reserve, and had earned a bachelor's degree in business administration from NYU, later receiving the doctorate degree from the same institution. He worked in the business office and proved to be a fiscal expert on whom Laffin and Cipriani relied heavily for financial advice. Monaco was instrumental in establishing fiscal accountability, gaining respect from SUNY Central. Cipriani learned of the casual management of money at the close of registration one evening when Monaco brought him to a back room and showed him three new fifty-five gallon bags containing cash and checks amounting to tens of thousands of dollars. It was clear that armed guards and an armored car service had to be hired to transport the money to a bank each night. Also, a new pre-registration and prepayment system had to be put in place for evening students.

Cipriani's early work gained the respect of the faculty and administrative staff. Dr. Laffin moved him to the position of assistant to the president in 1965 and next to dean of administration in 1968, a title that was changed by SUNY to vice president for administration. In this capacity, he managed public matters and was "the first line of intervention" for the president. Laffin was conscious of the public image of the college, and the need to manage that image. Cipriani was instrumental in recommending Frank Elkins to be the new public relations officer in 1966. Although Elkins lacked a college degree, he had achieved an impressive career working at *The New York Times* for more than twenty years. He helped to create a more positive public image of the college.

Cipriani functioned as a "troubleshooter" to Laffin and was asked to deal with numerous complaints about ongoing campus problems. For example, many students, parents, and faculty complained about the inadequate delivery of health services. After guidance from Bert Willenbrock, dean of students and Cipriani's wife Judy, who was a registered nurse teacher, insurance benefits were increased and a free taxi service was established to transport students to the local hospital when the campus infirmary was closed. Furthermore, an extra part-time nurse was hired, liability was reduced to the college, and filling the vacant full-time physician's line with five different doctors each to serve one day a week on campus resulted in increased services. All these benefits increased student insurance costs by only $5 a year, allowing the college to remain within budget. An agreement was also made with nearby Mid Island Hospital to provide student emergency and outpatient care. Laffin was pleased with the results and took Cipriani to lunch at the Rotary Club where he asked him to fix the "bookstore mess."

FIGURE 8-2. The 1975 graduation ceremonies were conducted in Nold Hall. Parents and friends attended to honor the 1891 graduates, a proud day for all.

Figure 8-3. Professor Robert Stockbridge, Chairman of the Agriculture Department, assists children as they pet animals during the 52nd Annual Open House program. Before the Agriculture program ended in 1987, thousands of children visited the campus farm to enjoy educational tours.

The college bookstore was a "mom and pop" operation that had been run by the Faculty Student Association (FSA) for decades. When student enrollments exploded in the 1960s, the old way of selling books became inefficient and expensive. The bookstore was poorly organized with long lines of students waiting to purchase books. There were never enough books to sell because they were bought on a ten-day consignment, meaning if they were not paid for within ten days, more supplies could not be purchased. To ensure a constant flow of books, the FSA borrowed money for a ninety-day period and included interest in the cost of the books. Cipriani secured the aid of Leonard Riggio, an NYU colleague and Brooklyn Tech alumnus, who had just become the new CEO of Barnes and Noble and who was asked to revamp the bookstore operation. In exchange for a five-year contract, Riggio provided $180,000 in upfront physical improvements of the bookstore, guaranteed there would be no long waiting lines, prices for books would be competitive, and there would be no shortage of books. The FSA also would receive 10 percent of net sales. This was the first SUNY bookstore operation contracted by Barnes and Noble, and it was extended to the university centers. Laffin was pleased with the results and expanded Cipriani's responsibilities.[6]

During these years, Cipriani assumed the position of secretary of the College Council, which met monthly on Saturday mornings. Locke James, who served in this capacity dating back to Knapp's time, advised Cipriani that his new responsibilities as secretary would include arranging meetings, recording, and distributing the minutes. Laffin and the council, especially Chairman Mortimer Gleeson, a vice president of Morgan Guarantee Trust, appreciated his work in summarizing data and his professional demeanor. It was Cipriani who later as president recommended that the first building to be constructed during his tenure be named after Gleeson. Gleeson Hall's financing included federal funding with mandates requiring accommodations for the physically disabled. The building also was designed to be energy efficient to combat the energy crisis.[7]

Throughout these early years, Cipriani witnessed firsthand the unique place that Farmingdale had within the SUNY system. In his many travels with Laffin to Albany and throughout the state to participate in conferences and meetings, he became familiar with the structure and function of public higher education. Laffin relied on him for his advice in advancing the mission of the college during this period of increased student enrollments, hiring new faculty, initiating new programs, maintaining an aging physical plant, reforming the administrative structure, putting new buildings in place, and contending for state funding. Laffin often expressed his frustration when seeking financial support. He was an honest, hard-working, and cautious executive who believed he, his staff, and faculty were not being properly rewarded for their accomplishments. But he worked within the system, achieving what was possible under dire circumstances, and accomplishing what was practical.

When Cipriani assumed the position of assistant to the president, the job represented a civil service line that was occupied by Locke James, a professor of poultry science. Cipriani was allowed to pursue a tenured faculty rank because Laffin did not want to lose this faculty line. Therefore, Cipriani had to qualify as a full professor and be evaluated by the faculty, a process that required consultation and agreement from the academic department to which he would be assigned. He thus met for more than two hours with Dr. Maurice Case, chairman of the General Education Division. Case later became dean of the School of Arts and Sciences, and seventy faculty members answering their questions. The division to which he sought acceptance included the departments of Mathematics, Sciences, English, Social Sciences, History, Economics, and Political Science. The next day, Dr. Case notified him that he had been unanimously approved for the tenured rank of professor. Two years later, in 1968, he was promoted to vice president of administration when SUNY Central approved two new vice presidential positions, one for administration and the other for student affairs.

After Laffin's untimely death in 1976, Jack Purcell and Mauro Zulli acted as president until 1978. Cipriani applied for the presidency, stressing his educational background and his administrative experience at the college. College Council members Chairman Walter A. Lynch Jr., Bob Ench, Anthony Mastroianni, Leon Applewaite, and Edythe Layne, all familiar with his work, advanced his candidacy. Although some of its members would have preferred an off-campus candidate, the SUNY Board of Trustees supported the College Council's recommendation and appointed him president April 28, 1978. Cipriani learned of his appointment while chairing a meeting of the Environmental Quality Council at Dr. Lee Koppleman's Hauppauge office in Suffolk County. In the days that followed, he received congratulations from campus colleagues, especially from Professor Casimir Rakowski who came to his office with joyful tears in his eyes, to tell him how pleased he was and that his prayers had been answered. Cipriani and Rakowski were both graduates of Brooklyn Technical High School.[8]

Cipriani called a Cabinet meeting for the following Wednesday to inform the members that he intended to honor the traditions of the past, but that his goal was to lead the college toward a radically new era. To achieve a new mission for the college, he needed the support of the administrative staff, and he welcomed all at the meeting to remain in their positions. Only Paul Bedell, vice president for student affairs, requested to return to the classroom, which he did eighteen months later. Mauro Zulli, vice president of academic affairs, who had worked closely with Laffin to set in motion a new era, stayed on for more than five years to assist the new president. Because Zulli was a respected senior academic and administrative leader, Cipriani valued his support. Two other Cabinet members on whom Cipriani relied heavily in the next two decades were Joseph Monaco and Noel Palmer.

Cipriani's official installation took place Sunday, May 7, 1978, at Roosevelt Hall. College Council Chairman Lynch guided the ceremony. Morris Shapiro, president of the Suffolk County Board of Rabbis, gave the invocation, and student government leaders Valerie DeSalvo and Harry Kuhlman presented selected readings. Professor Kathleen Hawryluk, chair of the Faculty Executive Council, delivered the Salutation. SUNY Board of Trustees Chairman Donald M. Blinken presented the new president, and Lynch read the charge and oath of office. Cipriani addressed the audience and stated the challenges that lay ahead, calling for constructive change in order to become a relevant institution of higher learning and necessary to prepare future generations to become productive citizens. He said, "We must be the architects of change or else we will become the victims of change." In his inaugural address, he mentioned for the first time his hope that four-year programs in the applied sciences and technologies be established at Farmingdale, insisting he could not accomplish this vision without the help of the campus community.[9]

In his inaugural presidential address, Cipriani stated that he "believed Long Island and the State were entering into a new era that would be a challenge to all of us." He listed his objectives:

1. To improve programs that were currently offered and already central to the mission as we redefined and refocused it.
2. To develop programs that were appropriate to the new mission and to the new technologies that were evolving from the scientific discoveries of research on Long Island and in New York State.
3. To raise standards while downsizing both in total numbers of students and state dollar requirements.
4. To re-engineer all of the academic offerings to incorporate as much of the learning technology that we could develop ourselves or afford to acquire.
5. To permit the faculty to reinvest in expanding their individual and departmental roles to incorporate more elements of scholarship, public services, applied research, and personal student contacts.
6. To streamline and downsize administrative functions and consolidate as many nonacademic operations as possible.
7. To ensure continuity of access to, and quality of, all academic offerings both new and traditional.

He was so committed to these objectives that he repeated them before the New York State Senate Committee on Higher Education meeting at the SUNY Stony Brook campus in 1996.[10]

During summer 1978, Cipriani met with his academic deans and assistants. He laid out plans and requested their support. In September, he met directly with the entire faculty and staff in Nold Hall gymnasium explaining clearly his vision for the future so that there be no misunderstanding of his intentions. Cipriani was aware that political, individual, and institutional concerns might arise that could oppose his strategy. He explained that to develop baccalaureate degrees, certain lower level programs would have to be eliminated, programs the community colleges would prefer to have. They included mortuary science, recreation supervision, and community service assistant. Cipriani believed that Farmingdale had the necessary financial resources and the superior faculty in the arts and sciences and technologies necessary to insure success in upper-division programs. Long Island needed advanced technologists in aerospace, engineering, and health sciences. Although the traditional agricultural curriculum was in decline and would be ended a decade later, the separate successful ornamental horticultural program would continue; it remained a $1 billion industry and ecologically critical to Nassau and Suffolk counties. He stressed his vision by pointing out he would first concentrate on establishing baccalaureate programs in aviation and mechanical engineering technology. He expected opposition from the Consortium of Independent Colleges and Universities, the lobbying group representing the private institutions on Long Island.[11]

Cipriani assumed the presidency at a critical time in the modern history of the college. Laffin had instituted changes, but he died as the process was just getting underway. Maintaining administrative continuity posed a challenge. Managing ongoing student unrest during the late 1960s and early 1970s was particularly stressful. At the same time, Gov. Carey (1975–1982) brought an end to the favored position of SUNY that Gov. Rockefeller had established. Rockefeller had been able to remove the SUNY campuses from the restrictive policies of the Board of Regents, which had favored the private colleges and universities. In fact, Carey insisted that only one new building be built in the SUNY system during his administration, and that would be Gleeson Hall on the Farmingdale campus. The Vietnam War had produced profound social change, especially affecting youth and academia. By 1979, there were still one-hundred acres of agricultural land under cultivation on campus, and new buildings such as Greenley Hall Library and Nold Hall Sports Complex coexisted with the original educational program and with the expanding technologies. The Long Island Educational Opportunity Center (LIEOC) also waas making an impact. In the 1979–1980 school year, total enrollment had grown to 16,652, including 6,156 full-time and 7,232 part-time evening students, along with 3,264 students studying at the LIEOC. New faculty members were hired with advanced academic credentials. Although gains had been made under Laffin's leadership, the College Council remained wary of its speed and impact on the college. But Laffin often stated "that Farmingdale's tradition was not something locked in the past but that the institution's history was one that anticipated change and needed to be continually assessed and addressed," according to College Council member Anthony Mastroianni.[12]

Major problems persisted, including inadequate salaries, lack of funding for new programs and physical plant maintenance, as well as SUNY Central's failure to understand fully Farmingdale's role within the system. Finally, managing the college in the New York City metropolitan area was especially difficult because of the high cost of living and competition from nearby colleges. Cipriani was aware of these issues, but he believed that if the college did not look to the future and reinvent itself, it would not survive.

When Cipriani assumed the presidency in 1978, he continued the policies of Laffin, focusing on student outreach and the college's emphasis on modern technological education. He impressed upon the College Council and faculty that the college would "wither away if it continued in the cluster of Ag and Tech Colleges." It was the only "Aggie" school that did not exist in a rural setting. Except for the ornamental horticultural curriculum (and the emerging Long Island wine industry), the original agricultural mission was no longer needed. Cipriani pointed out that Nassau and Suffolk Community Colleges, the two largest community colleges in New York State, were duplicating most of the programs offered at Farmingdale. A new strategy was imperative. He believed that the college's long tradition of adapting to economic and technological trends placed it in an advantageous position to adjust to the needs of Long Island's high-tech industries.

Mauro Zulli, who served as Laffin's academic vice president, directly witnessed these events. Knapp had hired Zulli as a laboratory assistant in physics at the Conklin Street School in 1955. He worked under Allee and Medesy. He assisted Laffin and Cipriani by researching and writing reports justifying the transition to a four-year technical college. Zulli typified the support that grew among the faculty and non-teaching professional staff to advance the college to a higher level.[13]

The LIEOC represented one of the most successful outreach programs during the Laffin and Cipriani years. Their combined leadership in this endeavor was prompted by Governor Rockefeller's mandate to make education available to all persons, regardless of race, gender, or status. The mission of the LIEOC was to offer tuition-free, non-degree education opportunities to disadvantaged persons and minorities who were not eligible to enter college. It prepared students to complete secondary school diploma requirements that enabled them to enter college or seek gainful employment through vocational and college preparatory courses. Courses in English as a Second Language for the foreign-born accelerated progress in the program. The LIEOC further served the community through public service programs. Three centers on Long Island provide academic and counseling services: Farmingdale campus (at Hooper Hall), Hempstead, and Brentwood. LIEOC students who achieve success are recommended to the Educational Opportunity Programs sponsored by New York State at participating SUNY units, and to the Higher Educational Opportunity Programs at private colleges. Farmingdale serves as the host institution for the college community on Long Island.[14]

The person who guided the successful development of the LIEOC, and who earned the descriptive title, "A Voice for the Disadvantaged," was Noel Palmer. Laffin hired Palmer in August 1966 as assistant to the president for special programs at a time when Laffin had inaugurated an initiative to meet the needs of the "educationally underserved minorities and women of the State." Palmer was born on the Caribbean island of Jamaica, graduating there from Union Theological College in Kingston (1954), majoring in religion. He entered William Penn College, Oskalooosa, Iowa (1956) where he received a bachelor's degree in religion with a minor in education. He obtained a bachelor's of science degree at Columbia University's Teacher College (1957), and continued his studies there to receive a master's degree two years later. Palmer encompassed a wide variety of professional experiences and accomplishments: Society of Friends (Quaker) minister, biology teacher, superintendent of the Five Towns Community House on Long Island. These credentials prepared this teacher-counselor-administrator for the impending tasks of guiding the LIEOC.

Palmer was inspired by Chancellor Samuel Gould's message to a 1968 meeting of SUNY college presidents in Buffalo mandating that SUNY campuses be equal-opportunity institutions. Palmer helped to create and lead important initiatives regarding assistance to the disadvantaged. The Long Island Chapter of the Congress of Racial Equality demanded educational programs must be made available for young black men. Early attempts to establish training courses at local colleges had failed, but Farmingdale offered a skills program on campus called Wider Opportunity at Farmingdale for black students that summer. Palmer then instituted a weekend tutoring program in 1969 for black youth. At the same time, the Work Incentive Program was begun on campus. Farmingdale participated in the Long Island Consortium of Colleges whose goal was to coordinate financial assistance and educational programs for disadvantaged students. These programs led to the establishment of the LIEOC in 1973, as stipulated and financed by New York State. Students who completed their training were able to achieve high school-equivalent degrees, advanced skills, basic adult education, work and language skills, and college preparation.[15]

Palmer, with logistical support from the administration and fiscal expertise of Joseph Monaco, applied his skill in securing funding from Albany. Money for hiring staff and to rent facilities such as classrooms, labs, and counseling offices, was provided by the university's vice chancellor for finance and business, service organizations, and local government agencies. Palmer lobbied directly to key leaders in the SUNY Central Office who then turned to both the state attorney general and comptroller to convince them of the importance of the special programs. He even persuaded the public school system in Roosevelt, Long Island to sponsor and fund a weekend residential college experience for high school juniors. The educational Urban Centers he opened on the Farmingdale campus, Hempstead, and Brentwood were working so well that the two public community colleges complained that the centers were violating their turf, even though they had been duplicating many of Farmingdale's programs. There was also criticism by those who had envisioned a less expensive way to serve the disadvantaged and minority students. Yet implementing the LIEOC concept achieved a positive impact on region's diverse population. "Dr. Laffin led the way, and Noel Palmer plotted the course to meet that challenge" of Gov. Rockefeller's and Chancellor Gould's mandate, commented Cipriani. During his career, Palmer also held the title of vice president for student affairs. He retired in 1991.[16]

Reginald "Tye" Marshall, who came to Farmingdale in 1973, replaced Palmer in 1991 as dean of the LIEOC. Marshall also was a successful educator/administrator. He served as the director of the LIEOC, and was the recipient of the SUNY Chancellor's Award for Excellence in Professional Service (1989) and the UUP Excellence Award (1990). It is important to mention the distinguished career of Veronica Henry who succeeded Marshall as dean/director of the LIEOC. She was one of the first students to graduate from the LIEOC and symbolized Farmingdale's equal-opportunity success story. She continued her studies in the Farmingdale nursing program (AAS), graduated from Stony Brook (BS, MS), Adelphi University (MS), and Columbia University (Ed.D). She has served as professor of nursing, dean of the LIEOC, and was appointed executive assistant to President W. Hubert Keen in 2009.[17]

The college continued to focus on its important function of educating a new generation of students under the guidance of a dedicated faculty. A Middle States Accrediting Committee recommended a student publication be established at a time when *The Rambler*, the college newspaper, had been shut down for several years. The recommendation came at the time when the college was planning to become a four-year institution. Professor James Friel of the English/Humanities Department (1970–2007) initiated the founding of *Humanities/AITIA* magazine, working with a small group of educators to advance teaching of philosophy and the humanities. Friel, who has continued as editor, met in 1972 with other scholars from cooperating institutions (Nassau Community College, New York Institute of Technology, CUNY, William Paterson College) and received a grant from the Matchette Foundation to hold a series of conferences and to support the magazine. *Humanities/AITIA* is an ongoing professional publication emphasizing

FIGURE 8-4. Students and faculty built the second Log Cabin at the northern section of the campus in the 1950s. Social gatherings took place there until a fire destroyed it in 1979, ending a campus tradition.

FIGURE 8-5. President Frank A. Cipriani is joined in College Convocation with Nobel Laureate Dr. James Watson of Cold Spring Harbor Laboratory, left, and Thomas Kelly, right, who guided the construction of the Grumman Lunar Excursion Module that landed on the moon.

teaching of philosophy and humanities by focusing on improving the environment, the individual's role in the community, and articulating citizenship values. AITIA means responsibility, as defined in *Greek Philosophical Terms* by F. E. Peters. The publication, courses, and conferences have provided a humanistic base for the increasing importance of technology.[18]

Covering a span of six decades, from the Knapp administration to the Cipriani administration, the construction of two log cabins provide an example of cooperation between students and faculty. The purpose of the log cabins was to hold social functions there for the campus community. The original cabin was built in the years 1924 to 1927. John F. "Chick" Meehan, popular coach of the NYU football teams (1925–1931) that used the campus for preseason practice, contributed expenses for this log cabin. The players slept in campus dormitories and ate in the dining hall; in return for these services and facilities, NYU donated $1,200 annually to the school. In the 1950s, the building, because of its small size and age, was razed and the Faculty Association with the support of Knapp decided to build a new one. In this instance, the Brooklyn Dodgers professional football team also used the campus facilities for practice and donated money to cover the cost of the new log cabin. Professors Don Waite, Guy Mowry, Carl Strohlein, and Horton Amidon began the log cabin project in spring 1953. Students assisted in the work and gained practical experience in construction techniques, including plumbing, carpentry, and electrical work. Students from the Agriculture Department built picnic tables and outdoor fireplaces. The Horticultural Department landscaped the grounds. The Long Island Lighting Company donated 1,600 feet of underground cable connecting to the power plant. Mrs. MacDougall, Knapp's secretary, was in charge of securing furniture and fixtures. To guarantee completion of the log cabin, the Classes of 1954 and 1955 contributed $7,500.[19]

The new log cabin was used for social functions, meetings, and a special place for students to escape from the pressures of schoolwork. Students of that period were "devoted to the memory" of the log cabin and they felt it was "an icon that was part of their experience on the college campus; it was a great place for people to just be themselves," said Director of Alumni Affairs Eileen Hasson. It was at the log cabin that Stefan Mansella (Class of 1966) met Annette LaRocca (Class of 1967) and became engaged. "We married on May 6, 1968," reminisced Mansella. The cabin was the place for chicken barbeques. The chickens were fresh from the campus barn, and fire pits were dug outside the cabin. Although Farmingdale was a secular school, religious services were held there. Seder, the Jewish ceremonial meal eaten during Passover, was often conducted there. This icon of college history suffered from two fires, but the second one was so catastrophic in 1979 that it was completely destroyed. Although alumni have discussed rebuilding a new log cabin, all attempts have failed.[20]

Despite his attempt to modernize the college, Cipriani sought to preserve the record of the past. No other institution on Long Island could match its long history because of its uniqueness, reflecting in many ways the region's development. He presided over the celebration of the "70th Anniversary Ball, 1912–1982," and soon followed with the appointment of a Historical Committee to highlight the seventy-fifth anniversary of the college. In the afternoon of October 11, 1986, the president chaired the ceremony in the Little Theater of Roosevelt Hall, while Professor Kay Wilson conducted a video presentation of the college history and an exhibit in the lobby. A dedication of the historical marker citing the founding year of 1912 was completed earlier in the day at the Melville Road entrance to the college. Presentations were made to the honorees who had served the college over the years: Professors Horton Amidon, Norman Foote, Gerald Allard, Robert Stockbridge, Anne Senyk, and Pearl Brod. Historical Committee Professors Michael Abbatiello, Frank J. Cavaioli, and Eugene O'Neill presented talks on the contributions the college had made to public education. The president requested all interested persons to record historical vignettes and to collect memorabilia as an important way to preserve the college history.[21]

As part of the seventy-fifth anniversary celebration, the Farmingdale College Foundation selected John O'Brien to receive The Ram's Horn Award at the Diamond Jubilee Ball, on March 14, 1987, for distinguished service. O'Brien, an alumnus and supporter of Farmingdale, joined the Grumman Aerospace Corporation in 1954 and worked his way upward through the ranks to become president and chief operating officer in the 1980s. The Ram's Horn symbolizes the qualities of integrity, strength, valor, and courage. It is the highest honor bestowed on an individual by the Farmingdale College Foundation. Previous Ram's Horn Award Recipients include Robert Ench (1983), president of Flower Time, Inc.; Lawrence S. Hanson 1985), senior vice president of Irving Trust Co.; and Robert F. Peyser (1986), senior vice president of Norstar Bank.[22]

Advances were made during the 1980s concerning the establishment of a cooperative educational venture with the Republic of China, a link that would be expanded under the leadership of President W. Hubert Keen (2007–). After preliminary negotiations, Chinese Professor Pei arrived on campus for the 1981 fall semester to teach electrical engineering technology courses. Professor Herb Zipper of Farmingdale's Electrical Engineering Technology Department served as his host. There were other main land Chinese educators who participated in the cultural exchange program during the 1980s. Professor Leon Taub sponsored Professor Tang, who taught construction engineering technology courses. Professor Chow, sponsored by Professor Nick Romanelli, taught in the same department. In return, Professor Hall Brennan and Dr. Dash Petrela went to teach at the University of Xi'an in 1987. Professors Taub and Zipper went there the following year.[23]

In October 1985, the presidents of both institutions signed a formal cultural exchange arrangement between Farmingdale and Xi'an Aerotechnical College of the Peoples Republic of China. In the same month, Cipriani made a ten-day trip to Xi'an Aerotechnical College. Professor Dominick Pugliese, assistant to the president for international programs, and Dr. Martha McCoy, College Council member, accompanied the president. Dr. McCoy acted as interpreter and advisor. Mrs. Anne Ip also accompanied the group to act as back-up interpreter and travel advisor

FIGURE 8-6. This panorama view, taken from Laffin Hall, of Ralph Bunche Plaza in the late 1970s shows a reception for grads, family, friends, and faculty following graduation ceremonies. Knapp Hall is at right. Hale Hall is at top left. Greenley Library has not yet been built.

throughout the China visit. They visited Xi'an Northwestern University, Stomotologic Hospital, Electrical Engineering Manufacturing Company of Xi'an, Polytechnic College of Xi'an, Science and Technology Commission of Xi'an, Chinese Dance-Drama Theater, Xi'an, and Ministry of Aviation, as well as the Aerotechnical College of Xi'an. Professors Pei and Cao, two of the first exchange scholars to Farmingdale, greeted them and provided them with vital technical assistance; Pei was now a vice president of the college and Cao was dean of academic affairs. College president Pei and vice president Fan hosted the American visitors. The American delegation also traveled to Hangzhou, the ornamental horticulture capital of China, Shanghai, and Beijing. President Cipriani offered a formal farewell to his hosts, President Fei and colleagues at Xi'an Aerotechnical College. He expressed "regrets" of having to leave but looked forward with "renewed enthusiasm and high hopes for the future of our joint endeavor." The "seeds of hope" that were planted five years ago, "have been nourished by caring individuals on both sides of the world." Cipriani thanked his hosts for their unequalled hospitality."[24]

Several other goals were achieved as a result of the China trip. A cooperative agreement was made concerning the Chinese Gardens of the Orient and the Queens Botanical Gardens. Another agreement provided for economic cooperation involving the Small Business Development Center of Farmingdale. The most important mission, however, was to continue the exchange of professors to lecture on planned subjects between Xi'an Aerotechnical College and the Farmingdale campus. In this regard, Professors Xiaoping Xue and Yaping Qi concluded an 18-month teaching visit at Farmingdale in December 1989. Professor Xue taught in the Electrical Engineering Technology Department and Professor Qi taught in the Computing Graphics Technology Department. Terry Smith, associate dean for the School of Engineering Technologies stated the Visiting Professor Program was "a very successful cultural and educational exchange since its inception in the fall of 1981." Cipriani considered the program an integral part of transforming the college to upper division status.[25]

Professor Herb Zipper of the Electrical Engineering Technology Department was a direct participant as an exchange scholar to China and host to a Chinese exchange scholar. As a respected teacher, advisor, and counselor, he had a special affinity for the college during his four decades of participation in all facets of campus life. He and his wife Maureen were permanent residents of Farmingdale Village. He said, "We had six children in a six-year time period, so we thought it would be economically smart for each of them to start their college careers at Farmingdale. SUNY Farmingdale also prepared them very well for whatever endeavors they chose." They went on to receive advanced degrees and secure professional positions. Zipper believed Farmingdale differed from other institutions because it "is a very caring school with qualified and interested faculty. Small classes also make it more personal." Many other faculty members shared their faith in a Farmingdale education by sending their children to the college.[26]

Another important individual who contributed to the advancement of the college was Patricia Hill Williams, who was hired in 1980 by Cipriani as assistant to the president for Alumni

FIGURE 8-7. Director Halsey B. Knapp was honored for his contribution and dedicated service to the College with this historical marker in the Greenhouse Gardens, placed there May 21, 1981 in a ceremony led by President Frank A. Cipriani.

Affairs, a newly created SUNY position. As time went on she assumed a greater administrative role as chief advancement officer with responsibilities involving public relations, college foundation, affirmative action, and government relations. A recipient of numerous awards, her two-year W. K. Kellogg Fellowship in international leadership allowed her to evaluate and implement projects in Latin America and the Caribbean. She is chairperson of the Inter-American Board of Partners of the Americas, one of the largest private voluntary organizations in the Western Hemisphere. Its Long Island chapter is linked to St. Vincent and the Grenadines and was brought to Farmingdale by Noel Palmer. The Long Island chapter provides aid and training in youth leadership programs in other Caribbean islands. She is particularly proud of her long service on

FIGURE 8-8. Campus Plant Manager Fred Harrison, left, guides the placing of a time capsule in the Ralph Bunche Plaza, 1987. Faculty and dignitaries look on.

the Suffolk County Human Rights Commission and the National Coalition of 100 Black Women. Her success in women's issues, civil rights, and education earned her four presidential appointments by Ronald Reagan, George H. W. Bush, Bill Clinton, and George W. Bush. She was instrumental in establishing a Ralph Bunche Society on campus and donated a bust of the late diplomat and Nobel Peace Prize winner for display in the University Club. Her public service has brought considerable esteem to Farmingdale. Dr. Williams was appointed vice president of external affairs in 2000. She retired four years later. In 2006 Gov. George Pataki appointed her to the Farmingdale State College Council.[27]

As these developments were contributing to the progress of the college, the process of implementing new programs, expansion of successful ones, and establishing a baccalaureate-granting institution remained difficult, complex, and challenging. Not only would creative leadership be necessary, but also the cooperation of faculty and staff. Opposition from local colleges would have to be overcome. The higher education bureaucracy in Albany needed to be persuaded. The road ahead would not be easy.

NINE

Transition and Transformation

> The State University Board of Trustees yesterday gave the go-ahead for the State College of Technology at Farmingdale to become a full-fledged four-year college, completing its transformation from an agricultural school with livestock and its own dairy to an institution that trains students in high-technology occupations.[1]

THE PROGRESS MADE IN THE LAST QUARTER OF THE TWENTIETH CENTURY was significant as the college struggled to achieve the status of a forward-looking institution without neglecting its traditions. Its history embraced change. Obstacles were confronted and overcome with new sources of energy and creativity since its chartering in 1912. Throughout the years, a dedicated faculty and staff sustained the college. To achieve its proper role in the SUNY remained a challenge. The Industrial-Technical Division, founded after World War II, was an important beginning. The addition of new programs and the increase in student enrollment affirmed Farmingdale's ability to adapt to society's changing needs.

From 1912 to 1976, three leaders had a major impact on the school at Farmingdale: Albert A. Johnson, Halsey B. Knapp, and Charles W. Laffin Jr. Johnson guided the formative years of the institution's focus on agricultural and horticultural education. He shaped the original physical layout of the campus. Knapp arrived at a critical time to save the school's existence, nurture its growth, and create new programs in technology. His thirty-three-year tenure gained him and the school wide respect. Laffin put the faculty on a professional schedule. He advanced his policies by hiring a highly qualified faculty and talented administrative staff. He believed the college should reach out to educate disadvantaged populations. He sought to expand its mission to adapt to an emerging technologically based society. His death in 1976 was sudden and devastating; his plans for a complete transformation of the college were cut short, but not silenced.

The stage was set for the presidency of Dr. Frank A. Cipriani (1978–2000) to apply his leadership skills to continue the process of growth and expansion. Having gained experience at several administrative positions since arriving on campus in 1964, and being influenced by Laffin's policies, he accomplished much during his years as president. But one fundamental goal remained: transforming the college into a four-year baccalaureate-granting institution, while simultaneously retaining successful programs. By 2000, Cipriani had successfully guided the establishment of the innovative Broad Hollow Bioscience Park at the northeastern part of the campus. As an academic/industrial park, this endeavor created collaboration with New York State, Cold Spring Harbor Laboratory, and Farmingdale. An ambitious faculty and administrative staff supported the changes.

The college's involvement in such a program at this time exemplified how it adapted to industrial-technical transformation by building an aviation curriculum. Aviation had a long tradition on Long Island. The campus location helped. Long Island may be considered the cradle of aviation, beginning even earlier than Charles A. Lindberg's heroic solo nonstop flight from Roosevelt Field (named for Theodore Roosevelt's son Quentin Roosevelt) to Paris in 1927. Pioneer Glenn H. Curtiss completed the first sustained flight of sixteen miles in 1909 across the Hempstead plains. Pilot Lawrence B. Sperry was the founding father of aviation manufacturing in Farmingdale before 1920. After his death in a 1923 plane crash, his wife and silent film star Winifred Sperry leased their South Farmingdale factory to Sherman Fairchild. Grumman Aircraft and Republic Airport also have long been associated with the development of aviation in the region, and the college exploited the opportunity to be a part of this important industry.[2]

As part of the national preparedness program in World War II, pilot training as initiated at Farmingdale helped to provide a foundation on which to build a future aviation curriculum. On the campus itself at the time, planes took off and landed on a grass strip that is now covered by the college's athletic facilities. Students learned about the airframe and power plant of the aircraft, maintenance, meteorology, movement of people and cargo, airport management, and other aspects of the aviation industry. The program ended with World War II.[3]

Laffin realized the importance of aviation on Long Island. In 1969, he hired Lou Howard to chair the Aerospace Technology Department. Howard secured three planes, hired faculty, and remembered teaching ten students at MacArthur Field in Suffolk County where there was a wooden tower at the far side of the field before moving on to Republic Airport in Farmingdale. Howard received a bachelor of science degree from Springfield College, and a certificate of advanced study from Hofstra University in Hempstead. He served four years in the U.S. Army Air Force. Howard was widely respected throughout New York State and applied his aviation expertise in developing a curriculum that was practical as it was current. A popular figure on Long island, Howard served as mayor of the Village of Amityville, teacher and football coach at Amityville High School, leading his school to nine straight football championships. He published the *Amityville Record* and the *Suffolk County News*, was a former member of the New York State Assembly, and presiding officer of the Suffolk County Legislature. Howard was appointed to the SUNY Board of Trustees in 1997, and later to the Stony Brook University Council. Laffin valued Howard's considerable influence that could be exerted in providing support for the aerospace program.[4]

FIGURE 9-1. This 1960 aerial scene shows a placid campus on the verge of expansion. Thompson Hall, with cupola, is at top center, off the Circle, with partially covered Hicks Hall and Cutler Hall to its right. The Director's Cottage is in foreground. The Ornamental Horticulture Teaching Gardens are at right. Part of Ward Hall can be seen at upper extreme left. The farm complex is in the background. Route 110, not shown, is at right.

Cipriani, a past navigator-instructor in the army, appreciated the link between the college's growth and the aviation industry. Early in his administrative position as vice president, he benefited from the contacts he had made with Long Island's commercial interests. With the encouragement of Dr. Laffin, he attended meetings of the Aircraft Owners and Pilots Association at Islip's MacArthur Airport. The group was concerned with preserving aviation facilities that were being dismantled at Long Island's four counties. Flushing Airport, Zahn's Airport in Amityville, and Grumman's facility in Bethpage would soon succumb. Also at risk were Floyd Bennett Field in Brooklyn, Suffolk County Air Force Base in Westhampton, and Grumman's Air Field in Calverton. Roosevelt Field was already being converted into a shopping mall. Mitchel Field became the home of Nassau Community College, the Coliseum, Marriott Hotel, and office buildings. Demand for real estate for housing and commerce was great. The college administration carefully monitored this situation as it sought to preserve and expand its program at Republic Airport in Farmingdale. Aviation was a growth industry and the college wanted to provide educational support. A coalition of business and aviation interests, with the cooperation of the college, managed to get New York State to acquire Republic Airport through the Metropolitan Transportation Authority with a stipulation that a 3.5-acre portion of the site fronting on Route 110 be set aside for Farmingdale's aerospace program.

By 1989, the college offered a two-year aerospace technology curriculum that granted an associate in applied science (AAS). Howard retired in 1988. The program recognized the burgeoning aviation industry that required skilled technicians in positions of flight control, air carrier operations, airport management, and related government capacities. At this time, the flight portion of the aerospace program charged a nominal student fee, and the college owned seven single-engine aircraft, five GAT simulators, and was accredited by the FAA for both flight and ground training. Upon graduation, students qualified for private pilot licenses. Related to the aerospace curriculum was the aircraft maintenance mechanical technology course, which also granted the AAS degree, preparing students for FAA certification as aviation maintenance technicians. All instruction was taught at the main campus and at the Aerospace Education Center located at Republic Field, 1.5 miles south of the campus. The college and Suffolk County Boards of Cooperative Educational Services III jointly sponsored the latter program.[5]

At the same time that Long Island's oldest public institution of higher learning celebrated its eightieth anniversary, ground was broken for its new Aviation Center at Republic Airport on April 15, 1993. Amid a group of public officials, leading industrialists, and educators Cipriani conducted the ceremony. The new 20,000-square-foot educational aviation facility was built at a cost of $3.2 million, with financing approved and bonded by the New York State University Construction Fund. Because the facility was located less than two miles from the main campus, the architects, Siris/Coombs, designed the building to be a self-sufficient "campus-off-campus," an academic village containing an airplane maintenance hangar, electrical fabrication and engine labs, classrooms, administrative offices, flight simulation lab, and a flight control and navigation center. Farmingdale's own fleet of seven Cessnas and one de Havilland "Beaver" flew in formation over the site during the ceremony.[6]

The aerospace program was revitalized five years later when three new training airplanes arrived at the Republic Airport facility for the 1997 fall semester. Professor and Chairman LaMarr O. Stanford, with the support of the administration, believed that these fuel-efficient aircraft with a high-technology satellite navigational device (global positioning system) upgraded the program to retain and increase the 220 students already in the program. Competition for outstanding college students in aviation remained intense. By September 1998, the name of the Aerospace Technology Department had been renamed the Department of Aviation, which was then under the chairmanship of Dr. Victor Bellard. Today the Aviation Department offers a bachelor of science degree in aeronautical science, professional pilot and a bachelor of science degree in aviation administration. It is recognized as the premier collegiate aviation program on Long Island, and the region.[7]

A critical development emerged in early 2003 when Republic Airport leaders and officials of the Long Island Business Aviation Association (LIBAA) protested the proposal of Stew Leonard's, Inc. to erect a 35-foot-high, two-story 120,000-square-foot supermarket in the runway protection zone at the northeast end of Republic Airport runway 14-32, about one-thousand feet from where airplanes touch down on the runway. Republic Airport Director Hugh. D. Jones and LIBAA Chairman William Mc Shane requested the Stew Leonard Company relocate eight-hundred feet away from the flight path. The site in question was located at the southwest corner of Route 110 and Conklin Street. Cipriani entered the fray to save the Republic Airport facility as a safe entity from being bulldozed into a massive shopping mall. As a member and vice president of the Babylon Airport Council, Cipriani was able to generate political and community support from the council, the Aircraft Owners and Pilots Association, the Long Island Association of Commerce and Industry, and the general and commercial aviation interests on Long Island. Emeritus Professor Lou Howard continued to support the aviation curriculum for the college, and in turn, used his own political contacts to save Republic Airport. College Council member Anthony

Mastroianni, Farmingdale Class of 1950, offered critical support. As the respected Suffolk County public administrator and political leader, Mastroianni joined the lobbying effort to achieve the same goal. With the victory won, Farmingdale's aerospace aviation program was secured nearby on Route 110.[8]

Such events helped to contribute to establishing Farmingdale as a four-year baccalaureate-granting institution. Patience was paramount. Laffin acknowledged toward the end of his presidency that the educational benefits of the G.I. Bill had been exhausted and the addition of new

FIGURE 9-2. President Cipriani conducts a faculty meeting in Nold Hall in the early 1990s to discuss reduced New York State funding. To his left are: George P. LaRosa, Vice President for Administration and Finance; Michael J. Vinciguerra, Provost; and Joseph Monaco, Deputy President. They were all appointees of President Charles W. Laffin, Jr.

public colleges would create competition for students. The traditional agricultural curriculum was attracting fewer and fewer students, and its costs were escalating. With the agreement of his administrative staff, Laffin believed that Farmingdale should find a special niche that would insure its future. Therefore, he wanted the institution to expand its mission by becoming an upper-division college, simultaneously retaining two-year programs. After Laffin's death, his plan was temporarily put on hold until a new president could be installed. SUNY Central watched and waited to see if Farmingdale could achieve the high standards expected of it.

When Cipriani was appointed the college's sixth president in 1978 his close association with Laffin influenced him to expand the mission of the college. To achieve the goal of establishing four-year programs, he believed Farmingdale had to take advantage of its unique geographical location and extend its historical tradition. His knowledge and experience with the business community and local political leaders helped him in this endeavor. He was aware of the research facilities at the University Center at Stony Brook, Cold Spring Harbor Laboratory, and the Brookhaven National Laboratory. The emergence of new high-tech-related industries also motivated him.[9]

It was difficult for SUNY Central to accept the proposed two-plus-two concept. Chancellor Clifton Wharton took a neutral position, while Jerry Komisar, vice president academic affairs and university provost, displayed opposition. Komisar had come from a SUNY arts and sciences college and believed that Farmingdale should continue to serve as a feeder college. He and others regarded Farmingdale as just another "two-year community college" that happened to have a resident student population. Upon Wharton's resignation, Bruce Johnstone, former president of Buffalo's Arts and Sciences College, became chancellor and was more agreeable to the proposed change of Farmingdale's status. However, new vice president for academic programs and Provost Joseph Burke was slow to recognize the importance of the Agricultural and Technical colleges, believing they should continue in their limited role.

Other issues arose. The rapid growth of the two local community colleges could not be stopped and the private four-year colleges opposed the change. The Consortium of Independent Colleges and Universities, representing Adelphi, Dowling, Hofstra, Molloy, New York Institute of Technology, and St. Joseph's, expressed its concern through a well-financed lobbying force fighting to protect their interests. The new State College at Old Westbury also offered competition as it mimicked some of the courses at Farmingdale, and even recruited some of Farmingdale's faculty. With the exception of Stony Brook, the only true engineering university on Long Island, the other public colleges remained silent. Stony Brook President John Marburger not only saw the value of supporting Farmingdale's initiative but also believed a future collaborative venture between the two campuses was possible. There also emerged in the post Rockefeller era a belief that SUNY had been overbuilt, and was too expensive to run. Gov. Hugh Carey's administration (1975–1982) and subsequent administrations attempted to consolidate campuses and reduce costs. SUNY budgets were slashed and Carey floated the idea that Farmingdale should be downsized, the agricultural curriculum be dropped, and 225 campus acres of the 380 be sold. As stated earlier, it was estimated that one acre of land on Route 110 was valued at nearly $1 million and could be used for housing and commercial ventures. These critical issues led Cipriani to enlist direct support of local legislators, including four Republican state senators and two Democratic and two Republican assemblymen.[10]

Reduced support for the entire SUNY system caused serious problems, but Farmingdale, little understood and traditionally under funded, was further weakened by cutbacks throughout the 1980s and 1990s. Unmatched inflationary costs eroded the quality and quantity of educational capabilities. At the same time, the transitional process to achieve upper-division status led to some temporary negative effects on curriculum and enrollment, even when consolidation and change were being planned. Farmingdale programs that were the least technologically reliant were eliminated. The Mortuary Science Department was transferred to Nassau Community College (NCC) in 1993, completing two years for the shift to take place. Other programs at Farmingdale eliminated due to budget cuts were recreational supervision, community service assistant, computer graphics, graphic communications (printing), early childhood education, veterinary science technology, and office management. Enrollment in the criminal justice program declined. Referring to mortuary science, Salvatore Rotella, NCC's academic vice president, stated, "This program will be identical to the nationally accredited one that has been offered by Farmingdale." The four professors in Farmingdale's mortuary science program—Chairman John Lieblang, Charles Metzroth, Marcus Gray, and Marijude Lofaro—became members of NCC's faculty. They benefited from NCC's high pay scale by nearly doubling their salaries.[11]

The administrations of the agricultural and technical colleges had frequently called for the expansion of their educational mission. To deal with this issue, SUNY followed up with a special study, *Final Report of the University Commission on Purposes and Priorities* (1976). In addition to associate and certificate degrees, the commission recommended a limited number of baccalaureate programs be offered at the agricultural and technical colleges. Thus, a new era was beginning in the 1980s for these institutions. For example, in 1985, the SUNY Board of Trustees granted

Farmingdale the authority to offer two four-year bachelor's degrees in electrical technology and manufacturing technology. Two years later, because of fiscal priorities, the agricultural program ended when the last class graduated in May. "The Call of the Farm," a verse in the school's 1920 *Yearbook*, no longer appealed to the young. The campus farm is "one of the last remaining resources to children in the area to see farm animals," said Maurie Semel, Farmingdale Class of 1942 and Cornell University entomology professor at the Riverhead research station. The campus farm provided an opportunity for thousands of visiting school children to see cows, pigs, sheep, chickens, and other animals in a real farm setting. Such a pivotal event acknowledged that the college was moving toward a more active involvement in national and global economic developments, recognizing the increasing importance of applied sciences and technology. Although some bemoaned the demise of the college's long tradition in agriculture, the ornamental horticultural curriculum remained vibrant. At the same time, the SUNY Board of Trustees sought to achieve greater efficiencies in the system.[12]

In 1988, SUNY commissioned consulting firm National Center for Higher Education Management Services (NCHEMS) to conduct a comprehensive analysis of how SUNY should address technical needs of the region and New York State. Following a two-year study, NCHEMS recommended a totally new SUNY strategy for the Long Island region, essentially affirming the strategy that Farmingdale had been pursuing for the past decade. It was found that Farmingdale was unique among the region's colleges by virtue of its location on Long Island in serving local students and technical industries, its difference compared to the community colleges, and its emphasis on baccalaureate degrees in applied technology. In February 1990, the SUNY Board of Trustees moved forward again by approving upper-division bachelor of science programs in aviation administration and aeronautical science (professional pilot). Farmingdale became the first public college in New York State to offer these programs. In April 1990, as a result of the NCHEMS recommendations, the SUNY Board of Trustees approved a resolution to make Farmingdale a baccalaureate degree-granting institution that offered degrees in applied sciences and technologies; the comprehensive array of associate degree programs would continue. The action further expanded the mission of Farmingdale and separated it from other colleges on Long Island.[13]

The SUNY Board of Trustees' action received high praise. SUNY Provost Joseph Burke expressed enthusiastic support of the planning exhibited by Cipriani and campus Provost Michael Vinciguerra. Burke indicated that the public colleges in the region had cooperated in the change because there would be no duplication of courses. The new mission gave Farmingdale the mandate to educate students in biotechnology, aerospace, computers, and other high-technology occupations with programs "so new that there may not even be a vocabulary to describe them," according to Cipriani. James LaRocca, president of the Long Island Association, the region's largest business group, praised the new mission, "Farmingdale's evolution from agriculture to a technology university reflects the change that has occurred and is occurring in this economy." Long Island planner Lee Koppelman, chairman of Farmingdale's Small Business Development Center, pointed out the "quality of the applied sciences and technology program makes Farmingdale an extremely good parallel to the research center at Stony Brook." Additionally, upper-division courses in the humanities and social sciences would be taught, but Farmingdale would not offer a bachelor of arts degree, and Cipriani insisted the "humanities [and social sciences] not be diminished."[14]

Finally, in April 1993 SUNY Farmingdale was officially designated a four-year college of technology by a unanimous vote of the New York State Board of Regents, even though the year before the Regents had opposed the change. The Albany bureaucracy had also delayed the final decision. Gov. Mario Cuomo's political support of the four-year program at Farmingdale contributed to the Regents' decision. The reality was that the college had been accepting students into bachelor of technology degree programs since 1985 based on the established policy of the SUNY Board of Trustees. The action also removed the requirement that every baccalaureate program be subject to a Master Plan amendment. At the same time, the Regents approved two new bachelor of technology programs to be added to the college curriculum, visual communication and industrial technology. Related to this development was the official opening of the Technology Transfer and Utilization Center (TTUC) in December 1993. Vinciguerra explained that the purpose of the TTUC was to serve as a gateway for industry access to the college resources. TTUC's addition to Lupton Hall symbolized Farmingdale's commitment to bridging the gap between theory and application, and to expand the college's effort in technology utilization. The TTUC initiative was made possible through the efforts of Long Island's State Sen. Ralph Marino. He obtained funding in 1984 for more than $1 million to fund the reconstruction of Lupton Hall's old foundry. The official opening of this facility occurred at a ribbon-cutting ceremony on December 3, 1993, featuring remarks by Cipriani, Vinciguerra, and Marino. Faculty from the schools of Business and Engineering Technologies presented a play demonstrating how computer-aided manufacturing can solve technology-application problems. Also, faculty from the Advertising and Art and Design Department presented a multimedia presentation on the uses of technology in industry.[15]

FIGURE 9-3. The beautiful Ornamental Horticulture Teaching Gardens are located behind Thompson Hall and Hicks Hall. The curriculum is one of the oldest and most popular. Students plan and maintain the Gardens.

The actual process of transforming the college to a four-year institution was difficult during a period when its resources were being stretched. Some two-year programs were eliminated as indicated above, and a few were modified. In 1992, seventeen tenured faculty and four untenured positions also were. The average campus salary was more than $15,000 below that of teachers in the local Farmingdale public school system. This fact was based on a long-held belief that the Farmingdale College faculty lacked the high standards found in upper-division colleges. Traditionally, salaries at SUNY two-year technical schools were the lowest in the system. But Farmingdale, located downstate, had to contend with a higher cost of living, a condition that Albany leaders had ignored since the school's founding. The college lacked money to maintain its physical facilities as its buildings, laboratories, and grounds were decaying. New York State's new 1995–1996 budget dealt a severe blow to the entire SUNY establishment. The SUNY trustees were forced to trim all campus outlays for the new academic year, but Farmingdale suffered an 11 percent reduction, the highest of all statewide campuses. Stony Brook lost 3 percent, while Old Westbury lost 4.1 percent. The SUNY trustees also increased undergraduate student tuition by $750. Gov. George Pataki's budget had actually called for a much larger SUNY budget reduction—39 percent—but the legislature restored most of the funds that would have been lost under the proposed cuts.[16]

The result of these developments was a drop in enrollments. In the fall term of 1994 all Long Island public colleges increased enrollments with the exception of SUNY Farmingdale (its new title), which plunged 13 percent from the previous year. Enrollments in real numbers year over year went from 7,730 to 6,717. In the previous four years, Farmingdale had experienced a dramatic 40 percent decline in enrollments. The only other public institution to decline, with less than one percent, was NCC. A combination of factors led to this decline: elimination of some two-year curricula while preparing for new four-year technology programs, tuition increases, tightening admissions requirements, and weak recruiting procedures. Cipriani and Vinciguerra accurately predicted that when the college's new mission was fully operational the trend in enrollments would stabilize and eventually increase. Also disquieting was a series of new titles adoptions for the institution during its transformation. In 1966, its new title became Agricultural and Technical College at Farmingdale. It was changed to SUNY College of Technology at Farmingdale in 1987 when the agriculture curriculum was ended. It 1993, it became SUNY Farmingdale, and in 2002 it was changed again to its present and permanent name, Farmingdale State College.[17]

Another factor explaining the enrollment decline was confusion over which specific programs were being offered. By the end of the 1990s, with all the changes taking place, the college experienced a lack of clarity in projecting its new educational mission. Felice Solomon, director of guidance for the Plainview-Old Bethpage School District, summed up the problem, "Our students used to go to Farmingdale for air conditioning, veterinary, pre-engineering and drafting. Then Farmingdale got out of a lot of those programs." Questioned about the new programs, she said, "People don't know about them, and when people don't know, they don't go." As a result, enrollment numbers worsened, dropping below 4,000 in 1999. Simultaneously, the SUNY Board of Trustees placed limitations on the college's ability to act, and New York State slowed the transitional process to four-year status through bureaucratic micromanaging approval of new bachelor degrees, among other issues. Vinciguerra said, "We were Stealth University. Because of those restrictions we were hiding programs and nobody could find them." Even Cipriani, addressing the Senate Higher Education Committee in 1996, commented that "from past experience all change in this state comes slowly and, perhaps painfully. What has taken more than fifteen years could have been easily accomplished in half the time, and with far less pain and dislocation."[18]

Despite these growing pains, the faculty and administration expressed optimism that the new mission would be successful and that the college would be prepared to serve future educational needs of the region. Accordingly, the difficult realignment of personnel and resources was essentially accomplished during the 1990s, but not without pain. Stability resulted and growth lay ahead. Transition was complete. Transformation was accomplished.

FIGURE 9-4. The Wall of Honor, at Ralph Bunche Plaza, was dedicated September 6, 1997. Alumni and friends of the College could be honored through the purchase of a brick for $100 or $300. Funds were used for student scholarships.

Cipriani, not to be satisfied, expanded his vision in seeking to establish a Bioscience Park on the northern section of campus land that was no longer used for agriculture. He believed that a new breed of technologists would enhance the more sophisticated industries being spawned on Long Island. Such an educational park would help develop the bioscience curriculum and nurture start-up companies. In 1996, he commissioned Dr. Pearl Kamer, senior economist of the Long Island Association, to do an economic evaluation of the president's re-engineering plan. The following year the SUNY Board of Trustees met at the college. With Cipriani and Vinciguerra in attendance, Kamer, presented a plan to allow Cold Spring Harbor Laboratory lease campus land for an incubator research center. She indicated that companies were leaving Long Island because of a lack of adequate research and development facilities. Cipriani commented, "By 1997 SUNY's System Administration's opposition went from being quietly hostile to watchfully cynical."[19]

Along with this development, the Farmingdale Foundation offered its support. It had been reorganized from Laffin's earlier efforts. Although financial contributions were not significant at the beginning, community good will was earned that could not be measured in dollars. During the 1990s, Horst Sahlbach, president of USA Festo, led the foundation. He was associated with Nobel Laureate James Watson, of the Cold Spring Harbor Laboratory, a research institution staffed by the world's leading scientists. Dr. Watson had received an honorary doctorate degree from the college a decade earlier. He delivered the convocation address at the college "Convocation and Colloquy" commemorating the twentieth anniversary of Cipriani's term in office, September 15, 1998. After release of the Kamer Report, and following a meeting with Watson, Vinciguerra, and Cipriani, an agreement emerged whereby the evolving incubator at the Cold Spring Harbor Laboratory would lease a section of land at the college to be the site for a collaborative enterprise. Each institution would benefit enormously.[20]

The challenge was how to get New York State to complete the arrangement between Farmingdale and the Cold Spring Harbor Laboratory. An opportunity surfaced when College Foundation member Michael Posillico secured a meeting for Cipriani with College Council Vice President Anthony Mastroianni, and Empire State Development Corporation Commissioner Charles Gargano, a confidante of Pataki who was concerned about economic growth. They convinced Gargano that the proposal was not just another incubator program but an innovative center that would be built by the state and help fledgling companies become tenants and pay rent on a graduated scale. These companies would establish incubators in biotechnology, software, and other emerging technologies on Long Island. State Sen. Norman Levy of Long Island entered as a major player in the proceedings; he was convinced of the importance of the proposal and introduced an enabling bill in the legislature. Upon Gargano's advice, Pataki supported the plan. The SUNY Board, state senate, and assembly added their support.

The New York State legislature appropriated $22 million for Long Island's economic development, of which $14 million went to Farmingdale. The Broad Hollow Bioscience Park established a collaborative venture between Farmingdale and Cold Spring Harbor Laboratory on a twenty-acre site at the northern section of the campus along Route 110. The State University Construction Fund built the first structure, a 63,500-square-foot building. OSI Pharmaceuticals became the anchor tenant along with start-up companies, Helicon Therapeutics and Immuno-Rx, each paying annual rents. Groundbreaking took place in summer 1998. Another $20 million was allocated for a second building to provide six more start-up companies, classroom, and laboratory space for the college's new bioscience program. A nonprofit Board of Directors was selected, half appointed by Cipriani and half by Watson. Degree programs in biotechnology, production, and informational technology would thus be expanded. New programs were planned. Scientific symposia would benefit faculty, and internships and career opportunities would be available to students. The Broad Hollow Bioscience Park validated the official 1993 mission change under Cipriani's leadership.[21]

As Cipriani had stated on numerous occasions, the success of transforming the college from a two-year technical-agricultural institution to a four-year college of technology depended on faculty support and a dedicated staff. He credited the following individuals who applied their talents with long hours of hard work: Provost Michael Vinciguerra; Deputy President Joseph Monaco; Vice President for Academic Affairs Nancy C. Thomson; Vice President of Administration George LaRosa; Academic Deans Robert V. Mark in Arts and Sciences, Dashimir Petrella and Terry Smith in Engineering Technologies, Frank Del Bene in Business, and John Burkhart in Health and Human Services. Nearly all these individuals also held academic positions at Farmingdale and understood the needs and implications of the transformation. With these accomplishments behind him, Cipriani decided to retire, confident that the leaders who followed would continue the work he had started.

After twenty-two years as president (1978–2000) and spending thirty-six years (1964–2000) on campus, from professor to administrative positions, Cipriani decided to exit academic life as of January 2000.

The college he left in 2000 offered approximately forty academic programs ranging from baccalaureate degrees, associate degrees, and one-year certificates. They included liberal arts and sciences, health sciences, engineering technologies, business, and specialized programs in aviation, security systems, and visual communications. Nearly two-hundred full-time and adjunct faculty taught nearly six-thousand residential and commuting students in full-time and part-time study. The honored tradition of small classes allowed students to receive individual attention. The college also administered the LIEOC on campus, annually providing 1,400 students with training necessary to achieve upgrading academic and vocational skills.[22]

FIGURE 9-5. An early computer science student is using a Stag ZL30 to program a logic device. This Logic Programmer unit is part of the College's transition to a high-tech educational institution.

Just as Albert A. Johnson, Halsey B. Knapp, and Charles W. Laffin Jr., altered the direction of the college, Cipriani's accomplishments were also significant. By overcoming seemingly insurmountable odds in bureaucratic-bound New York State, he changed the mission of the college saving it to remain relevant. Future benefits would also accrue to the Long Island region. His major achievements included the transformation of a traditional two-year agricultural and technical college to a four-year institution offering advanced technology programs. The establishment of a biotechnology partnership with Cold Spring Harbor Laboratory moved the college to the forefront of research. Other Cipriani accomplishments were construction of new facilities that included Gleeson Hall, the Halsey B. Knapp Horticultural Greenhouse, a child-care center, and the aerospace center. He provided a site for the University Club on campus. He initiated connections through international programs with several countries, main land China being one of them. He received the Legion of Merit Award from the Italian government for his efforts to develop business and academic collaborations. He initiated the on-campus Small Business Development Center, a TTUC, and a business incubator. In all of these endeavors his faculty, staff, and College Council supported him.

During his presidential tenure, Cipriani was active in Long Island and New York State affairs. He was widely recognized for his sensitivity to environmental, economic, and educational matters. He served with distinction on the Long Island Regional Planning Board, the Long Island Power Authority, chaired the Suffolk County Environmental Council, chaired the Kings Park Psychiatric Center Advisory Panel, chaired the Long Island Regional Ashfill Board, was coordinator of evaluations for the Centers for Advanced Technology for New York State Science and Technology, chaired the Suffolk County Environmental Council, chaired the Long Island Regional Advisory Council on Higher Education, and chaired the Board for the Regional Industrial Technical Partnerships Council.[23]

In 2000, a nationwide search was begun to select a new president. Mary A. Fallon, chair of the Farmingdale College Council, headed a broad-based committee that followed SUNY Board of Trustees guidelines. In the meantime, the Board of Trustees appointed Vinciguerra to serve as acting president. As the campus provost, Vinciguerra was assured by the SUNY chancellor that being in the role of acting president did not remove him from being considered for the position of permanent president. Following his temporary appointment as president, he called a campus-wide meeting to specify his goals: to increase enrollment, expand academic programs, improve campus grounds and residence life, reach out to alumni, increase fund raising, and maintain contacts

Figure 9.6. Patricia Hill Williams served in key administrative positions at Farmingdale (1980–2004). Governor George Pataki appointed her to the College Council in 2006. She poses here with President George H. W. Bush. Her leadership skills led to four presidential appointments by Ronald Reagan, George H. W. Bush, William Clinton, and George W. Bush.

with government officials. He also announced that Patricia Hill Williams would assume the new title of vice president for external affairs, expanding her role in fund raising and public relations, in addition to her governmental and alumni work. Upon completing his address to faculty and staff, he received a standing ovation. As a new millennium emerged, the college embarked on a new course of educational development quite different from its original mission. A new future lay ahead for the institution.[24]

TEN

Into the Twenty-First Century

> From its rural and humble beginnings, Farmingdale has been transformed into a leading college of technology, educating students and developing the regional workforce that is critical to the economic development of the region.[1]

THE FIRST DECADE OF THE TWENTY-FIRST CENTURY WITNESSED remarkable growth as those leaders who succeeded Frank A. Cipriani after 2000 continued the policies that were put into effect. Farmingdale State was now a college of technology offering baccalaureate degrees with strong components of the humanities and social sciences. Building on its new mission, the college developed new intercollegial relations and international educational programs. Its outreach agenda conducted through the LIEOC added a new campus in Riverhead, broadening its services to the underserved population. Recognizing Long Island's aviation origins and its farsighted planning, the college has developed one of the most advanced programs in its Aviation Department consisting of aeronautical science, professional pilot training, and aviation administration. Enrollments, which were static during the period of transition, began to increase at the same time student academic profiles rose. As a specialized college, its faculty and staff embarked on a challenging future of innovation and creativity.

New leadership was put in place. The SUNY Board of Trustees, upon the recommendation of the College Council, officially appointed Michael J. Vinciguerra on April 25, 2000, to serve as acting president until a permanent replacement could be found. He was assured at first that because of his position on campus he would not be excluded from consideration, a similar promise that had been made to Cipriani when he also applied for the presidency, although the latter was not serving as acting president. Vinciguerra was a physical chemist holding a PhD, completing postgraduate studies at Harvard University. He began his academic career at Farmingdale in 1970, advancing through the ranks as professor of chemistry (1987), chairman of the Division of Arts and Sciences Department (1976–1979), assistant vice president for academic affairs (1979–1983), vice president for academic affairs (1983–1987), and served as provost (1998–2000) to the time of his appointment as acting president (2000–2001). Vinciguerra chaired the Broad Hollow Bioscience Park Board of Directors. He guided the campus-wide strategic planning that transformed Farmingdale to its new role as a baccalaureate-granting institution. His experience involved extensive fiscal and enrollment management responsibilities, and was widely respected by his colleagues and knowledgeable about Farmingdale and New York State educational matters.[2]

Nevertheless, the SUNY Board of Trustees passed on Vinciguerra and appointed Jonathan C. Gibralter, a former Long Islander who held the position of interim president at upstate Corning Community College. Although having promised to give full consideration to Vinciguerra, SUNY Chancellor Robert L. King stated that Vinciguerra had "put the interests of the college above his own when deciding to continue to serve as acting president rather than becoming a candidate for the presidency during the search process." Despite King's statement, Vinciguerra had been led to believe that he would be considered for the position. One faculty member stated Vinciguerra had given long service to the college and had done a good job, "even in his acting [presidential] role." This statement expressed the sentiments of a large segment of the campus, one of their own having been rebuffed. Adding to this conflicted situation, an unidentified SUNY spokesman in Albany said it was the system's policy not to consider acting presidents for the highest campus position. Thus, an outsider was brought in. King praised Gibralter as an "outstanding educator and administrator." SUNY Board Chairman Thomas Egan said Gibralter had "excelled in every position he has held."[3]

Vinciguerra now looked beyond Farmingdale to secure a presidential position. His broad experience within the SUNY system qualified him to secure the leadership appointment at St. Francis University in Joliet, Illinois, a private Catholic institution of nearly five-thousand students in June 2002. The members of the House of Representatives of the Illinois 92nd General Assembly honored him by passing a Resolution wishing "Michael J. Vinciguerra well as he assumes his duties as the eighth president of the University of St. Francis."[4]

Assuming the Farmingdale presidency under such circumstances made Gibralter work that much harder to cultivate a rapport with campus personnel. His leadership skills achieved a successful working relationship with faculty and staff. Gibralter was born in New Hyde Park and spent the first twelve years of his life there before moving with his family to Bayside, Queens.

He earned his PhD in human development from Syracuse University (1996), master's in counseling psychology from NYU (1982), and bachelor's in psychology from SUNY Binghamton (1978). He participated in the League for Innovation in Community Colleges and attended the Harvard Graduate School of Education Leadership Institute. In addition to his position as interim president and dean of academic affairs at Corning Community College, he was dean of the Rome Campus of Mohawk Valley Community College, and associate dean of the School of Liberal Arts at the SUNY Morrisville College of Agriculture and Technology.

Gibralter became the college's seventh president, taking office on June 1, 2001 at the age of forty-four. His official installation took place November 2, 2001 at Nold Hall. Professor Stanley Mehlman led the academic procession as grand marshall. Mary Fallon, chair of the College Council, gave the welcome address. The New York State Fraternal Order of Police Honor Guard presented the Colors. Rabbi Marc Gellman offered the Invocation. Farmingdale Emeritus Professor Lou Howard, SUNY Board Trustee from Amityville, introduced King who made the Presentation of the President's Medallion to Gibralter, who then gave the Inaugural Address. He was pleased to return to Long Island, pointing out that Farmingdale was "poised to contribute to the economic development of the region. My vision is to cultivate partnerships that will enhance the College's ability to reach its full potential."[5]

While in office, Gibralter set in motion a number of priority task forces for dealing with campus issues such as student retention, marketing, facility planning, and strategic planning. He focused on student life, especially revitalizing dormitories. He initiated an Annual Giving Campaign, and engaged the alumni and foundation organizations to establish technical support for increased giving. He also planned for a Capital Campaign to begin in spring 2002. He reached out to the corporate community by taking an active role on the Board of the Advancement for Commerce, Industry, and Technology, and creating the Presidential Advisory Council with a number of Long Island's leading decision makers. He sought to move the college forward to adjust to changing national and global realities.

During his first visit to the Farmingdale campus, on an evening when it was raining heavily, Gibralter asked his taxi driver to tour the grounds for him. He saw "a mix of dilapidated buildings and modern facilities" on the sprawling campus bordered by Route 110 and Melville Road. The taxi driver was familiar with the campus because he had graduated from Farmingdale; he was a professional musician, temporarily unemployed, who had taken on the part-time job. It would be a familiar experience for the new president to meet numerous alumni on Long Island because nearly fifty-thousand students had graduated from the college since 1919. Gibralter also would be confronted with references to the "Aggie" school because of nearly seven decades of agricultural education, despite the school's history of technical education since 1946 and officially becoming a four-year college of applied technology in 1993. Nevertheless, the hard work of the previous administration in transitioning and transforming the curriculum was already making its mark. Gibralter would not only benefit from the change, but he would also build on it.[6]

FIGURE 10-1. President Frank Cipriani, center, joins friends of the College in the ground breaking ceremony for the 20,000 square foot Aerospace Training Facility at Republic Airport April 15, 1993. The facility will house the aviation program in a "campus-off-campus" about a mile south of the main campus.

Figure 10-2. This building at Republic Airport houses a complete academic village. The Aviation curriculum leads to a Bachelor of Science degree in Aeronautical Science - Professional Pilot, and a Bachelor of Science degree in Aviation Administration.

During his years as president, he hired a vice president for marketing to develop a comprehensive marketing plan and it contributed to an increase in student enrollment of 25 percent, from 5,100 to 6,400. This larger student body necessitated establishment of an effective Student Success Center. At the same time, entrance requirements were raised because of the advanced programs. Among new bachelor's degree programs launched during this period were bioscience, technology studies, computer programming and information systems, and applied mathematics. He maintained strong campus ties with Long Island's business leaders, creating forums on banking, bioscience, health care, horticulture, hospitality tourism, engineering, and manufacturing. Gibralter began a Major Gifts Campaign in 2003, setting a goal of $10 million. In May 2004, the college initiated a kickoff celebration to build on nearly $3 million in donations, pledges, and in-kind contributions. In the process of connecting with industry leaders, Gibralter served as a board member of the Long Island Forum for Technology, the Long Island Life Sciences Initiative, and the Fair Media Council. He was chairman of the Broad Hollow Bioscience Park. As with previous presidents, he served on the Middle States Commission on Higher Education. He helped secure funding for laboratory equipment for the second Broad Hollow Bioscience Park building and for acquiring new aircraft for the Farmingdale Professional Pilot Program at Republic Airport.[7]

In 2006, Gibralter resigned from his position at Farmingdale and assumed the presidency at Frostburg State University in Alleghany County in western Maryland. Farmingdale's previous leaders had historically held their positions for extended periods of time. Although Gibralter's tenure was comparatively short, his strength focused on establishing strategic planning, which included themes of sustainability, engagement, academics, and leadership. He applied these themes hoping to guide Farmingdale State's growth in meeting goals set by the Middle States Commission on Higher Education. In 2003, he also generated a ten-year capital plan that eventually included $133 million in campus upgrades. Projects included constructing new buildings, among them a $20 million dormitory and a $7.5 million athletic complex, renovating older buildings; and demolishing a field house, five dormitories, and several barns. Allard Field House was demolished in 2011; only two dormitories were demolished instead of the projected five. A second building of 50,000-square-feet at the Broad Hollow Bioscience Park was subsequently constructed under a $20 million appropriation from the State University Construction Fund. Fourteen new airplanes, at a cost of nearly $3 million, were to be added to the college's fleet of eleven aircraft at Republic Airport. The fifty-year-old fieldstone and brick building, Lupton Hall, was renovated under a $12-million appropriation. Lupton Hall housed the engineering technologies programs, which replaced the technical facilities at the Conklin Street School in the 1950s. Future projects included a $25 million student activities center (now called the Campus Center) near Thompson Hall. Hicks Hall and Cutler Hall, two of the original campus buildings, now closed, are slated to be restored to their previous stately appearance. As of this time, these buildings have not undergone renovation. They had housed the horticultural and agronomy programs, and were each built in 1914 at a cost of $63,629. The *New York Times* pointed out that Gibralter was "continuing and expanding the vision of his predecessor, Dr. Frank A. Cipriani."[8]

With Gibralter's resignation as president in the midst of plans to improve the campus infrastructure and implement its new mission, the challenge for Farmingdale, the College Council, and the SUNY Board of Trustees was to fill the position with a knowledgeable educator committed to the institution. Upon completion of a thorough search, a unanimous decision was made to appoint Provost W. Hubert Keen as the college's eighth president on January 11, 2007. SUNY Chancellor John R. Ryan thanked the College Council and the Search Committee for bringing forward a strong list of candidates. He also thanked Farmingdale Senior Vice President and Chief Financial Officer George LaRosa who had served as officer-in-charge of the campus since August 2006. SUNY Board Chairman Thomas F. Egan indicated that SUNY had been successful in hiring presidents from across the country; however, "we will recognize internal talent and are very pleased to be promoting Hubert within the University." Keen had been serving as Farmingdale provost and vice president for academic affairs since 2005 and enjoyed wide support among the College Council, faculty, and external constituents.[9]

Keen possessed the necessary credentials for the office. From 1999 to 2005, he served as special assistant to system provost in SUNY where he was responsible for initiatives in teacher education and collaboration with K–12 schools. He was liaison for the SUNY Urban Teacher Education Center in New York City. Before joining the system administration, he served from 1998 to 1999, as interim president at SUNY College at Old Westbury. From 1994 to 1998, he held the position of provost and vice president for academic affairs at York College of CUNY. He began his career as assistant professor at SUNY Cortland, moving up the ranks to professor, coordinator of the environmental cience program, chairman of the Department of Biological Science, and dean of arts and sciences from 1976 to 1994. His teaching and research were concentrated in the areas of ecology, environmental science, evolutionary biology, aquatic biology, and biostatistics. He was awarded with grants from the University of Virginia's Biological Station Research Program, National Science Foundation, SUNY Research Foundation, Fulbright Commission, U.S. Public Health Service, and German Academic Exchange Service. Keen received a bachelor's in biology and German from Pikeville College, an MS in physiological ecology from Eastern Kentucky, and a PhD in ecology from Kent State University.

The presidential inauguration ceremony of W. Hubert Keen took place in Nold Hall May 11, 2007. Fallon presided, Brian Maher of the Educational Opportunity Center was master of ceremonies and Professor Lloyd Makarowitz led the academic procession as grand marshall. Kathryn Burke, bioscience student, sang the national anthem and Sister Elizabeth McGarvey, OP, gave the invocation. Vice president George LaRosa acknowledged guests. SUNY Chancellor John R. Ryan made the presentation and installation of the president. In his Inaugural Address, President Keen quoted Danish philosopher Soren Aabye Kierkegaard (1813–1855) who said, "Life must be understood backward, but we must never forget that life must be lived forward." He offered a thoughtful observation of the college's history when he continued, "We must understand the current status of this institution by looking backward. But we can only succeed here by going forward. Otherwise we are regressive." He observed that tradition had to be respected but the future would be different. Dr. Keen cautioned, "The path is not easily attained. Our primary areas of focus are our students, ourselves, and our community." His previous two years as provost and vice president for academic affairs at Farmingdale State allowed him to gain knowledge of the college's unique past and to acquire administrative experience in the present to implement the promise of Farmingdale's changed mission.[10]

In an interview with the *Long Island Business News* the month following his appointment, Keen indicated that one of his goals was to continue to increase the number of quality programs, such as those recently developed (applied economics, applied psychology, and software technology). He noted that the college was undergoing an ascendant trend. He expected it to continue to grow at a moderate pace, and believed such growth would be manageable. Today's students arrive at college with experiences different from earlier generations because they have been exposed to more varied technology. Services for students would be expanded; in fact, implementation of the President's Students First Initiative began in 2010. Also, Keen planned to work with the business community "because we are truly embedded in that community here. . . . We'll invite business leaders from particular sectors that relate to what we provide here in academic programs."[11]

With the recent inauguration of Keen as president, a review of commencement exercises, past and present, provides an interesting historical perspective of this important part of the college's past. During the early years, graduation exercises were a weeklong series of events. In April 1919, some of those events included a military and athletic field day, students providing entertainment, a baccalaureate sermon, student demonstrations of their work, class-day exercises, senior dance, faculty reception, and the final graduation ceremony featuring a prominent public figure presenting a keynote address. Students did not wear caps and gowns until 1949, up to the time when their education was considered to be primarily vocational. Even though the State

FIGURE 10-3. Professors C. Dick Thomson, Raynor Wallace, and Edwin F. Ore, of the English Department, composed Farmingdale State College's inspiring tribute, *Alma Mater*.

FIGURE 10-4. Professor Edwin F. Ore continued to express his devotion to Farmingdale State College in 1984 by writing words and music to the *Fight Song.*

FIGURE 10-5. Dr. W. Hubert Keen presents the Presidential Inaugural Address during his installation as the College's eighth president May 11, 2007. The Platform party included distinguished academic leaders.

Education Department had created the Division of Technical Institutes in 1948, Farmingdale had used the title of "Institute" as early as 1924. With the formation of SUNY in 1948, Farmingdale and the other agricultural institutes would begin an upward trend leading to full status of granting four-year degrees in applied sciences and technology. However, because Farmingdale was originally an agricultural school, the academic calendar revolved around the growing season. Over the years commencement exercises have therefore become more elaborate in conforming to a more academic tradition. This important event has been held in various campus locations: barn; gymnasium; Old Hangar, which was disassembled at the Conklin Street School and reassembled on the main campus; Allard Field House; and the campus lawn. Some notable individuals who have presented graduation addresses were Col. Theodore Roosevelt Jr., Alfred University President Boothe C. Davis, Hofstra University President John Cranford Adams, State Education Commissioner Lawrence L. Jarvie, Halsey B. Knapp, Socialist presidential candidate Norman Thomas, Congressman Victor L. Anfuso, Hofstra University President Clifford Lee Lord, Suffolk County Executive H. Lee Dennison, Congressman Otis G. Pike, SUNY President Samuel B. Gould, State Assembly Speaker Perry B. Duryea, State Assembly Speaker Joseph F. Carlino, Gov. Nelson A. Rockefeller, State Supreme Court Justice Sol Wachtler, SUNY Chancellor Ernest L.

Boyer, Emeritus College Council Chairman Mortimer J. Gleeson, Board of Regents Chancellor Theodore M. Black, SUNY Chancellor Clifton R. Wharton Jr., Lt. Gov. Mario M. Cuomo, Professor Raynor W. Wallace, Congressman Thomas J. Downey, Class of 1978, NASA astronaut Fernando Caldeiro, Sister Rose Elizabeth Thering, New York State Attorney General Eliot Spitzer, Sen. Charles Schumer, and Cold Spring Harbor Laboratory President Bruce Stillman.[12]

An examination of student matriculation reveals significant findings. After enrollments dropped precipitously following curriculum changes and demographic shifts, they once again began to rise. Such a trend was expected during the transition period leading to four-year programs. Since 2000, enrollment numbers have steadily risen. In fall 2010, the official total head count of full- and part-time students rose to 6,861. The peak attendance year during this era occurred in 2009 with 6,992 students. The schools of Arts and Sciences, Business, Engineering Technology, Health Sciences, and Undeclared Majors all benefited from this growth. The latest official totals reflect this upward trend (see Table 10.1).

Furthermore, of the 2010 enrollment, 5,126 students were classified as full-time and 1,735 as part-time. The decrease in enrollment from 2009 to 2010 was due to the planned increase in the percentage of students who attend full-time versus part-time. Approximately 500 students

Table 10.1. Recent Enrollment History

YEAR	TOTAL
2000	5,045
2001	5,449
2002	5,798
2003	5,949
2004	5,881
2005	6,047
2006	6,253
2007	6,447
2008	6,872
2009	6,992
2010	6,861

resided on campus at this time. This figure represents one of the smallest residential populations at Farmingdale, down from a maximum of 1,200 students in 1970. The number of students living on campus is expected to increase as older dormitories are refurbished and Orchard Hall reaches its full capacity. Orchard Hall was opened in 2005 and is the newest residence hall.

Enrollment figures indicate that Farmingdale was one of the fastest growing colleges in New York State. By 2010, enrollment targets were surpassed, and applications surpassed nine thousand, an increase of 72 percent since 2000. Entering freshmen achieved a high school grade point average of at least 87. As of 2011, there were twenty-seven bachelor's programs; the BS in telecommunications and sports management technology were the last to be established. Additionally, there were ten associate degree programs and fourteen certificate programs as of 2011. Additionally, the Undeclared Major Program accommodates students for two-semesters who meet admissions requirements but are undecided about a career. Nearly one-hundred international students reside on campus. Tuition for full-time New York State residents was $4,970. Tuition for out-of-state students was $12,870. Recent numbers of graduates confirm the growth of the college. From July 1, 2008 to June 30, 2009, there were 1,221 students who received degrees; from 2009 to 2010 there were 1,275 who received degrees; and from 2010 to 2011 the number of graduates increased to 1,371.[13]

In the 2007–2008 year, the college initiated efforts to expand the relationship with its alumni through a comprehensive communications and re-invigoration program by establishing an Alumni Association Board. Judith McEvoy (Class of 1961) led in this strategic endeavor. Eileen Hasson was appointed director of alumni affairs, and the *Alumnus Newsletter* was relaunched. At its 2008 annual dinner, more than two-hundred graduates and campus leaders joined in honoring Robert L. Van Nostrand (Class of 1977), Robert C. Meyer (Class of 1964), Dr. Lee Anne Xippolitos (Class of 1975), and Gary R. Johnson (Class of 1990). One-hundred attendees participated in the Alumni Garden Party at the Annual Garden Festival. Also, two-hundred alumni and their families watched Keen throw out the ceremonial first pitch when the Long Island Ducks baseball team hosted a reception for Farmingdale State College Alumni and Friends. These ongoing events represent efforts to benefit from the talent and resources of graduates, who also have the opportunity to express pride in their alma mater.[14]

Farmingdale State College continued its partnerships with industry and the community as it played a leading role in economic development and creative enterprise. The faculty, known for its commitment to student success in the classroom, was now engaged in more advanced research.

The National Institutes of Health awarded the first grant to the college, and two U.S. patents were awarded for research related to hydrogen fuel cell technology. The college, building on its tradition of protecting the environment for nearly a century, has pledged to "go green" and established the motto, "Green then, Green now." It has led to efforts in search of alternative sources of energy. Campus vehicles run on electric and flex fuel power; half of its motor pool uses power sources other than fossil fuels. The college is proud of its Solar Energy Center, which has more than $1million worth of photovoltaic units and provides energy to the campus. Students learn about the solar energy field, leading to employment opportunities in related technologies. The new Green Building Institute (GBI) at the college encourages and assists in the design and construction of buildings that will reduce or eliminate the negative impact on the environment. The GBI makes Long Island a center for research in the advancement of economic enterprises relating to green buildings. Continuing its green movement, Farmingdale has opened a new sustainable garden that serves as an outdoor classroom for students in the ornamental horticulture program at its four-acre Teaching Gardens. The Science and Technology Education Program involving K–12 students strengthened the college's commitment to the community, along with mentoring programs for disadvantaged high school students and hosting science competitions. The nursing program has affiliated with Winthrop University Hospital and the Parker Jewish Geriatric Institute to expand its mission. Workforce training programs have been established with such companies as Forest Laboratories, Estee Lauder, and North Shore-Long Island Jewish Health System. The college also assists emerging companies on Long Island through its Small Business Development Center.[15]

A further examination of developments highlights growth of the college. The original $133 million construction commitment of 2003 was increased under Keen's leadership to an unprecedented $185 million plan that provided greater improvements for campus facilities and for enrichment of academic programs. A $25 million Campus Center near historic Thompson Hall will provide an important focal point for student activity. It will include a bookstore, modern dining facilities, offices, meeting spaces, lounges, and a spacious auditorium that will feature academic lectures and concerts. A $2.5 million renovation of the Dental Hygiene Center was completed to make it one the most technologically advanced learning centers in the nation. State Sen. Charles J. Fuschillo Jr. and Assemblyman Robert Sweeney, along with the entire Long Island legislative delegation, were able to secure an appropriation of nearly $55 million for a new School of Business building. In 2011, the $1 million purchase of two Piper Warriors and one Piper Arrow expanded Farmingdale's fleet to twenty-two planes and increased the capacity for the professional pilot track to 125, the only such aviation program at a public college in the state. With the continued legislative support of Fuschillo and Sweeney, Farmingdale acquired a $90,000 Frasca Model 142 flight simulator. Other allocations included $1 million for a Center for Applied Mathematics, $1 million for an Information Commons that will integrate library and support services for students, and more than $7 million for a new child-care center serving the needs of the faculty, administration, students, and public. An expansion of the Broad Hollow Bioscience Park was completed in 2008. Orchard Hall was the first residence life building constructed in thirty-five years at Farmingdale. The new state-of-the-art one-thousand-seat baseball stadium features artificial turf, lights, dugouts, press box, batting cages, and bullpens. It is an integral part of a comprehensive renovation of athletic facilities. Restoration of Nold Hall is in the planning stage; it houses a pool, racquetball and squash courts, indoor track, basketball courts, a golf simulator, and weight room. The complex includes an outdoor eight-lane track surrounding a synthetic turf field for lacrosse and soccer competition. All of these physical additions advance the academic programs.[16]

FIGURE 10-6. The Farmingdale State College baseball team celebrates after winning its first-ever Skyline Conference Baseball Championship in June 2008. The men's basketball team and women's soccer team also won conference championships in the same year.

Figure 10-7. Chief Financial Officer George LaRosa, left, and Athletic Director Mike Harrington, right, surround President W. Hubert Keen and State Senator Charles F. Fuschillo, Jr. at the ribbon-cutting ceremony of the new athletic field, 2008. This state-of-the-art facility contains a synthetic-turf lacrosse/soccer field surrounded by an eight-lane track.

The seminal achievements under Keen's new administration began to receive attention. He was named to the "Long Island Power List" in 2008 and 2009, the annual ranking of Long Island's most influential leaders published by the *Long Island Press*. In 2008, he was one of only three college presidents named for this distinction, and was ranked 39th out of 51 individuals from the fields of academia, business, government, health care, not-for-profit, and public sector.

He is credited with propelling Farmingdale forward in the areas of academic programs, scientific research, infrastructure improvements, and vision for the college. Keen has reorganized his administrative team to promote the college's initiatives in key areas that include fundraising, internal and external communications. He has restored the *Campus Times*, a monthly publication, and the *Alumnus Newsletter*, a biannual publication, in order to improve communications with important constituencies. In 2008, *Networking* magazine presented Keen with the "David Award" for exceptional achievement in his chosen field, the first Farmingdale president to receive the award. Additionally, the Long Island Association's Small Business Council honored Keen the following year as the "2009 Education Advocate" and for the college's role as an "economic engine" in the region. These represent the esteem he received for making an impact in the educational and economic spheres.[17]

On April 4, 2008, friends, family, and colleagues attended a ceremony in Lupton Hall honoring Professor Herb Zipper who spent forty-six years in the Department of Electrical Engineering Technology. The Digital System Memorial Laboratory was dedicated in his name. The facility was part of a renovation of classroom and laboratory space on the second floor of Lupton Hall. A much-admired professor, Zipper symbolized the commitment made to his students, an important characteristic of the college faculty. He died in 2005.[18]

Significant trends emerged as the college advanced to the forefront of higher education. Farmingdale has always been known for its graduates' success in employment and income. This fact was confirmed in 2009 when the college received national attention because its graduates ranked 88th in earning power among more than two-hundred colleges and universities. According to *Payscale.com*, Farmingdale's graduates received a starting median salary of $46,100 and a mid-career median salary of $80,500. In August 2009, *US News & World Report* credited Farmingdale with being one of the top baccalaureate colleges in the northeast. Finally, in 2010, the online publication *The Daily Beast* ranked Farmingdale the fifth safest campus in the nation. Available raw data were collected from nine-thousand schools for the latest three years in the study (2006–2008) revealed that the campus high in security and low in crime. Figures compiled by the college and reported to federal authorities, revealed no arson offenses, no robberies, three burglaries, and one forcible sex offense. "We strive to insure the well-being of our students," stated Keen.[19]

Director Lee E. Koppelman and Chief Economist Pearl M. Kamer, of the Long Island Regional Planning Board, published results of a five-year special study on the Long Island economy in 1993, "The Long Island Regional Strategic Economic Development Plan," that essentially coincided with Farmingdale State College's own strategic plan that was predictive of the future. It forecast the future and challenges that lay ahead. The study concluded that Long Island "is at an economic crossroads." After examining the status of the economy and providing projections to the year 2010, the study offered "a positive outlook." They pointed out that all the region's colleges and universities contributed materially to economic development in wages, goods, and services, and to the skills of its labor force. The future depended on the competitive advantages Long Island offered in "advanced materials, electronics and information systems, future manufacturing systems, and the life sciences." The region already possessed much of the infrastructure to generate new growth for the future.[20]

This timely report merged well with the transformation of the college going into the twenty-first century. By 2010, Farmingdale State had emerged as an increasingly vital economic force for Long Island, producing more than a $1 billion impact on the regional economy. Additionally, the college's direct operating and capital expenditures increased Long Island's earnings to an estimated $343 million and led to more than ten-thousand secondary jobs. These were the findings of a twenty-six-page study again conducted by Dr. Pearl M. Kamer of the Long Island Association, the area's largest business organization consisting of more than five-thousand members from business, labor, government agencies, civic groups, not-for-profits, and institutions of higher learning. The study was titled, "Fueling the Long Island Economy: The Regional Impact of Farmingdale State College." Although agriculture had served its purpose in an agrarian society, future success lay in technological education, according to the study.[21]

The New York State School of Agriculture on Long Island, founded in 1912 to train boys and girls from New York City and nearby counties, has evolved into a different institution today. It has assumed many titles through the years as it has advanced into the only public college on Long Island to offer a comprehensive foundation in the applied sciences and technology. Its directors/presidents have achieved a record of effective leadership in developing innovative educational programs. With all the change that has taken place, they stabilized the institution in maintaining its viability. A dedicated faculty and staff also contributed to the overall success of the institution.

Albert A. Johnson (1913–1923), the school's first director, focused on the campus infrastructure, some of which has stood the test of time. Based on his agricultural and educational background, he engaged in curriculum development and applied his administrative skills to establish a firm foundation for the young institution. Continuous curriculum modifications resolved issues in attempting to achieve goals set down in its original charter: "to furnish training in agricultural science." Practical, hands-on education was stressed. Military routine and instruction prevailed during the World War I era. Service to the community was paramount. Female students enrolled because of the school's equal opportunity policy. Minority students also benefited, but it would take several generations for barriers in the general society to fall for all to achieve complete equality of opportunity. Johnson was directly involved in all these matters. He was forced to resign as director when issues arose challenging his leadership style.

The school was on the brink of collapse when Halsey B. Knapp (1923–1956) was appointed the new director. Because of its early record of graduating few students, questionable educational standards, and allegations of misuse of funds, there were attempts to close the school. Knapp took charge and put the school on a new path that prevented its demise. He stamped out a campus Ku Klux Klan cell when he arrived to assume the directorship, despite the fact that the Klan was a powerful force on Long Island. This un-American organization reached its peak of power in the 1920s, but declined soon after. Hard times continued throughout the Great Depression and the critical years of World War II. Knapp clung to the agricultural curriculum but was farsighted in establishing the industrial-technical division, which pointed to the educational future. He had a loyal following among his staff and faculty. Toward the end of his tenure, however, criticism arose aimed at his domineering personnel policies. At the same time, the school grew under his leadership and gained public respect. His vision of educational policy, as well as complete devotion to the school, was unparalleled. During his thirty-three-year tenure as director, he left an indelible imprint on the institution. Knapp Hall is a visual reminder of the man.

Dr. Charles W. Laffin, Jr. (1961–1976) guided the college during a period of national turmoil. His presidency was cut short by his premature death. The first leader to take the title of "president," he put the campus on a professional schedule, and his vision sought to expand the college's mission and its academic programs. During his tenure a new institutional title was adopted. The designation "institute" was replaced with the official title of Agricultural and Technical College at Farmingdale in 1966. He hired faculty with advanced degrees; he appointed talented assistants who put many ideas of his vision into play. In a new age of labor relations, he pursued a democratic administration. He developed programs to aid women, minorities, and the disadvantaged. Although Laffin was able to secure some public funding for new buildings and programs, he was often frustrated by a lack of adequate support from New York State and SUNY. His ambitious plans far outpaced SUNY's willingness to understand the needs of Farmingdale and its valued place in the system. His attempt to make Farmingdale a four-year institution was cut short by his death.

Dr. Frank A. Cipriani (1978–2000) succeeded Laffin as president and was greatly influenced by him. Hired in 1964, he assumed all the important administrative positions in the next fourteen years to gain experience to prove his ability before he became president. He adhered to, and extended the vision of his predecessor, especially in programs involving minorities, in addition to environmental and technology matters. Cipriani believed that for Farmingdale to survive it had to "re-engineer" itself to be different from the other institutions of higher education on Long Island and within the SUNY establishment; it had to play a key role in the region's economic development. His service on local civic boards, involvement in economic associations, and contacts with political leaders enabled him to implement his plan for the college. He was guided by the age-old principle that "all politics is local." His achievements were many and important. Perhaps the most important was establishing four-year programs in the applied sciences and technology.

It was Cipriani, with the support of the SUNY Board of Trustees, who realized that the time had arrived to end the agricultural program in 1987 because it attracted fewer and fewer applicants, and cost more than the combined Nursing and Dental Hygiene departments. Except for the importance of the ornamental horticulture curriculum, agriculture was yielding to an expanding commercial-industrial economy and a suburban society that had to adapt to increased taxes, services, and land values, and to meet the needs of technically trained graduates. Additionally, the college advanced to create and feature four research centers: Institute of Research and Technology Transfer, Solar Energy Center, Applied Mathematics Center, and Social Science Research Center.

Another important educational achievement under Cipriani's leadership was the creation of the Broad Hollow Bioscience Park, whose purpose is biotechnology research. The college collaborates with the Cold Spring Harbor Laboratory, a leading institution on genetics. The Broad Hollow Bioscience Park is located on the northeastern section of the Farmingdale campus. In April 2011, Gov. Andrew Cuomo signed into law a bill sponsored by Fuschillo and Sweeney allowing the college to enter into lease agreements to expand the Broad Hollow Bioscience Park. The park's anchor tenant since 2002 is OSI Pharmaceuticals, now owned by Astellas Pharma Inc., a multinational corporation. Farmingdale State College offers a bachelor of science degree in bioscience and the Broad Hollow Bioscience Park provides internships and scholarships for students. The purpose of the new law is to have the Broad Hollow Bioscience Park and the college lead in the development of the biotech industry and grow the Long Island economy.

Thus, in looking back at a century of existence, Farmingdale survives and thrives today as a full-fledged institution of higher learning. Its first two twenty-first-century presidents—Jonathan C.

FIGURE 10-8. At the Melville Road south entrance of the campus this prominent sign welcomes visitors to the College. The title of Farmingdale State College, a Campus of the State University of New York, is the institution's tenth and final name.

Gibralter and W. Hubert Keen—have provided informed leadership consistent with past leaders. By 2012, it had established its position as the largest college of technology in the SUNY system. It is an important factor in the local economy. It educates students to meet the needs of an ever-changing world. Its mission is distinctly different from what was stated in the original 1912 charter. One of sixty-four campuses within the SUNY system, its unique history is much more than a chronicle of growth, service, and achievement. Farmingdale State College has played a central role in the history of Long Island, New York State, and higher education. More than ever, the relationship between the college and the community has remained closely bound in confronting society's future challenges.

A milestone was achieved in 2011 when the college received a $1 million gift from entrepreneur Theresa Patnode Santmann, an alumna and Babylon (Suffolk County) resident. The gift provides funds for student scholarships and faculty research. Patnode Santmann founded the Little Flower Adult Home in Babylon in the 1960s before earning a nursing degree from Farmingdale in 1969. Four years later, she established the Little Flower Nursing Home in East Islip. In 1993, she founded the Petite Fleur Nursing Home in Sayville. By 2000, her nursing home business was ranked as the fourth largest female-owned business on Long Island. The $1 million gift is the largest in the college's history. The School of Health Sciences will be named in honor of Theresa Patnode Santmann.[21]

Notes

Chapter 1. Chartering the New York State School of Agriculture on Long Island

1. Ralph Henry Gabriel, *The Evolution of Long Island* (Port Washington, NY: Ira J. Friedman, 1921), p. 134.

2. Edwin L., Dunbaugh, "New York to Boston via the Long Island Railroad," *Evoking A Sense of Place*, ed. Joann Kreig, (Interlaken, NY: Heart of the Lakes Publishing, 1988), p. 75.

Stan Fischler, *Long Island Railroad* (St. Paul: MN; Voyageur Press, 1997), pp. 13–19.

Today the LIRR uses the designation "Railroad" as two words in its title, "Long Island Rail Road."

3. Sean Kass, "The Long Island Railroad and Its Promotion of Long Island, 1900–1930," *Long Island Historical Journal*, 17 (Fall 2004/Spring 2005): 85, 89–90.

Jacqueline Overton, *Long Island's History* (Garden City, NY: Doubleday, Doran, 1920), pp. 230–235.

See also Ron Ziel and George Foster, *Steels to Sunrise* (New York: Hawthorne Books, 1965).

4. S. Kass, pp. 84–90.

5. *New York Times*, 11 May 1912.

6. Charles L. Sachs, *The Blessed Isle, Hal B. Fullerton and His Image of Long Island, 1897–1929* Interlaken, NY: Heart of the Lakes Publishing, 1991), pp. 52–56.

See also Anne Nauman, *The Junior Partner: Edith Loring Fullerton, Long Island Pioneer* (Las Vegas, NV: Scrub Oak Pres, 1997); and Natalie A. Naylor, "Edith Loring Fullerton's Partnership with Hal. B. Fullerton," *Nassau County Historical Society Journal* 63 (2008): 28–42.

7. "Roosevelt to the Farmers," *New York Times*, 24 August 1910.

8. "Long Island Farming," *New York Times*, 6 October 1912. C. L. Sachs, pp. 64–65. *Long Island Agronomist* 4 (February 1911): 4. *Long Island Agronomist* 5 (April 1912):1–2.

9. C. L. Sachs, pp. 60–61. Chet Chorzempa, "The Fullertons and the Experimental Farms of the Long Island Railroad," *Long Island Historical Journal,* 6 (Spring 1994): 245–253. "As an Early Boost for L.I., He Had a Vision of Utopia," *New York Times*, Long Island Section, 8 July 1990, p. 2. Suffolk County Historical Society Exhibition, "The Blessed Isle: Hal B. Fullerton and His Image of Long Island," 1990; and Exhibition, "Edith Loring Fullerton: The Lady of the Garden," 2011.

10. *Long Island Agronomist* 2 (March 1909): 1. *Long Island Agronomist* 7 (April 1912): 1–4. *Long Island Agronomist*, 5 (March 1912): 2.

11. United States Department of Justice, *2000 Statistical Yearbook of the Immigration and Naturalization Service*, 2002.

12. Samuel Eliot Morison, Henry Steele Commager, and William E. Leuchtenburg, *The Growth of the American Republic*, Vol. II (New York: Oxford University Press, 1980), pp. 141–143. James W. Darlington, "Agriculture," *The Encyclopedia of New York State*, Ed. Peter Eisenstadt (Syracuse, NY: Syracuse University Press, 2005), 28–36.

13. J. Overton, p. 243. Peter Ross, *History of Long Island*, Vol. III (New York: Lewis Publishing, 1902), p. 295. "The Brooklyn Institute of Arts and Sciences," *The Columbia Encyclopedia*, Sixth Edition, 2008. Ellwood P. Cubberley, *Public Education in the United States* (Boston: Houghton Mifflin, 1934), pp. 629–630.

14. Franklin W. Hooper, "Industrial Museums for Our Cities," *Proceedings of the Eighth Annual Meeting of the American Associations of Museums*, June 1913, pp. 10–15.

15. S. E. Morison, H. S. Commager, and W. E. Leuchtenburg, pp. 127–131. David M. Ellis, James S. Frost, and William B. Fink, *New York, The Empire State* (Englewood Cliffs, NJ: Prentice-Hall, 1989), pp. 163–165, 184–186, 246–248. Harold S. Wechsler, "Higher Education," *The Encyclopedia of New York State*, Ed. Peter Eisenstadt (Syracuse, NY: Syracuse University Press, 2005), pp. 714–716.

———, "State University of New York," *The Encyclopedia of New York State*, Ed. Peter Eisenstadt (Syracuse, NY: Syracuse University Press, 2005), pp. 1471–1473.

Frank J. Cavaioli, "Chartering the New York State School of Agriculture on Long Island," *Long Island History Journal* 21 (Fall 2009): 1–22. See also Dennis Seven Nordin and Bertrand N. O. Walker, *Rich Harvest A History of the Grange, 1867–1900* (Jackson, MS: University Press of Mississippi, 1974).

16. Leroy Douglas, "At the Door of the Metropolis, The Struggle to Locate the New York State School of Agriculture on Long Island," *Long Island Forum* 16 (Winter 2002): 16–30.

"Our Agricultural School," *The South Side Signal*, 19 April 1912.

Agricultural Education Association, *Free Winter School of Agriculture*, Winter, 1912. FSC Archives.

Franklin W. Hooper, "Letter to the Officers and Members of Agricultural Organizations, Boards of Trade, and other Organizations: To Taxpayers, and to Citizens Generally in the Southeastern Quarter of the State of New York," 9 April 1912. FSC Archives.

17. *New York Tribune Farmer*, 15 April 1912.

J. W. Darlington, "Agriculture," pp. 28–29.

18. New York State, "*Chapter 319*," *Laws of New York*, 1912, pp. 637–639.

19. *Long Islander*, 9 September 1914.

20. Leroy Douglas, "Serving Community and Country: The New York State School of Agriculture at Farmingdale, 1914–1919," *Nassau County Historical Journal*, 57 (2002): 13–27.

Questions have arisen whether the New York State School of Agriculture on Long Island (now Farmingdale State College) was established in 1912 as a "Land Grant College" under federal legislation, the Morrill Land Grant Act of 1862. It was not. The only land grant college that was established in New York State was at Cornell, and it is now known as the New York State College of Agriculture and Life Sciences at Cornell University. Source: Patricia Mazzaferro, Assistant in Higher Education, The State Education Department, State University of New York, letter to the author, 13 August 1986. See also Gould Colman, "New York State College of Agriculture and Life Sciences at Cornell University," *The Encyclopedia of New York State*, Ed., P. Eisenstadt (Syracuse, NY: Syracuse University Press, 2005), p. 1995. See also Frank J. Cavaioli, *State University of New York at Farmingdale* (Charleston, SC: Arcadia Publishing, 1999).

Chapter 2. Laying the Foundation

1. New York School of Agriculture on Long Island, *Bulletin*, February 1916, p. 7.

2. *Historical Population of Long Island Communities 1790–1980: Decennial Census* (Hauppauge, NY: Long Island Regional Planning Board), 1980, pp. 15–16.

3. "Roosevelt to the Farmers," *New York Times*, 24 August 1910.

4. New York State, "Chapter 319," *Laws of New York, 1912*, p. 639.

5. Leroy Douglas, "At the Door of the Metropolis, The Struggle to Locate the New York State School of Agriculture on Long Island at Farmingdale: 1911–1913," *Long Island Forum* 65 (Winter 2002): 16–30.

Franklin W. Hooper, "Expense Account," 28 February 1914. Farmingdale State College Archives. Hereafter FSC Archives.

"Twenty-five Years of Progress," 1941. FSC Archives.

Long Island Agronomist 5 (May 1912): 5.

"Benjamin Franklin Yoakum," www.fbhsli.org, 2010.

6. New York State, *The Red Book*, 1912, p. 135.

7. L. Douglas, "At the Door of the Metropolis, The Struggle to Locate the New York School of Agriculture on Long Island at Farmingdale," pp. 16–23.

8. New York State School of Agriculture on Long Island, (NYSSA), Board of Trustees Meetings, 8 June 1912; 29 June 1912. FSC Archives.

9. Paul Bailey, "Rogers, Stone and Bailey," *Long Island Forum*, Fiftieth Anniversary Edition, 51 (Spring 1988): 50–53. Reprinted from May 1960 issue. Bailey died in 1962.

10. Vincent F. Seyfried, *The Cross-Island Line, The Story of the Huntington Railroad Operation in Huntington, Melville, Farmingdale, Amityville* (Garden City, NY, 1976), pp. 755–756.

11. L. Douglas, "At the Door of the Metropolis, The Struggle to Locate the New York State School of Agriculture on Long Island at Farmingdale," pp. 16–26.

Babylon Leader, 17 January 1913.

"Farm School Directors Justify Their Selection of the Site at Melville for State College," *Amityville Record*, 17 January 1913.

12. Franklin W. Hooper, "Statement to the Board of Trustees," June 1912. FSC Archives.

13. New York State School of Agriculture on Long Island, *Bulletin*, February 1916.

Atlas of Long Island (New York: Sanborn Map Company, 1904).

Belcher-Hyde Atlas of Nassau County 1906 (New York: Sanborn Map Company, 1910, 1920, 1925).

14. "The New York State School of Agriculture," *Babylon Leader*, 17 January 1913.

15. *Long Island Agronomist*, 5, February 1912, pp. 2–3.

16. NYSSA, *Bulletin*, 1916, p. 11.

17. Edwin Voorhis, *Master Plan of Village of Farmingdale*, Vol. I (Rockville Center, NY, 1959).

18. Frank J. Cavaioli, "The State University of New York at Farmingdale: The Foundation Years," *Long Island Forum* 64 (Winter 2001): 28.

New York Times, 21 June 1963.

"Albert Aaron Johnson," *The National Cyclopedia of American Biography*, Vol. A (New York: James T. White, 1924), pp. 483–484.

Lawrence A. Cremin, *The Transformation of the School, Progressivism in American Education, 1876–1957* (New York: Alfred A. Knopf, 1961), pp. 46–48.

The Albert Aaron Johnson Papers are deposited at the University of Wisconsin, Madison WI.

19. Albert A. Johnson and Franklin W. Hooper Correspondence, 13 January–27 December 1913. FSC Archives.

20. A. A. Johnson and F. W. Hooper Correspondence, 8 November 1913. FSC Archives.

21. Farmingdale Board of Trustees, "Minutes," 12 December 1912, 28 December 1912, 4 January 1913, 8 February 1913. FSC Archives.

"Lewis F. Pilcher, Architect, Was 70," *New York Times*, 16 June 1941.

22. Albert A. Johnson, "Statement," n. d. FSC Archives.

23. "Land or Appurtenances, Year Built or Purchased, Cost," n. d. FSC Archives.

24. "State School Cannot Open," *Amityville Record*, 28 May 1915.

"Farmingdale School is Open for Work," *Amityville Record*, 3 March 1916.

25. Leroy Douglas, "Serving Community and Country: The New York State School of Agriculture at Farmingdale, 1914–1919," *Nassau County Historical Society Journal* 57 (2002): 6–17.

NYSSA, *Bulletin*, February 1916, pp. 7, 31.

"City Boys Will Become Farmers," *Amityville Record*, 28 January 1916.

"Farm School Ready," *Suffolk County News*, 28 January 1916.

26. Samuel Eliot Morison, Henry Steele Commager, and William Leuchtenburg, *The Growth of the American Republic*, Vol. I (New York: Oxford University Press, 1980), pp. 198–200, 222–223.

27. NYSSA, *Bulletin*, February 1916, pp. 4–6.

James W. Darlington, "Agricultural Organization and Education," *The Encyclopedia of New York State*, Ed. Peter Eisenstadt (Syracuse, NY: Syracuse University Press), pp. 34–36.

28. Ellwood P. Cubberley, *Public Education in the United States* (Boston: Houghton Mifflin, 1934), pp. 598–599.

L. A. Cremin, *The Transformation of the School: Progressivism in American Education, 1876–1957*, pp. 52–57, 884–85.

29. NYSSA, *Bulletin*, October 1917, pp. 17–18.

30. NYSSA, *Bulletin*, February 1916, pp. 8–11.

31. NYSSA, *Bulletin*, October 1917, pp. 12–13.

32. NYSSA, *Bulletin*, October 1917, p. 16.

C. Dick Thomson, "From Idea to Reality," n. d. FSC Archives.

33. "Farm Boys Are Up in Athletics," *Amityville Record*, 20 October 1916.

"1st Game in 1919, Aggies Won, 28–0," *Alumnus*, May 1964.

34. F. J. Cavaioli, "The State University of New York at Farmingdale: The Foundation Years," p. 31.

L. Douglas, "Serving Community and Country: The New York State School of Agriculture at Farmingdale, 1914–1919," pp. 18–31.

35. *1917–1918 Budget*. FSC Archives.

36. C. Dick Thomson, Edwin F. Ore, and Raynor Wallace, *Alma Mater*, 1984. FSC Archives.

Chapter 3. Albert A. Johnson, 1913–1923

1. *Furrow*, November–December 1921, back cover. FSC Archives.

2. "Preparing for Food Harvest on Long Island Acres," *New York Times*, 6 May 1917.

"The First World War," *The Cricket History of Calderdale and Kirless*, www.cricketheritage.org.uk, 2009.

C. Dick Thomson, "From Idea to Reality," n. d. FSC Archives.

3. *NYSSA Yearbook*, 1919. The title "NYSSA" was used from 1919 to 1928.

4. "Professor Franke Still Finds Pleasure in Teaching After 40 Dedicated Years," *Alumnus*, January 1961.

NYSSAN Yearbook, 1930. The title "NYSSAN" was used from 1929 to 1947. From 1948 to the present the new title for the yearbook has been "*Islander*."

5. *NYSSA Yearbook*, 1919.

6. *NYSSA Yearbook*, 1919.

"The Institute in War Time," n. d. FSC Archives.

7. Frank J. Cavaioli, "The State University of New York at Farmingdale: The Foundation Years," *Long Island Forum* 64 (Winter 2001): 28–29.

8. *NYSSA Yearbook*, 1919 and *NYSSA Yearbook*, 1920.

C. D. Thomson, "From Idea to Reality," n. d. FSC Archives.

New York State Department of Health, A Special Report on the Mortality from Influenza in New York State During the Epidemic of 1918–1919, 1923.

9. "The Country Life Program," n. d. FSC Archives.

"The Nassau–Suffolk Share of the Population of New York State and of the United States," *Census '70*, Vol. I, Tables 1, 3.

Frank J. Cavaioli, "Ethnic Population Patterns on Long Island," *Ethnicity in Suburbia: The Long Island Experience*, Ed., Salvatore J. LaGumina, (Garden City, NY, 1980), p. 20.

10. "New York State Egg Laying Contest," n. d. FSC Archives.

11. "A Boost for Long Island Poultry Men," *Suffolk County News*, 14 May 1920.

12. NYSSA *Yearbook*, 1919.

"Farmers Fifteen in First Class Initial Graduation Exercise for Its First Pupils," *Amityville Record*, 4 April 1919.

13. C. D. Thomson.

F. J. Cavaioli, "The State University of New York: The Foundation Years," pp. 30–31.

NYSSA *Yearbook*, 1920.

NYSSA *Yearbook*, 1921.

NYSSA *Yearbook*, 1922.

NYSSA *Yearbook*, 1923.

14. "Twenty-five years of Progress." FSC Archives.

"History of the Alumni Association, 1921–1955." FSC Archives.

The Alumni Association charter members were: Bertrand Anderson, Albert Berg, Wilfred Brenzel, Bernard Cavallaro, Paul Donley, Walter Eidt, Abraham Ginsberg, Charles Glass, Wesley Graff, Bess Hamilton, Judy Hara, Russell Harned, Joseph Horak, Albert A. Johnson, Edward Kowalsky, Julio Laguette, Edward Leitner, Lancaster Lordly, Fred Moss, John Nicolai, Eric Patterson, Oliver Patterson, Willis Pignol, William Powers, Gerald Rawlins, Thomas Rome, Maude Schaeffer, Herbert Scheffer, Herbert Schmidt, Charles Schroeder, Abe Southard, Fred Stang, and Morton Stowe.

15. "The Early Days: '21 Alumnus Recalls." FSC Archives.

16. "Farming for Soldiers, Lectures at Upton to Help Men Find Places After the War," *Amityville Record*, 10 January 1919.

Carl E. Van Horn and Herbert A. Schaffner, Eds. *Work in America, An Encyclopedia of History, Policy and Society*, Vol. I, (Santa Barbara, CA: ABC-CLIO, 2003), pp. 163–164.

17. Frank J. Cavaioli, "The Memorial Oak Tree at Farmingdale" *Long Island Forum* 66 (Winter 2003): 18–23.

18. "Heroes' Oak Planted in Battlefield Soil," *New York Times*, 5 June 1921.

"President [*sic*] A. A. Johnson Cordially Invites You to Send A Representative to Both Luncheon and Ceremony," n. d. FSC Archives.

Charles Lathrop Pack, "The Memorial Tree," *American Forestry*, (July 1921): n. p.

19. Michelle Robbins, "Rooted in Memory," *American Forests*, (Spring 2002): 1–6.

20. "A Tablet, The Gift of the Class of '27," *1933–34 Freshman Manual*, p. 23. FSC Archives.

21. Halsey B. Knapp, "Letter to Faculty and Staff," 12 April 1956. FSC Archives.

22. Arthur Brisbane, "A School That Creates Farmers," *New York American*, 20 July 1920.

23. "Legislative Probe for Farm School," *Suffolk County News*, 1 March 1918.

24. NYSSA *Yearbook*, 1922.

NYSSA *Yearbook*, 1923.

25. *New York Evening Post*, 22 May 1922–29 December 1922.

26. Col. Forbes Asks Miller for Inquiry at Farmingdale," *New York Evening Post*, 27 April 1922.

"Soldier Students To Go," *New York Times*, 7 November 1927.

27. *Resolution Passed by the N. Y. State Federation of Farm Bureaus at a Regular Meeting Held at Syracuse*, 7 July 1922. FSC Archives.

28. Charlotte Scharf, "Ward Hall: A Look Back," *Campus Times*, (Winter 1998), p. 4.

"Rear Admiral Ward Is Dead at Roslyn," *New York Times*, 6 July 1918.

Two other U. S. Navy ships were named in honor of Rear Admiral Ward.

29. William A. Niles, "Letter to Hilda Ward," 14 October 1920. FSC Archives.

L. A. Wilson, "Letter to Miss Hilda Ward,"6 December1920. FSC Archives.

30. Hilda Ward, "Statement of Hilda Ward," 24 May 1922. FSC Archives

31. *New York Evening Post*, 7 April 1922; 26–29 April 1922; 1–5 May1922.

The Moreland Act was passed by the New York State Legislature and signed into law by Governor Charles Evans Hughes in 1907. Republican leader Sherman Moreland introduced the bill in the Assembly.

32. "Dean Resigns at Farmingdale," *Suffolk County News*, 19 May 1922.

33. "State Farm School Shake-Up Is Advised," *New York Times*, 1 September 1922.

34. *Johnson on Long Island, Excerpts from the Testimony Given During the Investigation of the Management and Affairs of the State Institute of Applied Agriculture at Farmingdale, L. I., Before Special Commissioner Edward G. Zimmer*, 1922. FSC Archives.

35. William M. Baldwin, "Statement to the Press, With Reference to the Farmingdale Matter," September 1922. FSC Archives.

"Trustees Make Answer," *Suffolk County News*, 15 September 1922.

36. "Another Fiasco," *Oyster Bay Guardian*, 23 June 1922.

"L. I. Press Association Want Director Johnson as Farm School Head," *New York Evening Post*, 16 December 1922.

37. "Student Petition," 19 October 1922. FSC Archives.

Harry J. Fisher, Telegram to Miss Hilda Ward, 19 October 1922. FSC Archives.

38. "Farm School Head Quits, Ending Four Years of Criticism," *New York Tribune*, 19 December 1922.

"Johnson Resigns Post as Director of Farm School," *Brooklyn Eagle*, 19 December 1922.

"Resigns Under Fire From Farm Institute," *New York Times*, 19 December 1922.

39. "Johnson Is Hooted After Resignation," *The Standard Union*, 19 December 1922.

40. "Farmingdale Trying to Get Principal Travis," *Suffolk County News*, 9 February 1923.

"Bricker Opposes Travis," *Suffolk County News*, 16 February 1923.

"Faculty Meeting," 2, 14 May 1923. FSC Archives.

"Bricker Quits State Farm," *New York Times*, 24 August 1923.

41. *New York Times*, 1 June 1963.

The Albert Aaron Johnson Papers, (Madison, Wisconsin: Wisconsin Historical Society, 2009).

"Albert Aaron Johnson," *National Cyclopedia of American Biography* (New York: James T. White and Company, 1924), pp. 483–484.

42. Albert A. Johnson, Letter to Locke James, April 1962. FSC Archives.

43. Karen A. Gelles, Interview with Fred Harrison, 30 September 2009. FSC Archives.

Frank A. Cipriani, Letter to the author, 17 September 2009. *New York Times*, 1 June 1963.

Chapter 4. Halsey B. Knapp, 1923–1956

1. Halsey B. Knapp, "Statement at Director's Luncheon, Country-Life Open House Program," 23 February 1956. FSC Archives.

2. *Suffolk County News*, 9 and 16 February 1923.

3. Henry Isham Hazelton, *The Boroughs of Brooklyn and Queens, Counties of Nassau and Suffolk, Long Island*, Vol. 4 (New York: Lewis Historical Publications, 1924), pp. 23–24.

4. *The Standard Union*, 26 September 1923.

5. Berne A. Pyrke, Letter to Halsey B. Knapp, 20 September 1923. FSC Archives.

Dow Beekman, Letter to Halsey B. Knapp, 24 October 1923. FSC Archives.

Arthur R. Mann, Letter to Halsey B. Knapp, 21 September 1923. FSC Archives.

6. Halsey B. Knapp, Letter to William M. Baldwin, 27 August 1923 and 4 September 1923. FSC Archives.

Edmund R. Lupton, Letter to Halsey B. Knapp, 29 August 1923. FSC Archives.

Frank J. Cavaioli, "Halsey B. Knapp," Part 1, *Long Island Forum* 48 (April 1985): 68–74.

7. H. I. Hazelton, p. 24.

8. H. B. Knapp, "Statement at Director's Luncheon."

9. Frank J. Cavaioli, "The Ku Klux Klan on Long Island," *Long Island Forum* 42 (May 1979): 100–106.

Jane S. Gombieski, "Klokards, Kleagles, Kludds, and Kluxers: The Ku Klux Klan in Suffolk County, 1915–1928," *Long Island Historical Journal* 6 (Fall 1993): 41–62.

Frank J. Cavaioli, "Mid-1920s Crisis at Farmingdale," *Long Island Forum* 50 (February 1987): 38–41.

Alfred E. Smith, Letter to H. B. Knapp, 23 March 1923. FSC Archives.

Edward J. Smits, *Nassau, Suburbia, U.S.A* (Garden City, NY: Doubleday, 1974), pp 145–147.

10. H. B. Knapp, "Statement at Director's Luncheon."

Joseph Petrick, "From Schools of Agriculture to Colleges of Technology: A Century of Evolution," *SUNY at Sixty, The Promise of the State University of New York*, Eds. John B. Clark, W. Bruce Leslie, and Kenneth P. O'Brien, (Albany, NY: SUNY Press, 2010).

11. *New York Times*, "Close Farmingdale, Gov. Smith Advises," pp. 21, 23 March 1926.

F. J. Cavaioli, "Mid-1920s Crisis at Farmingdale," pp. 38–41.

12. Alfred E. Smith, Letter to H. B. Knapp, 4 June 1926. FSC Archives.

"Agriculture On Long Island," *New York Times*, pp. 26, 23 March 1926.

13. Halsey B. Knapp, Letter to Governor Alfred E. Smith, 3 June, and 9 June 1926. FSC Archives.

14. *New York Times*, 4 May 1927.

15. *Long Islander*, 19 March 1926.

Brooklyn Eagle, 24 March 1926.

Farmingdale Post, 26 March 1926.

Albany Evening News, 3 April 1926.

16. "State School Safe for Present," *Nassau Weekly*, 26 March 1926.

"Sees Asylum Plan as Danger to Girls in Industrial School," *Brooklyn Eagle*, 31 March 1926.

New York Times, 23 March, 23 April 1926, and 4 May 1927.

17. *1925–1926 Freshman Handbook.*

1932 Freshman Manual.

18. Halsey B. Knapp, "For Better Country Life," *LIRR Bulletin 1931*, pp. 10–14.

www.nysagsociety.org/presidents, 2010. www.autonnews.com/FarmingdaleObserver/2005/07/1opinion, 2010.

www.Rotary.org, 2010.

19. Frank J. Cavaioli, "Halsey B. Knapp," *Long Island Forum*, Part I, 48 (April 1985): 72–73.

20. "Personnel Service, 1934–1935." FSC Archives.

21. Alumnus, January 1961.

22. Carl E. Van Horn and Herbert A. Schaffner, Eds. *Work in America, An Encyclopedia of History, Policy, and Society*, Vol. I (Santa Barbara, CA: ABC-CLIO, 2003), pp. 163–164.

23. F. J. Cavaioli, "Halsey B. Knapp," Part I, pp. 73–74.

24. Natalie A. Naylor, "The Legacy of New Deal Art on Long Island," *Long Island Historical Journal* 17 (Fall 2004/Spring 2005): 41–70.

Basil R. Northam, Letter to Kathryn Coley, 12 February 1999. FSC Archives.

25. Frank J. Cavaioli, "George L. Thompson and the College at Farmingdale," *Long Island Forum* 55 (Spring 1993): 4–6.

26. C. Dick Thomson, "From Idea to Reality," n. d. FSC Archives.

"G. Thompson Dies, 76," *New York Times*, 2 September 1941.

27. C. D. Thomson.

28. "Country Life Program Boasts Several New and Interesting Features," *Aggazette*, 6 February 1946.

29. C. Dick Thomson, Letter to Professor Eugene O'Neill, n. d. FSC Archives.

30. "Stony Kill Farm," 1955, pp. 1–9. FSC Archives.

"Stony Kill Environmental Education Center," New York State Department of Environmental Conservation, 2009, pp. 1–10.

31. Unsigned Document, "Institute History," n. d., pp. 7, 28. FSC Archives.

NYSSA Yearbook, 1922.

32. "A Tablet, The Gift of the Class of '27," *1933–34 Freshman Manual*, p. 23.

33. "Horton Amidon Report," February 1954. FSC Archives.

Frank J. Cavaioli, "Halsey B. Knapp," Part II, Conclusion, *Long Island Forum* 48 (May 1985): 89–90.

34. Halsey B. Knapp, "Knapp Memo," 9 June 1947. FSC Archives.

"Report of the Policy Committee for the Administration of Instructional Personnel," 10 November 1947. FSC Archives.

35. Halsey B. Knapp, "Halsey B. Knapp Address to Technical-Industrial Faculty," 15 September 1949. FSC Archives.

F. J. Cavaioli, "Halsey B. Knapp," Part II, Conclusion, pp. 90–93.

36. "A Report on Personnel Policies," 1 December 1952. FSC Archives.

37. Betty Mountain, Telephone interview with author, 1 August 1984.

Michael Abbatiello, Interview by author, 2 August 1984.

38. Michael Abbatiello, Interview by author, 2 August 1984.

39. H. B. Knapp, "Statement at Director's Luncheon."

40. "Halsey B. Knapp Dies Tuesday," *Farmingdale Post*, 9 September 1976.

"Dr. H. B. Knapp, Ex-College Head," *Long Island Press*, 8 September 1976.

41. Peter John Tedesco, *Remembering*. Memoir presented to the author by Priscilla Tedesco Hancock, 4 May 2010

Chapter 5. The World War II Era

1. William Penn, quoted by Halsey B. Knapp, *NYSSAN Yearbook*, 1945.

2. "NYSIA in Nation's Service," *NYSSAN Yearbook*, 1943.

"Total Number Who Served and Were Killed in Action," 29 October 1945. FSC Archives.

3. Locke James, "Wartime Services at the State Institute of Agriculture, Farmingdale," n. d. FSC Archives.

C. Dick Thomson, "Activities in World War II," n. d. FSC Archives.

"Institute History," n. d. FSC Archives.

4. "Faculty Tintypes, Our Director," *Aggazette*, January 1937. The *Aggazette* was a student publication covering the years 1923–1948.

Graduating Class of 1949, Letter to Director Knapp, 21 November 1948. FSC Archives.

Frank A. Cipriani, email message to author, 9 September 2009.

Sara Howitt, "The World War II Homefront: The Farmingdale Experience," *Long Island Forum* 58 (Summer 1995): 24–25.

5. *1950–1951 Student Handbook*.

1955–1956 Student Handbook.

6. "Enrollments in All Classes, 1916 to 1945." FSC Archives.

Daniel Hart Horton, "Institute History, Poultry," June 1945. FSC Archives.

"Number of Graduates Based on Community Programs, Yearbooks, and Annual Reports," n. d. FSC Archives.

7. "The 1940 Annual Country Life and Home Show." FSC Archives.

8. C. Dick Thomson, "From Idea to Reality," n. d. FSC Archives.

9. C. Dick Thomson, "Achievements," n. d. FSC Archives.

10. *1942 Catalog*. FSC Archives.

11. Frank J. Cavaioli, "The Campus Village at Farmingdale," *Long Island Forum* 45 (March 1982): 44–46.

12. F. J. Cavaioli, "The Campus Village at Farmingdale," pp. 44–46.

13. Halsey B. Knapp, "Memorandum to Messrs. Amidon, Hallock," 7 April 1955. FSC Archives.

14. Oliver Cromwell Carmichael Jr., *New York Establishes a State University* (Nashville, TN: Vanderbilt University, 1955), pp. v, 1–40.

Office of University Affairs and Development, *Sixty-four Campuses* (Albany, NY: State University of New York, 1985), pp. 1–9.

15. Harold S. Wechsler, "State University of New York," *The Encyclopedia of New York State*, Ed. Peter Eisenstadt, (Syracuse, NY: Syracuse University Press, 2005), pp. 1471–1473.

Joseph Petrick, "From Schools of Agriculture to Colleges of Technology: A Century of Evolution," *SUNY at Sixty, The Promise of the State University of New York*, Eds. John B. Clark, W. Bruce Leslie, and Kenneth P. O'Brien, (Albany, NY: SUNY Press, 2010), pp. 80–83.

16. H. S. Wechsler, p. 473.

17. O. C. Carmichael Jr., pp. 132–135, 228, 231–232, 267–268.

18. Halsey B. Knapp, "Statement at the Annual North Atlantic Regional Conference-Agricultural Education" 6–9 April 1948. FSC Archives.

19. O. C. Carmichael Jr., pp. 273–274, 293–294.

20. David C. Hammack, "Nonprofit Sector," *The Encyclopedia of New York State*, Ed. Peter Eisenstadt, (Syracuse, NY: Syracuse University, 2005), pp. 1116–1118.

H. S. Wechsler, p. 1473.

21. Halsey B. Knapp, "Memorandum to Messrs. Merritt, Wedell, Davidson, Rissmeyer, Foote, James, Stockbridge, McLaughlin, Allee, Willenbrock, Griffith, Roberts, Judd, Coogan, Bowman, Amidon, Raymaley, Hallock, Hallahan, Floyd, Roesch, Rogers," 16 January 1950. FSC Archives.

22. Frank A. Cipriani, "Re-Engineering SUNY Farmingdale," Unpublished memoir, 2009, pp. 1–12. A copy was presented to the author.

H. S. Wechsler, p. 1473.

23. New York State Supreme Court, Appellate Division, Second Department, *Frank J. Cavaioli, et al., Plaintiffs-Appellants, Against Board of Trustees of the State University of New York, et al., Record of Appeal*, 29 January 1985.

Isaac Kaplowits and Daniel Galinson, *Brief of Plaintiffs-Appellants*, 4 February 1985. *Class Action Suit Determination*, 21 April 1988. FSC Archives

24. "Minutes of the Faculty Executive Committee," SUNY College of Technology at Farmingdale, 16 October 1987. FSC Archives.

Chapter 6. The Industrial-Technical Division

1. Bernard Palmer, "*The Conklin Street Story*," 1956. FSC Archives.

2. John S. Brubaker and Willis Rudy, *Higher Education in Transition*, 4th ed. (New Brunswick, NJ: Transaction Publishers, 1997), pp. 161–164.

Edward L Desnozka and David E. Kapel, revised edition by David E. Kapel, Charles S. Gifford, and Marilyn Kapel, *American Educators' Encyclopedia* (New York: Greenwood Press, 1991), pp. 122–123, 569.

Joseph Petrick, "From Schools of Agriculture to Colleges of Technology: A Century of Evolution," *SUNY at Sixty, The Promise of the State University of New York*, Eds. John B. Clark, W. Bruce Leslie, and Kenneth P. O'Brien, (Albany, NY: SUNY Press, 2010), pp. 83–84.

3. "*Technical Education*." FSC Archives.

4. Frank J. Cavaioli, "Halsey B. Knapp," *Long Island Forum*, Part II, 48 (May 1985): 90.

5. Halsey B. Knapp, "Statement at Director's Luncheon, Country Life-Open House Program," 23 February 23. FSC Archives.

6. Richard Hofstadter and C. DeWitt Hardy, *The Development of Higher Education in the United States* (New York: Columbia University Press, 1952), pp. 144–145.

7. Frank J. Cavaioli, "The Conklin Street Campus," *Long Island Forum* 46 (May 1983): 90–92.

8. Christine Wilkens, Ed., "Nazareth Trade School," *Farmingdale's Story, Farms to Fligh*t, Farmingdale Village Bicentennial Issue, 1976.

9. Frank J. Cavaioli, "David W. Allee and the College of Technology at Farmingdale," *Long Island Forum* 51 (Summer 1988): 62–63.

10. F. J. Cavaioli, "David W. Allee and the College of Technology at Farmingdale," pp. 62–66.

11. Long Island Agricultural and Technical Institute," *Bulletin 1946*.

12. F. J. Cavaioli, "David W. Allee and the College of Technology at Farmingdale," pp. 62–66.

F. J. Cavaioli, "The Conklin Street Campus," pp. 90–94.

13. David W. Allee, Telephone interview by author, 3 January 1983.

F. J. Cavaioli, "David W. Allee and the College of Technology at Farmingdale," p. 64.

14. F. J. Cavaioli, "The Conklin Street Campus," pp. 90–95.

15. Anthony Mastroianni, Letter to author, 5 October 2009.

16. Casimir Rakowski, Interview by author, 3 January 1983.

17. Anthony Vitale, *Escalate* (Evening College newspaper), February 1977, p. 6.

Farmingdale State College, *Catalog 2009/2010*, pp. 74–79.

18. F. J. Cavaioli, "The Conklin Street Campus," pp. 90–95.

19. "Celebrating 75 Years . . . and Tomorrow," 1987. FSC Archives.

"R. Wallace, 91, Professor," *Newsday*, 8 November 2008.

20. *College Catalog 2009/2010*, pp. 66–68.

21. "Long Island Institute Graduates First Industrial Class," *Institute News Item*, 28 June 1948. FSC Archives.

"Graduation Statistics," Farmingdale State College, 1948. FSC Archives.

22. Bernard Palmer, "The Conklin Street Story," 1956. FSC Archives. Bernard Palmer did not sign his name to the article. He was identified as the author by Professor C. Dick Thomson of the English Department in an undated letter to Dr. Eugene O'Neill, dean of instruction. Palmer was a member of the English Department from 1952 to 1960.

23. "Farmingdale Institute to Present Country Life-Open House Program," *News Release*, 1951. FSC Archives.

24. Halsey B. Knapp, "Memorandum to R. C. Davidson," 7 August 1952. FSC Archives.

Halsey B. Knapp, "Memorandum to Horton Amidon," 28 January 1953. FSC Archives.

Halsey B. Knapp, "Memorandum to Horton Amidon," 5 February 1953. FSC Archives.

25. "Memorialization of Director Allee," *Alumnus*, Winter, 1987.

"David W. Allee Dedication," *Campus Times*, September 1994. *Alumnus* (1961–Present) and the *Campus Times* (1980–Present) are official college publications.

William A. Medesy, "Report on Placement and Progress of Graduates," 1956. FSC Archives.

Chapter 7. The Charles W. Laffin Jr. Years, 1961–1976

1. Anthony Mastroianni, Letter to the author, 5 October 2009. Mastroianni, Class of 1950, served on the Farmingdale College Council from 1967 to 2000.

2. Scott Ennis, "William A. Medesy, A Lifelong Advocate of Education," *Congressional Record*, Vol. 146, 14 February 2000, pp. 133–134.

3. William Medesy, Letter to the Editor, 15 April 1956.

4. Agricultural and Technical Institute, *News Release*, 4 May 1957. FSC Archives.

"Dedication Pamphlet," 30 May 1959. FSC Archives.

5. "The Faculty of State University Agricultural and Technical Institute at Farmingdale Petition to Director William A. Medesy, Dean Lawrence L. Jarvie and the SUNY Board of Trustees." FSC Archives.

6. "William Adelbert Medesy, 90, Died February 1," *Rocky Mountain News*, 8 February 2000.

7. "Dr. Charles W. Laffin, President Passes Away," *Escalate*, February 1977.

8. "The Farm is a Classroom," *New York Sunday News*, 9 August 1970.

"A Pilot Program, Aerospace Technology Curriculum Unique at Farmingdale University," *New York Sunday News*, 11 January 1971.

Frank J. Cavaioli, *State University of New York at Farmingdale* (Charleston, SC: Arcadia Publishing, 1999), pp. 8, 78–80.

"Profile of SUNY at Farmingdale," 9 August 1972. FSC Archives.

9. "Electronics Blends with Farming on L. I. College," *New York Times*, 6 June 1962.

10. Albert A. Johnson, Letter to Locke James, 6 April 1962. FSC Archives.

11. F. J. Cavaioli, *State University of New York at Farmingdale*, p. 78.

12. A. Mastroianni, Letter to author, 5 October 2009.

13. Charles W. Laffin Jr., "President's Message to Graduates of June 1963," *Islander*, 1963, p. 2.

Samuel Eliot Morison, Henry Steele Commager, and William E. Leuchtenburg, *The Growth of the American Republic*, Vol. II (New York: Oxford University Press, 1980), pp. 760–762.

14. Frank A. Cipriani, "Re-Engineering SUNY Farmingdale," 2009, pp. 55–62.

15. Charles W. Laffin Jr., "Evaluating the Performance of Non-Teaching Professionals," Paper presented at Colorado State University, Fort Collins, Colorado, 16–19 June 1975, pp. 1–15.

Christine E. Murray, "Taylor Law," *The Encyclopedia of New York State*, Ed. Peter Eisenstadt, (Syracuse, NY: Syracuse University Press, 2005), pp. 1536–1537.

16. A. Mastroianni, Letter to author, 5 October 2009.

New York Times, 6 June 1972.

17. Kathryn Coley, "Biographical Information for William Fichtner," 7 June 2000. FSC Archives.

"Farmingdale State's Class of 2008 Begins a New Journey," *Campus Times*, June 2008.

18. "Tri-Semester Planned," *Rambler*, 27 March 1962. *1965–1966 Annual Report*.

State University Agricultural and Technical College at Farmingdale, "First Trimester Class Graduates," *Alumnus*, March 1965.

"Profile of SUNY at Farmingdale," 9 August 1972. FSC Archives.

19. Charles W. Laffin Jr., "Letter," 6 April 1966. FSC Archives.

20. State University of New York, *The Master Plan, Revised* (Albany, NY, 1964), pp. xi, 1, 11, 15–17, 28–29.

21. "600 'Aggie' Grads Become Alumni," *Alumnus*, July1974.

John W. Wydler, "Commencement Address, State University Agricultural and Technical Institute, Farmingdale, NY," *Congressional Record*, 89th Congress, First Session, 22 June 1965.

F. J. Cavaioli, *State University of New York at Farmingdale*, pp. 81, 84, 110.

22. "SUNY Farmingdale Intercollegiate Athletic Program." FSC Archives.

"George E. Nold, 72, A Physics Professor," *New York Times*, 23 July 1971.

23. *Catalog 2009/2010*, p. 36.

24. Agricultural and Technical College at Farmingdale, *Press Release*, February 1968. FSC Archives.

25. "Adams Chronicles Spurring College-by-TV," New York Times, 1 August 1976.

Frank J. Cavaioli, "Adams Chronicles," *Escalate*, March 1976. FSC Archives.

26. Robert C. Blank, Interview with the author, 9 September 2009.

Nell Ewing, "Phi Theta Kappa: Founded by Presidents," Letter to the author, 1 October 2009.

27. *Catalog 2008/2009*, p. 22.

28. *New York Times*, 6 June 1972 and 6 December 1976.

A. Mastroianni, Letter to author, 5 October 2009.

"Charles Laffin Dies," *Newsday*, 26 December 1976.

29. "Dr. Charles W. Laffin, President, Passes Away," *Escalate*, February 1977.

"Charles W. Laffin," www.Excelsior.edu, 2009.

"Leadership Spotlight, Dr. Charles W. Laffin Jr.," *Long Island Educational Review* 27 (September 1972).

30. "Mauro Zulli Acting President of SUNY Farmingdale," *Escalate*, February 1977.

31. "Ceremony Honoring the Memory of Dr. Charles W. Laffin Jr., President, 1961–1976, and Dedication of the Charles W. Laffin Jr. Administration Building," 14 May 1977. Document given to the author by Kevin R. Laffin (son) 5 May 2010.

Chapter 8. Dr. Frank A. Cipriani Heralds the Future, 1978–2000

1. Frank A. Cipriani, "75th Anniversary Presidential Message," 1987. FSC Archives.

2. Harold S. Wechsler, "State University of New York," *The Encyclopedia of New York State*, Ed. Peter Eisenstadt (Syracuse, NY: Syracuse University Press, 2005), pp. 1471–1473.

3. Frank A. Cipriani, "Re-Engineering SUNY Farmingdale," Unpublished memoir, 2009, pp. 1–4, 14–19.

Brooklyn Tech Alumni Foundation website, 2009.

4. F. A. Cipriani, "Re-Engineering SUNY Farmingdale," pp. 23–24.

5. *Catalog 2009/2010*, p. 32.

6. F. A. Cipriani, "Re-Engineering SUNY Farmingdale," pp. 19–37.

7. F. A. Cipriani, "Re-Engineering SUNY Farmingdale," pp. 33–38, 78.

8. F. A. Cipriani, "Re-Engineering SUNY Farmingdale," pp. 72–76.

9. "Installation Ceremony for President, Frank A. Cipriani, Ph. D.," 7 May 1978. FSC Archives.

Campus Times, May 1990.

Rev. Hugh McManus presented a prayer of dedication and Rev. Albert Palmer concluded the presidential installation ceremony with a benediction.

10. Frank A. Cipriani, "Testimony Presented Before the Senate Higher Education Committee Hearing on the 'Rethinking' SUNY Report by the New York Board of Trustees," 5 January 1996, SUNY Stony Brook Campus." FSC Archives.

11. F. A. Cipriani, "Re-Engineering SUNY Farmingdale," pp. 84–87.

12. *1979–1980 Annual Report*. FSC Archives.

Anthony Mastroianni, letter to author, 5 October 2009.

13. Mauro Zulli, telephone interview by author, 20 December 2009.

14. *Catalog 2008/2009*.

15. "A Voice for the Disadvantaged," *Campus Times*, November 1991.

Noel Palmer, "Let Each Become," Unpublished memoir, 1978. A copy was provided to the author. The title is taken from the motto of the State University of New York, "Let each become he is capable of being."

16. F. A. Cipriani, "Re-Engineering SUNY Farmingdale," pp. 39–44.

17. *Campus Times*, October 1991.

Catalog 2008/2009, p. 173.

18. James Friel, letter to author, 16 September 2009.

Humanities/AITA, various editions.

19. Frank Pyne, "New Log Cabin (Farmingdale)." FSC Archives.

20. Christy Hinko, "Cabin Fever." FSC Archives.

21. "The 75th Anniversary Historical Committee Program," 1 October 1986. FSC Archives.

22. *Campus Times*, December 1986.

"Diamond Jubilee Ball," Farmingdale College Foundation, 1987. FSC Archives.

23. Kathryn Coley, letter to the author, 14 June 2009.

Frank J. Cavaioli, *State University of New York at Farmingdale* (Charleston, SC: Arcadia Publishing, 1999), p. 109.

24. *Campus Times*, November 1986.

25. *Campus Times*, September 1986.

Campus Times, January 1990.

26. *Campus Times*, April 1994.

27. Patricia Hill Williams, letter to author, 14 April 2010.

Campus Times, May 2010.

Chapter 9. Transition and Transformation

1. "Farmingdale Graduates, College Completes Transition to 4-Year Institution," *Newsday*, 28 April 1990.

2. Leroy Douglas, "Republic Airport in History," *LI-Airport Historical Society Newsletter* (Summer–Fall 2008): 30–32.

3. "The Institute in Wartime," n. d. FSC Archives.

Frank A. Cipriani, "Statement at Groundbreaking Ceremony of New SUNY Farmingdale Airport Facility at Republic Field," 15 April 1993. FSC Archives.

4. Lou Howard, Telephone interview by author, 20 March 2010.

"Lou Howard," www.Stonybrook.edu, February 2010.

5. Frank A. Cipriani, "Re-Engineering SUNY Farmingdale," unpublished memoir, 2009, pp. 39–45.

6. "Groundbreaking Ceremony for Aerospace Facility," *Campus Times*, May 1993.

"SUNY College of Technology at Farmingdale News Release," 15 April 1993. FSC Archives.

7. Lorretta M. Donaldson, "Aviation Department," 16 September 1995. FSC Archives.

"New Planes Arrive at SUNY," *Farmingdale Observer*, 3 October 1997.

College Catalog 2009–2010, pp. 57–59.

8. L. Douglas, pp. 11–12.

F. A. Cipriani, "Re-Engineering SUNY Farmingdale," pp. 43–46.

9. "A Brief History of SUNY Farmingdale's Renewed Mission," *Campus Times*, May 1990.

F. A. Cipriani,"Re-Engineering SUNY Farmingdale," pp. 83–84.

10. *F. A. Cipriani,"*Re-Engineering SUNY Farmingdale, "pp. 77–87.

11. "Mortuary Science Program Is Now Administered by Nassau Community College," *Campus Times*, October 1991.

"Program Cuts at Farmingdale," *Newsday*, 11 December 1992.

12. "Student–Farmer Mourns Dying Trade," *Newsday*, 3 April 1986.

Joseph Petrick, "From Schools of Agriculture to Colleges of Technology: A Century of Evolution," *SUNY at Sixty, The Promise of the State University of New York*, Ed. John B. Clark, W. Bruce Leslie, and Kenneth P. O'Brien, (Albany, NY: SUNY Press, 2010), p. 85.

13. "A Brief History of SUNY Farmingdale's Renewed Mission," n. d. FSC Archives.

14. "Farmingdale Graduates, College Completes Transition to 4-Year Institution," *Newsday*, 28 April 1990.

15. "Baccalaureate Mission Approved," *Campus Times*, May 1993.

"TTUC Opens," *Campus Times*, December 1993.

"Seeds of Future Yet to Sprout," *Newsday*, 4 May 1992.

16. "Seeds of Future Yet to Sprout," *Newsday*, 4 May 1992.

"SUNY Cutbacks," *Newsday*, 21 June 1995.

17. "SUNY Farmingdale Enrollment Plunges," *Newsday*, 14 October 1994.

18. "Welcome to Stealth University," *New York Times*, 2 May 1999, Section 14, pp. 1, 17.

Frank A. Cipriani, "Testimony Presented before the Senate Higher Education Committee Hearing on the 'Rethinking' SUNY Report" by the New York Board of Trustees, Friday, 5 January 1996, Stony Brook Campus." FSC Archives.

19. F. A. Cipriani, "Re-Engineering SUNY Farmingdale," pp. 97–99.

20. "Biotechnology Park Is Funded," *SUNY Farmingdale News & Events*, 19 January 2000. FSC Archives.

21. "Biotechnology Park Is Funded," *SUNY Farmingdale News & Events*. 19 January 2000. FSC Archives.

22. "About SUNY Farmingdale," www.farmingdale.edu, 2000.

23. State University of New York at Farmingdale, "Convocation and Colloquy Commemorating the Twentieth Anniversary of President Frank A. Cipriani, Ph. D., 15 September 1998." FSC Archives.

24. "Michael A. Vinciguerra Appointed Acting President," *Campus Times*, May 2000.

Chapter 10. Into the Twenty-First Century

1. W. Hubert Keen, "Message from the President," *Farmingdale State College Annual Report 2008*.

2. "Michael J. Vinciguerra Appointed Acting President at Farmingdale State, 2010,

www.farmingdale.edu, 2010. "Michael J. Vinciguerra Appointed Acting President," *Campus Times*, May 2000.

3. "SUNY Farmingdale Gets President," *Newsday*, 28 March 2001.

4. "Resolution," Illinois General Assembly, *92-HR1014*, 1 June 2002.

5. "Inauguration of Jonathan C. Gibralter, Ph. D., President," 2 November 2001.

6. “Setting Higher Goals for Farmingdale State,” *New York Times*, 23 February 2003, Long Island Section, p. I14.

7. Jonathan C. Gibralter, “Vita,” 2006. FSC Archives.

Patricia Hill Williams, E-mail correspondence with the author, 14 April 2010.

8. “Farmingdale Campus Gets A $133 Million Upgrade,” *New York Times*, 15 June 2003.

9. “SUNY Names New President at Farmingdale College,” *Farmingdale Observer*, online edition, 19 January 2007.

10. “The Inauguration of W. Hubert Keen,” 11 May 2007. FSC Archives.

“W. Hubert Keen Installed as Farmingdale President,” *Farmingdale View*, Fall 200. FSC Archives.

11. “Interview with W. Hubert Keen,” *Long Island Business News*, 16 February 2007.

12. “Commencement Speakers,” 2010, FSC Archives.

“Commencement, Historical Perspective,” www.farmingdale.edu, 2010.

13. “Facts and Figures,” www.farmingdale.edu, 2007, 2010.

“Academic Programs,” “News,” www.farmingdale.edu, 2011.

“Commencement at Farmingdale State College,” 2008. FSC Archives.

“Enrollment Statistics,” Farmingdale State College Registrar, 10 October 2009. FSC Archives.

“Total Graduates 2008–2009: 2009–2010; 2010–2011,” Farmingdale State College Registrar, 23 July 2011. FSC Archives.

14. *Annual Report 2000*. FSC Archives.

15. *Annual* Report *2000*, FSC Archives.

“SUNY Farmingdale Major Priority for System,” *Long Island Press*, 10 July 2009.

“Solar Energy Center,” http://www.farmingdale.edu, 2010.

“The Green Building Institute at Farmingdale State College,” www.farmingdale.edu, 2011.

“Opening of New Sustainable Garden at Farmingdale State College,” www.farmingdale.edu, 24 March 2011.

16. “*Annual Report 2008*.” FSC Archives.

“Farmingdale State College to Benefit from $54.5 M Secured by State,” *Campus Times*, May 2008.

“Farmingdale State College’s Aviation Program Announces $1 Million Purchase of New Planes,” www.farmingdale.edu, 31 March 2011.

17. “Dr. W. Hubert Keen Named to LI Power List,” www.farmingdale.edu, 2008.

“Farmingdale State College President W. Hubert Keen Named Winner of David Award by *Networking Magazine*, www.farmingdale.edu, 8 September 2008.

“President Keen Honored by LIA Small Business Council,” www.farmingdale.edu, 2009.

Annual Report 2008. FSC Archives.

18. “Digital Systems Memorial Lab Dedicated to Herb Zipper,” *Campus Times*, May 2008.

19. “Farmingdale State College Nationally Ranked in Graduate Earning Power,” *Long Island Press*, 17 November 2009.

“Farmingdale State Named Fifth Most Safe College in the United States by *The Daily Beast*,” www.farmingdale.edu, 2010.

20. Lee E. Koppelman and Pearl M. Kamer, “Anatomy of the Long Island Economy: Retrospective and Prospective,” *Long Island Historical Journal* 6 (Spring 1994): 146–167.

“College Has $1 Billion Economic Impact on Region, According to LIA Study,” *Campus Times*, March 2009.

“Facts and Figures,” www.farmingdalew.edu, 2010.

Annual Report 2009. FSC Archives.

21. “$1 M Gift for Farmingdale,” *Newsday*, 22 September 2011.

Bibliography

Articles, books, interviews, memoirs, and websites.

"A Boost for Long Island Poultrymen," *Suffolk County News*, 14 May 1920.

"A Pilot Program, Aerospace Technology Curriculum at Farmingdale University," *New York Sunday News*, 11 January 1971.

Abbatiello, Michael. Interview by author. Farmingdale, NY, 2 August 1984.

"About SUNY Farmingdale," www.Farmingdale.edu, 2000.

"Adams Chronicles Spurring College-by-TV," *New York Times*, 1 August 1976.

Albert Aaron Johnson Papers. Madison WI: Wisconsin Historical Society Archives, 2009.

Allee, David W. Telephone interview by author. Farmingdale, NY, 3 January 1983.

"Another Fiasco," *Oyster Bay Guardian*, 23 June 1922.

Atlas of Long Island. New York: Sanborn Map Company, 1904.

Babylon Leader, 17 January 1913.

Bailey, Paul. *Long Island, A History of Two Great Counties, Nassau and Suffolk*. New York: Lewis Historical Publishing Co., 1949.

———. "Rogers, Stone and Bailey," *Long Island Forum*, Fiftieth Anniversary Edition, (Spring 1988): 50.

Belcher-Hyde Atlas of Nassau County 1906. New York: Sanford Map Company, 1910, 1920, 1925.

Blank, Robert C. Telephone interview by author, 9 September 2009.

"Bricker Opposes Travis," *Suffolk County News*, 16 February 1923.

"Bricker Quits State Farm," *New York Times*, 24 August 1923.

Brisbane, Arthur. "A School That Creates Farmers," *New York American*, 20 July 1920.

Brooklyn Eagle, 24 March 1926.

Brubaker, John S. and Willis Rudy. *Higher Education in Transition*. 4th edition. New Brunswick, NJ: Transaction Publishers, 1977.

Carmichael Jr., Oliver Cromwell. *New York Establishes A State University*. Nashville, TN: Vanderbilt University Press, 1955.

Carpenter, James W. *The Mineola Fair*. Uniondale, NY: Agricultural Societies of Queens, Nassau and Suffolk Counties, 1965.

Cavaioli, Frank J. "Chartering the New York State School of Agriculture on Long Island," *Long Island History Journal* 21 (Fall 2009): 1–19.

———. "David W. Allee and the College of Technology at Farmingdale," *Long Island Forum* 51 (Summer 1988): 62–66.

———. "Ethnic Population Patterns on Long Island." *Ethnicity in Suburbia: The Long Island Experience*. Ed. Salvatore J. LaGumina. Garden City, NY, 1980.

———. "George L. Thompson and the College at Farmingdale," *Long Island Forum* 55 (Spring 1993): 4–6.

———. "Halsey B. Knapp," Part I, *Long Island Forum* 48 (April 1985): 68–74.

———. "Halsey B. Knapp," Part II, *Long Island Forum* 48 (May 1985): 90–96.

———. "Mid-1920s Crisis at Farmingdale," *Long Island Forum* 50 (February 1987): 38–41.

———. *State University of New York at Farmingdale*. Charleston, SC: Arcadia, 1999.

———. "The Campus Village at Farmingdale," *Long Island Forum* 45 (March 1982): 44–46.

———. "The Conklin Street School," *Long Island Forum* 46 (May 1983): 90–92.

———. "The Ku Klux Klan on Long Island," *Long Island Forum* 42 (May 1979): 100–106.

———. "The Memorial Oak Tree at Farmingdale," *Long Island Forum* 66 (Winter 2003): 18–22.

———. "The State University of New York at Farmingdale: The Foundation Years," *Long Island Forum* 64 (Winter 2001): 22–33.

Cemetery Records-Veterans, Revolution to World War I, Westchester County. Albany, NY: New York State Archives, n. d.

"Ceremony Honoring the Memory of Dr. Charles W. Laffin Jr. Administration Building, 14 May 1977." Document presented to the author by Kevin R. Laffin (son), 5 May 2010.

"Cipriani, Frank A., Alumnus of the Year," www.BooklynTechAlumniFoundation.com, 2009.
Cipriani, Frank A. Email message to the author, 9 September 2009.
———. "Re-Engineering SUNY Farmingdale." Unpublished memoir, 2009.
"City Boys Will Become Farmers," *Amityville Record*, 28 January 1916.
"Commencement, Historical Perspective," www.farmingdale.edu, 2008.
Clancy, Ambrose. "Interview with W. Hubert Keen," *Long Island Business News*, 16 February 2007.
Clark, John B., W. Bruce Leslie, and Kenneth O'Brien, Eds. *SUNY At Sixty: The Promise of the State University of New York*. Albany, NY: SUNY Press, 2010.
"Col. Forbes Asks Miller for Inquiry at Farmingdale," *New York Evening Post*, 27 April 1922.
Coley, Kathryn. Letter to author, 14 June 2009.
Colman, Gould. "New York State College of Agriculture and Life Sciences at Cornell University," *The Encyclopedia of New York State*. Ed. Peter Eisenstadt. Syracuse, NY: Syracuse University Press, 2005.
Cremin, Lawrence A. *The Transformation of the School: Progressivism in American Education, 1976–1957*. New York: Alfred A. Knopf, 1961.
Cubberley, Ellwood P. *Public Education in the United States*. Boston: Houghton Mifflin: 1962. Revised and enlarged.
Darlington, James W. "Agricultural Organization and Education," *The Encyclopedia of New York State*. Ed. Peter Eisenstadt. Syracuse, NY: Syracuse University Press, 2005.
"Dean Resigns at Farmingdale," *Suffolk County News*, 19 May 1922.
Desnozka, Edward L. and Davis E. Kapel. Revised edition by David E. Kapel, Charles S. Gifford, and Marilyn Kapel. *American Educators Encyclopedia*. New York: Greenwood Press, 1991.
"Dr. Charles W. Laffin Jr., President of the College at Farmingdale Is Dead," *New York Times*, 26 December 1976.
"Dr. H. B. Knapp, Ex-College Head," *Long Island Press*, 8 September 1976.
"Dr. W. Hubert Keen Named to L. I. Power List," www.farmingdale.edu, 2008.
Douglas, Leroy. "At the Door of the Metropolis, The Struggle to Locate the New York State School of Agriculture on Long Island in Farmingdale, 1911–1913," *Long Island Forum* 65 (Winter 2002): 16–30.
———. "Serving Community and Country: The New York State School of Agricultural at Farmingdale, 1914–1919," *Nassau County Historical Society Journal* 57 (2002): 13–27.
———. "Republic Airport in History," *LI-Airport Historical Society Newsletter* (Summer–Fall 2008): 30–32.
Dunbaugh, Edwin L. "New York to Boston Via the Long Island Railroad," *Evoking A Sense of Place*. Ed. Joann Krieg. Interlaken, NY: Heart of the Lakes Publishing, 1988.
"Editorial," *Farmingdale Post*, 26 March 1926.
"Electronic Blends with Farming on L. I. College," *New York Times*, 6 June 1962.

Ellis, David M., James S, Frost, and William B. Fink. *New York, The Empire State*. Englewood Cliffs, NJ: Prentice-Hall, 1989.

Ennis, Scott. "William A. Medesy, A Lifelong Advocate of Education," *Congressional Record* (Vol. 146), 14 February 2002.

Ewing, Nell. Letter to author, 10 October 2009.

"Excelsior College," www.Excelsior.edu, 2009.

"Facts and Figures," www.farmingdale.edu, 2007.

"Farm Boys Are Up in Athletics," *Amityville Record*, 20 October 1916.

"Farm School Head Quits, Ending Four years of Criticism," *New York Tribune*, 19 December 1922.

"Farm School Ready," *Suffolk County News*, 28 January 1916.

"Farmers Fifteen in First Class, State Has Initial Graduation Exercise for Its First Pupils," *Amityville Record*, 4 April 1919.

"Farming for Soldiers, Lectures at Upton to Help Men Find Places After the War," *Amityville Record*, 10 January 1919.

"Farmingdale Campus Gets A $133 Million Upgrade," *New York Times*, 15 June 2003.

"Farmingdale Graduates, College Completes Transition to 4-Year Institution," *Newsday*, 28 April 1990.

"Farmingdale School Is Open for Work," *Amityville Record*, 3 March 1916.

"Farmingdale State College President W. Hubert Keen Named Winner of David Award by *Networking Magazine*," www.farmingdale.edu, 2008.

"Farmingdale State College Ranked Nationally in Graduate Earning Power," *Long Island Press*, 17 November 2009.

"Farmingdale State College's Aviation Program Announces $1 Million Purchase of New Planes," www.farmingdale.edu, 31 March 2011.

"Farmingdale Trying to Get Principal Travis," *Suffolk County News*, 9 February 1923.

Fischler, Stan. *Long Island Railroad*. St. Paul, MN: Voyageur Press, 2007.

Friel, James. Letter to author, 16 September 2009.

Fullerton, Edith Loring. *History of Long Island Agriculture*. New York: Long Island Rail Road, 1929.

"G. Thompson Dies," *New York Times*, 2 September 1941.

Gabriel, Ralph Henry. *The Evolution of Long Island*. Port Washington, NY: Ira J. Friedman, 1921.

"George E. Nold, 72, A Physics Professor," *New York Times*, 23 July 1971.

Gombieski, Jane S. "Klokards, Kleagles, Kludds, and Kluxers: The Ku Klux Klan in Suffolk County, 1915–1928,)," *Long Island History Journal* 6 (Fall 1993): 41–62.

Graves, Frank P. A *Student's History of Education*. New York: Macmillan, 1936. Revised edition.

"Halsey B. Knapp Dies Tuesday," *Farmingdale Post*, 9 September 1976.

Harrison, Fred. Interview by Karen A. Gelles. Farmingdale, NY, 30 September 2009.

Hazelton, Henry Isham. *The Boroughs of Brooklyn and Queens Counties of Nassau and Suffolk, Long Island*. Vol. 4. New York: Lewis Historical Publications, 1924.

"Heroes' Oak Planted in Battlefield Soil," *New York Times*, 5 June 1921.

Historical Population of Long Island Communities, 1790–1980: Decennial Census Data. Hauppauge, NY: Long Island Regional Planning Board. 1982.

Hofstadter, Richard and C. DeWitte Hardy. *The Development of Higher Education in the United States*. New York: Columbia University Press, 1952.

Hooper, Franklin W. "Industrial Museums for Our Cities," *Proceedings of the Eighth Annual Meeting of the American Associations of Museums*, June 1913.

Howard, Louis. Telephone interview by author, 20 March 2010.

———. www.stonybrook.edu, 2010.

Howitt, Sara. "The World War II Home Front: The Farmingdale Experience," *Long Island Forum* 58 (Summer 1995): 18–35.

"Johnson Is Hooted After Resignation," *Standard Union*, 19 December 1922.

"Johnson Resigns Post as Director of Farm School," *Brooklyn Eagle*, 19 December 1922.

"Jonathan C. Gibralter Named New President of Frostburg State University," www.USMD.edu, 2006.

Kaplowitz, Isaac and Daniel Galinson. *Brief of Plaintiffs-Appellants*, 4 February 1985.

Kass, Sean. "The Long Island Railroad and Its Promotion of Long Island, 1900–1930," *Long Island Historical Journal* 17 (Fall 2004–Spring 2005): 85–90.

"Knapp Visits Cobleskill," *Albany Evening News*, 3 April 1926.

Knapp, Halsey B. "For A Better Country Life," *LIRR Bulletin*, 1931.

Koppelman, Lee E. and Pearl M. Kamer. "Anatomy of the Long Island Economy: Retrospect and Prospective," *Long Island Historical Journal* 6 (Spring 1994): 146–167.

"Legislative Probe for Farm School," *Suffolk County News*, 1 March 1918.

Leslie, W. Bruce, John B. Clark, and Kenneth P. O'Brien, Eds. *SUNY At Sixty, The Promise of the State University of New York*. Albany, NY: SUNY Press, 2010.

"Lewis F. Pilcher, Architect, Was 70," *New York Times*, 16 June 1961.

"L. I. Press Association Want Director Johnson as Farm School Head," *New York Evening Post*, 16 December 1922.

Long Island Agronomist, 1907–1914 editions.

Long Island Rail Road. *Long Island, the Sunrise Homeland*. New York: Long Island Railroad. 1924.

Mastroianni, Anthony. Letter to author, 5 October 2009.

Mazzaferro, Patricia. Letter to author, 13 August 1986.

Medesy, William A. "Letter To the Editor," *Commentary*, 15 April 1956.

"Michael J. Vinciguerra Appointed Acting President at Farmingdale State," www.Farmingdale.edu, 2000.

Morison, Samuel Eliot, Henry Steele Commager, and William E. Leuchtenburg. *The Growth of the American Republic*. Vols. 1, 2. New York: Oxford University Press. 1980.

Morton, Louis G. *Mesa College, The First Fifty Years*. Grand Junction, CO: Mesa State College, 1982.

Mountain, Betty. Telephone interview with author, 1 August 1984.

Murray, Christine E. "Taylor Law," *The Encyclopedia of New York State*. Ed. Peter Eisenstadt. Syracuse, NY: Syracuse University Press, 2005.

"Nassau–Suffolk Share of the Population of New York and of the United States," U. S. *Census '70*, Vol. I, Tables 1, 3.

Naylor, Natalie A. "The Legacy of New Deal Art on Long Island," *Long Island Historical Journal* 17 (Fall 2004–Spring 2005): 41–70.

"New Planes Arrive at SUNY," *Farmingdale Observer*, 3 October 1997.

New York State. "Chapter 319," *Laws of New York State*. Albany, NY. 1912.

———. *The Redbook*. Albany, NY. 1912.

"New York State," www.2010.census.gov/2010.

"New York State Agricultural Society," www.NYSAGSociety.org, 2010.

New York State Supreme Court, Appellate Division, Second Department, *Frank J. Cavaioli, et. al., Plaintiffs-Appellants, Against Board of Trustees of the State University of New York, Record of Appeal*, 29 January 1985.

Nordin, Dennis Sven and Bertrand N. O. Walker. *Rich Harvest, A History of the Grange*. Jackson, MS: University Press of Mississippi. 1974.

Office of University Affairs and Development, *Sixty-Four Campuses*. Albany. NY: State University of New York, 1985).

"$1 M Gift for Farmingdale." *Newsday*, 22 September, 2011.

Overton, Jacqueline. *Long Island's History*. Garden City, NY: Doubleday, Doran, 1920.

Pack, Charles Lathrop. "The Memorial Tree," *American Forestry* (July 1921).

Palmer, Noel. "Let Each Become." Unpublished memoir. 1978.

Petrick, Joseph. "From Schools of Agriculture to Colleges of Technology: A Century of Evolution," *SUNY at Sixty, the Promise of the State University of New York*. Eds. W. Bruce Leslie, John B. Clarke, and Kenneth P. O'Brien. Albany, NY: SUNY Press. 2010.

"Preparing of Food Harvest on Long Island Acres," *New York Times*, 6 May 1917.

"President Keen Honored by LIA's Small Business Council," www.Farmingdale.edu, 2008.

"Program Cuts at Farmingdale," *Newsday*, 11 December 1972.

"R. Wallace, 91, Professor," *Newsday*, 8 November 2008.

Rakowski, Casimir. Interview with author. Farmingdale, NY, 3 January 1983.

"Rear Admiral Ward Is Dead At Roslyn," *New York Times*, 6 July 1916.

"Resigns Under Fire From Farm Institute," *New York Times*, 19 December 1922.

"Resolution 92-HR 1014," Illinois General Assembly, 1 June 2002.

Robbins, Michelle. "Rooted In Memory," *American Forests* (Spring 2003): 1–3.

"Roosevelt To the Farmers," *New York Times*, 24 August 1910.

Ross, Peter. *History of Long Island*. Vol. III. New York: Lewis Publishing, 1902.

Rosenthal, Joel. "Pride and Identity: The College Histories of the SUNY Campuses," *SUNY At Sixty, The Promise of the State University of New York*. Eds. John B. Clarke, W. Bruce Leslie, and Kenneth P. O'Brien. Albany, NY: SUNY Press, 2010.

Sachs, Charles L. *The Blessed Isle, Hal B. Fullerton and His Image of Long Island, 1897–1927*. Interlaken, NY: Heart of the Lakes Publishing, 1991.

"Seeds of Future Yet To Sprout," *Newsday*, 4 May 1992.

"Sees Asylum Plan As Danger to Girls in Industrial School," *Brooklyn Eagle*, 31 March 1926.

"Setting Higher Goals for Farmingdale State," *New York Times*, 23 February 2003.

Seyfried, Vincent F. *The Cross-Island Line, The Story of the Huntington Railroad Trolley Operation in Huntington, Melville, Farmingdale, Amityville*. Garden City, NY, 1976.

Smits, Edward J. *Nassau Suburbia, U.S.A.* Garden City, NY: Doubleday, 1974.

"Soldier Students To Go," *New York Times*, 7 November 1927.

Standard Union, 26 September 1923.

"State Farm School Shake-Up Is Advised," *New York Times*, 1 September 1922.

"State School Cannot Open," *Amityville Record*, 28 May 1915.

"State School Safe for Present," *Nassau Weekly*, 26 March 1926.

State University of New York. *The Master Plan, Revised*. Albany, NY, 1964.

"Stony Kill Environmental Education Center," New York State Department of Environmental Conservation, 2010.

"Student-Farmer Mourns Dying Trade," *Newsday*, 3 April 1986.

Suffolk County Historical Society Exhibition, "The Blessed Isle: Hal B. Fullerton and his Image of Long Island," 1990; and Exhibition, "Edith Loring Fullerton: The Lady of the Garden," 2001.

Suffolk County News, 9 and 16 February 1923.

"SUNY Board Names New President at Farmingdale College," *Farmingdale Observer*, online edition, 19 January 2007.

"SUNY Cutbacks," *Newsday*, 21 June 1995.
"SUNY Farmingdale Enrollment Plunges," *Newsday*, 14 1994.
"SUNY Farmingdale Gets President," *Newsday*, 28 March 2001.
"SUNY Farmingdale Major Priority for System," *Long Island Press*, 10 July 2009.
SUNY Office of University Affairs and Development. *Sixty-Four Campuses*. Albany, NY, 1985.
"The Central Branch: Farmingdale's Other Line," *Farmingdale-Bethpage Historical Vignettes*, 2010.
"The Cross-Island Trolley Line, 1909–1919," *Farmingdale-Bethpage Historical Society Historical Vignettes*, 2010.
"The Farm Is A Classroom," *New York Sunday News*, 9 August 1970.
"The First World War, The Cricket History of Calderdale and Kirless," www.cricketheritage.org, 2009.
"The Green Building Institute at Farmingdale State College," www.farmingdale.edu, 2011.
"Trustees Make Answer," *Suffolk County News*, 15 September 1922.
Van Horn, Carl E. and Herbert A. Schaffner. *Work in America, An Encyclopedia of History, Policy, and Society*. Vol. I. Santa Barbara: CA: ABC-CLIO, 2003.
Voorhis, Edwin. *Master Plan, Village of Farmingdale*. Vol. I. Rockville Center, 1959.
Ward, Hilda. *The Girl and The Motor*. Cincinnati, OH: The Gas Engine Publishing, 1908.
Wechsler, Harold S. "State University of New York," *The Encyclopedia of New York State*. Ed. Peter Eisenstadt. Syracuse, NY: Syracuse University Press, 2005.
"Welcome to Stealth University," *New York Times*, 2 May 1999.
Wilkens, Christine. "Nazareth Trade School," *Farmingdale's Story, Farms to Flight*, Farmingdale: NY: Bicentennial Issue, 1976.
"William Adelbert Medesy, 90, Died February 1," *Rocky Mountain News*, 8 February 2000.
Williams, Patricia Hill. Letter to author, 14 April 2010.
Wydler, John W. "Commencement Address, State University Agricultural and Technical Institute, Farmingdale," *Congressional Record*, 89th Congress, First Session, 22 June 1965.
"Yoakum, Benjamin Franklin," www.fbhsli.org, 2010.
Ziel, Ron and George Foster. *Steels to Sunrise*. New York: Hawthorne Books, 1965.
Zulli, Mauro, Telephone interview with author, 20 December 2010.

Farmingdale State College Archives

"A Report on Personnel Policies" December 1952.
"A Tablet, The Gift of the Class of '27," *1933–34 Freshman Manual*.
"Biotechnology Park Is Funded," *News and Events*, 19 January 2000.
Beekman, Dow. Letter to Halsey B. Knapp, 24 October 1923.

Budget 1917–1918.
"Celebrating 75 Years . . . and Tomorrow," 1987.
"Class Action Suit Determination," 21 April 1988.
Cipriani, Frank A. "75th Anniversary Presidential Message," 1987.
———. "Statement: Ground Breaking Ceremony of New SUNY Farmingdale Airport Facility at Republic Field," 15 April 1993.
———. "Testimony Presented Before the Senate Higher Education Committee Hearing on the 'Rethinking SUNY Report' by the New York Board of Trustees Friday, 5 January 1996, Stony Brook Campus."
Coley, Kathryn. "Biographical Information for William Fichtner," 9 June 2000.
"Commencement at Farmingdale College," 2008.
"Convocation and Colloquy Commemorating the Twentieth Anniversary of President Frank A. Cipriani, Ph. D., 15 September, 1998."
"Dedication Pamphlet," 30 May 1959.
"Diamond Jubilee Ball Program," 1987.
Donaldson, Loretta M. "Aviation Department," 16 September 1995.
"Dr. Charles W. Laffin Jr., President, Passes Away," *Escalate*, February 1977.
"Enrollments in All Courses, 1916 to 1945."
"Faculty of State University Agriculture and Technical Institute at Farmingdale Petition to Director William A. Medesy, Dean Lawrence L Jarvie, and the SUNY Board of Trustees," n. d.
"Faculty Meeting," 2, 14 May 1923.
"Farmingdale Institute to Present Country Life-Open House Program," 1951.
Fisher, Hardy J. Telegram to Miss Hilda Ward, 19 October 1922.
Freshman Handbook 1925–1926, 1932–1933.
Gelles, Karen. "Commencement Speakers," 2010.
Gibralter, Jonathan C. "Vita," 2006.
Graduating Class of 1949. Letter to Director Knapp, 21 November 1948.
"Graduation Statistics," 1948.
Graves, Frank P. Letter to William M. Baldwin, 31 August 1923.
Hinko, Christy. "Cabin Fever," n.d.
"History of the Alumni Association, 1921–1955," 1955.
Hooper, Franklin W. "Expense Account," 28 February 1914.
———. "Letter to the Officers and Members of Agricultural Organizations, Boards of Trade, and Other Organizations, to Citizens Generally in the Southeastern Quarter of the State of New York," 9 April 1912.

———. “Statement to the Board of Trustees,” June 1912.
“Horton Amidon Report,” February 1954.
Horton, Daniel Hart. “Institute History, Poultry,” June 1954.
“Inauguration of Jonathan C. Gibralter, President,” 2 November 2001.
“Inauguration of W. Hubert Keen,” 11 May 2007.
“Installation Ceremony for President Frank A. Cipriani, Ph. D.,” 7 May 1978.
“Institute in War Time,” n. d.
James, Locke. “War Time Services at the State Institute of Agriculture, Farmingdale,” n. d.
“Jobs of Tomorrow,” *Escalate*, February 1977.
Johnson, Albert A. “Proposed Plans for the Establishment of the State School of Agriculture on Long Island,” 11 December 1912.
Johnson, Albert A. and Franklin W. Hooper Correspondence, 13 January 1913–27 December 1913.
“Johnson or Long Island, Excerpts from the Testimony Given During the Investigation of the Management and Affairs of the State Institute of Applied Agriculture at Farmingdale, L. I., Before Special Commissioner Edward G. Zimmer,” 1922.
Johnson, Albert A. Letter to Locke James, 6 April 1962.
King, Shelly Galehouse. “The Early Days: ‘21 Alumnus Recalls,” n. d.
Knapp, Halsey B. ““Halsey B. Knapp Address to Technical-Industrial Faculty,” 15 September 1949.
———. “Knapp Memo,” 9 June 1947.
———. Letter to Faculty and Staff, 12 April 1956.
———. Letter to Governor Alfred E. Smith, 3 June, 9, 1926.
———. Letter to William M. Baldwin, 27 August, 4 September 1923.
———. “Memorandum to Horton Amidon,” 5 February, 28 January 1953.
———. “Memorandum to Messrs. Amidon, Hallock,” 7 April 1955.
———. “Memorandum to Messrs. Merritt, Wedell, Davidson, Rissmeyer, Foote, James, Stockbridge, McLaughlin, Allee, Willenbrock, Griffith, Roberts, Judd, Coogan, Bowman, Amidon, Raymaley, Hallock, Hallahan, Floyd, Roesch, Rogers,”16 January 1950.
———. “Memorandum to R. C. Davidson,” 7 August 1952.
———. “Statement at Director’s Luncheon, Country Life-Open House Program,” 23 February 1956.
———. “Statement at the Annual North Atlantic Regional Conference-Agricultural Education,” 6-9 April 1948.
Laffin, Charles W. Jr. “Evaluating the Performance of Non-Teaching Professionals,” paper presented at Colorado State University, 16–19 June 1975.

"Land or Appurtenances, Year, Built or Purchased, Cost," n. d.
"Long Island Institute Graduates First Industrial Class,"1948.
Lupton, Edmund R. Letter to Halsey B. Knapp, 29 August 1923.
Mann, Arthur R. Letter to Halsey B. Knapp, 21 September 1923.
"Mauro Zulli Acting President of SUNY Farmingdale," *Escalate*, February 1977.
Medesy, William A. "Report on Placement and Progress of Graduates," 1956.
"Minutes of the Faculty Executive Committee," SUNY College of Technology at Farmingdale," 16 October 1987.
"New York State Egg Laying Contest," n. d.
"New York State School of Agriculture on Long Island Board of Trustees Meeting, Minutes," 8, 29 June 1912; 12; 28 December 1912; 4 January 1913; 8 February 1913.
"News Release," 4 May 1957, 15 April 1993.
Niles, William A. Letter to Hilda Ward, 14 October 1920.
Northam, Basil R. Letter to Kathryn Coley, 12 February 1999.
"Number of Graduates Based on Community Programs, Yearbooks, and Annual Reports," n. d.
Palmer, Bernard. "The Conklin Street Story," 1956.
"Personnel Service, 1933–1935," 1935.
"Press Release," February 1968.
"Profile of SUNY at Farmingdale," 9 August 1972.
Pyne, Frank. "New Log Cabin," n. d.
Pyrke, Berne A. Letter to Halsey B. Knapp, 20 September 1923.
"Report of the Policy Committee for the Administration of Instructional Personnel," 10 November 1947.
"Resolution Passed by the New York State Federation of Farm Bureaus at a Regular Meeting Held at Syracuse," 7 July 1922.
Smith, Governor Alfred E. Letter to H. B. Knapp, 4 June 1926.
"State University of New York at Farmingdale Convocation and Colloquy Commemorating the Twentieth Anniversary of President Frank A. Cipriani, Ph.D.," 15 September 1998.
"Statement to the Press by William A. Baldwin with Reference to the Farmingdale Matter," September 1922.
"Stony Kill Farm," 1955.
"Student Petition," 19 October 1922.
"SUNY College Intercollegiate Athletic Program," n. d.
"The Early Years: "21 Alumnus Recalls," n. d.

"The 75th Anniversary Historical Committee Program," 1 October 1986.
Thomson, C. Dick. "Achievements," n. d.
———. "Activities in World War II," n. d.
———. "From Idea to Reality," n. d.
———. "Letter to Professor Eugene O'Neill," n. d.
Thomson, C. Dick, Edwin F. Ore, and Raynor Wallace. *Alma Mater*. 1984.
"Total Number Who Served and Were Killed in Action," 19 October 1945.
"Twenty-Five Years of Progress," 1941.
"W. Hubert Keen Installed as Farmingdale President," *Farmingdale View*, Fall 2007.
Ward, Hilda. "Statement of Hilda Ward," 24 May 922.
Wilson, L. A. Letter to Hilda Ward, 6 December 1920.

Farmingdale State College Publications

Aggazette, 1923–1948.
Alumnus, 1961–Present.
Bulletin, *Catalog*, 1916–Present.
Campus Times, 1980–Present.
Escalate, various.
Freshman Handbook, various.
Furrow, 1916–1922.
ISLANDER Yearbook, 1948–Present.
NYSSA Yearbook, 1919–1928.
NYSSAN Yearbook, 1929–1947.
Rambler, 1948–Present.
Student Handbook, various.

Index

References to photographs are indicated with **BOLD** page numbers.

2 year degrees and programs, 140, 142, 204
4 year degrees and programs, xiv, 139, 217, 222, 225–26, 263
  opposition to, 223–24

Abbatiello, Michael, ix, 68, 99, 108, 109, 211
Academic programs in 1940, 98
Acquisition of land, 25
Advertising Art and Design, 148
Aerial view of campus, 219
Aerospace. *See* Aviation
Agricultural and technical colleges, 130, 178, 205
Agricultural Education Association, 13, 14
Agriculture, School of, xiv, 139, 177–78, **185**, 194, 204, 225, 254
Agronomy Building. *See* Cutler Hall
Aircraft Maintenance and Operation Program, 148, 158, **161**, 220
Aircraft Manufacture Program, 148
Alfred, 2, 12, 13, 98, 141
Allard Field House, 148, 176, 180
Allard, Gerald, 46, 99, 180, 211
Allee, David W., ix, xiii, **144**, 146, 147, **151**, 153, 161–63, 168
Alma Mater, 48, 49, 243
Alumni Association, 58, 59, 102, 152, 263
Amidon, Horton, 102, **181**, 211
Amityville Record, 36
Andrews, William, 37
Apiculture, **32**
Applied sciences and technologies, 139
Arnold, W. C., 98

Athletic conferences, 180
Athletics, 45, 46, 99, 180
Attendance. *See* enrollment
Aviation, xiii, 114, 158, 170, 204, 218–21, 225, 235, **238**, **239**, 248–49
Aviation Center at Republic Airport, 220–21

Baccalaureate degrees. *See* 4 year degrees
Baker, 54
Baldwin, William H., 3
Baldwin, William M., 46, 71, 72
Bamforth, Jack, 52
Barnes and Noble, 200–201
Barron, Leonard, 123
Baseball, 46, 99, **249**
Baseball stadium, 249
Basketball, 46
  men's, **76**, **176**
  women's, **88**
Baumann, 54
Bausch, Adolph, 13
Beanies, **132, 136, 190, 191**
Becker, Walter G, 126
Bees. *See* apiculture
Bethpage State Park, xi, 23, 98
Biotechnology, 226
Blank, Robert C., 182, 184
Block, Murray, 191
Board of Trustees, 15–16, 22–23, 25, 27, 29, 67; 69, 70, 82, 83. *See also* College Council
Bookstore, administration of, 200–201
Boyer, Ernest L., 156
Bricker, Garland Armor, 73, 76, 77
Brisbane, Arthur, 64
Broad Hollow Bioscience Park, xi, xiv, 218, 230–31
Broadhollow Rd. *See* Route 110
Brod, Pearl, 171, 211
Brooklyn Institute of Arts and Sciences, xii, 2, 9, 10, 13, 22
Brooks, F. D., 57
Brown's Hotel, Farmingdale NY, 23
Bryant Library, Roslyn NY, x
Buff, Nellie, **33**
Building Construction Department, 148
Bulletin. See *College Catalog*
Bunche Plaza, 179, **212**, **229**
Bunche, Ralph, 179, 215
Burkart, John, 231
Button, H. F., 37
Byrne, James, 22
Byrne, William, 171

Camouflage courses, 115
Campbell, Thomas, **154**
Campus Center, 248
Campus unrest, 1960s, xiii, 172–73, 179, 204
Campus Village, xiii, 113, 123, **124**, 126, 127, 148
Canton, 2, 12, 13, 98, 141
Carey, Governor Hugh, 156, 194, 204
Carll, John A., 22
Case, Maurice, 201–202
Cavaioli, Frank J., vii, 182, 211
Chapter 319 of the Laws of New York 1912. *See* Harte-Thompson Bill
Chase, E. L., 37
Chicken barbecue, 190, 210
Childcare Center, 233
Chinese exchange program. *See* international education

Cipriani, Frank A., viii, ix, xiv, 132, **195, 209, 222, 238**
bioscience park, 230
biography, 196
campus unrest, 171–73
community organization involvement, 233
Dean of School of Continuing Education, 194
Inauguration, 202–203
Legion of Merit Award, 233
professorship, 201
retirement, 231
support for aviation, 218–22
Vice Presidency, 198, 202
Clabisforum, **162**
Close the college, threats to, 84, 85, 86, 87, 140
Cobleskill, 12
Cold Spring Harbor Laboratory, xii, xiv, 218, 223, 230
Cole, L. M., 37
Coley, Kathryn, ix
Collective bargaining. *See* Unions
College Archives. viii
College Catalog, 37, 38, 39, 42, 43, 46
College Council, 113, 152. *See also* Board of Trustees
Collingwood, H. W. *See* commencement speakers
Commencement, 245
1970s, **199**
1919, 57, 242
1920s, 58
1940s, 118, 119, **125,** 158, 242
1960s, 176
speakers, 58, 230, 245
Community Service Assistant, 203, 224
Computer Graphics, 224
Computer Technology, 226, **232**
Conklin Hall, 35, **89**
Conklin St. School, **143**, 146, 148, **150**, 161, 163
Conklin Stree campus. *See* Industrial-Technical Division, on Conklin Street
Conservatory. *See* greenhouses
Construction of first buildings, 35
Cooley, James, xii, 2, 12–14
Corbin, Austin, 3
Country Life Open House, xii, 56, **74**, 99, 109, 119, 120, 153, 160, **200**
Country Life Program. *See* Country Life Open House
Cox, Frederick, xii, 2, 12–14
Creedmoor State Hospital, 85–87
Criminal Justice, 224
Cuomo, Governor Mario, 194, 226
Cutler Hall, 35, 57, 240

Dairy barn, 35
Dairy Test Laboratory, **89**
DeForest, M. Henry and P., 98
Del Bene, Frank, 231
Delhi, 12, 86, 98, 141
Dental Hygiene Center, 248
Dental Hygiene Department, 68, 148, 156–58, **183**
Dew Drop Inn, 124
Dewey, Governor Thomas E., xv, 124, 127, 128
Dewey, John, 51
Diamond Jubilee Ball, 211
Diehl, Ann, 182
Director's Cottage, 15, **34**, 35, **219**
Diversity, xv, 52
Dix, Governor John Alden, 13, 14, 22
Dodge, H. A., 73
Dorm 2. *See* Hooper Hall

Dorm 3, 35
Dorm 4, 35
Dorm I. *See* Ward Hall
Dougher, Ronald, **181**
Drama Club, **174**

Early Childhood Education, 224
Eastern College Athletic Conference, 180
Educational Opportunity Center, 170, **189**, 198, 205–206, 235
Egan, Thomas F., 241
Electrical Equipment with Industrial Electronics, 148
Electrical Technology, 152, 225
Elkins, Frank, 171, 198
Ench, Bob, 202, 211
Enrollment, xiii, xv, 36, 56, 84, 92, 103, 109, 130, 142, 149, 170, 177, 204, 228, 239, 246–47
Entrance requirements, 39
Extension programs, 38, 99, 100, 115

Faculty research and grants, 248
Faculty Student Association, 200–201
Faculty, founding members of, 37
Fallon, Mary, 233, 237
Farm and Home Equipment Show. *See* Country Life Open House
farm complex, 177, **219**
Farmingdale Executive Committee. *See* Governance
Farmingdale Foundation, 230
Farmingdale Village School District, ix
Farmingdale, Village of, ix, 23, 24, 27, 91, 139. *See also* Location of college
Federal Board for Vocational Education, 59, 65–67. *See also* Johnson, Albert A. (investigations)
Female students, 43, 52, **117**, 118, **122**, 123, **137**, 197. *See also* Buff, Nellie; Freeman, Kathryn
Fichtner, William, 176
Fight Song, 244
Fiippen, E. O., 24
Flesch, Berthold, 22
Food Administration/Technology, 148, **188**
Football, **45**, 46, 99, **111**, 180
Foote, Norman H., 114, 211
Foreign exchange. *See* international education
Four-year school. *See* 4-year degrees
Franke, George, 53, **116**
Freedoms Foundation Award, 197
Freeman, Kathryn, 58
Freshman Manual, 90
Friel, James, ix, 208
Fullerton, Edith Loring, 4, 5, 26
Fullerton, Hal B., xii, 2, 4, 7, 9, 12, 14, 25, 26
funding problems, 85, 92, 130, 173–74, 194, 224, 227–28
Furrow. *See* Student newspapers
Fuschillo, Charles J., 248–49, **250**

Gardens, 227
Gargano, Charles, 230
Gelles, Karen A., viii
General Education Division, 102
Gibralter, Jonathan C., xiv
  appointment, 236
  biography, 235–36
  campus renovations, 240
  fund raising. 237, 240
  inauguration, 237
  resignation, 240
Gleeson Hall, 67, 201, 204

Gleeson, Mortimer J., 179, 190, 201
Goldstein, Jonathan, ix
Governance, 106, 107, 134
Graduates, 119, 121
Graduation. *See* commencement
Grange, 5, 21, 29, 47, **55,** 58, 92, 119
Graphic Communications (Printing), 224
Graves, Frank P., 70, 82, 87
Greenberg, David B., 37, 52, 54
Greenhouses, 97, 98, **214**
Greenley Hall, 123, 174, 179, 204
Grumman Aircraft, 149, 157–58
Gymnasia, 35, 179–80, 204, **222**

Hall, James, ix
Hancock, Pricilla Tedesco, ix
Hangar. *See* Allard Field House
Hansen, Viggo, 149
Harriman, Governor W. Averell, 194
Harrington, Mike, **250**
Harrison, Fred, **215**
Harte, Dennis J., xii, 2, 12, 14
Harte-Thompson Bill, 13, 14, 16
Harvey, Don, 176
Hasson, Eileen, ix, 247
Health services, 198–99
Hendrikson, J. K., 25
Henry, Veronica, 107
Hicks Hall, **17**, 35, **40**, 57, 167, 240
Hicks, Henry W., 61, 167
Highway and Bridge Construction Department, 148
Hoefer, Herman. *See* State Architect
Homecoming, **162**, **174**
Homecoming and Visitation Day, 59
Honor societies, 182–86
Hooper Hall, 35
Hooper, Franklin W., xii, 2, 9, 10, 11–14, 22, 25, 27, 30
Horticulture, xiii, 92, 121, 204, 225
Horticulture Building. *See* Hicks Hall
Horton Hall, 57, 95, **116**, 167
Horton, D. Hart, **94**, **95**, 126
Howard, Lou, ix, **161**, 218
Howell, Charles H., xii, 2, 12, 14
Hughes, Governor Charles Evans, 13
Humanities/AITIA, 208–209
Hungerman, J. C., 37
Hunt, M. E., 97

Industrial Chemistry, 148
Industrial Instrumentation, 148
Industrial Instrumentation, 153
Industrial Technology, 226
Industrial-Technical Division, 156
  founding of, xiii, 98, 102, 141, 142, 143
  in Lupton Hall, 161
  on Conklin Street, 118, **145**, 159
Influenza, 56
International education, 211

Jamaica. *See* Winter School of Agriculture
James, Locke, 100, 171
James, William, 51
Johnson, Albert Aaron, xii, **28**
  1923 commencement, 58
  A. A. Johnson Syndicate, 171
  and Russian students, 66
  and Soviet Union, 66, 77, 78
  biography, 27–29, 60, 80
  Chairman of American Commission for Near
    East Relief, 77

Johnson, Albert Aaron *(continued)*
death and burial, 80
Harold A. Little, 65
hired, 27, 29
investigations, 51, 64–67, 70, 71
letter to Locke James in 1962, 171
memorial plaque, **78**
on architecture and construction, 35
on learning-by-doing, 36
on salaries, 30
resignation, xii, 51, 73
student strike against, 66, 72–73
support of Arthur Brisbane, editor, 64
support of Board of Trustees, 70
support of Hal Fullerton, 72
support of William Baldwin, 71
travels, 77
Johnston, William J., ix

Kamer, Pearl, 230, 251, 252
Kaplan, Sylvia, 197
Keegan, Bob, **154**
Keen, W. Hubert, x, xiv, **245**
appointment, 241
awards and recognition, 250–51
biography, 241
campus renovations, 248
inauguration, 241–42
Students First Initiative, 242
Kelly, Thomas, 209
King, Robert L., 236, 237
Knapp Hall, xiii, **96**, 97, **117**, 179
radio station, 153
Knapp, Halsey B,., ix, xiii, **83, 94, 105, 124, 169**
and Campus Village, 126, 127
and Memorial Oak, 63
biography, 81, 82, 110, 111
correspondence with students who enlisted, 117
death, 110
hired, 81, 82
involvement with Rotary International, 92, 110
leadership style, 127, 165
memorial greenhouse plaque, **214**
on dedication of Knapp Hall, 97
on learning-by-doing, 91, 141
on race discrimination, 108
opposition to closing school, 85–87
pink and blue memos, 108
retirement, 109, 110, 165–66
speech to NYS Conference of Farm Organizations, 141
United Nations consultant, 110
Komisar, Jerry, 223
Koppelman, Lee E., 251
Ku Klux Klan, 84

Laffin Hall, 179, 190
Laffin, Jr., Charles W., ix, xiii, 131, **169, 189**
administrative hires, 171
awards, 187
biography, 168–69
building dedication, 190
campus unrest, 172–73
collective bargaining, 173
community college movement, 168–69, 171
community organization involvement, 186–87
death, 175, 186
Educational Opportunity Center, 170
faculty professional status, 170
hired, 168

SUNY Master Plan, 177
support for agricultural education, 177–78
support for aviation, 218
Vietnam War, 171–73
Laffin, Kevin R., ix
LaRosa, Georg, ix, **222**, 231, 241, **250**
Lazarus, M. M., 25
Learning-by-doing, concept of, 36, 37, 39, 48. *See also* Knapp and Johnson
Legislation, vetoed, 13
Lehman, Governor Herbert H., 97
Levine, Irving, ix
Levy, Norman, 230
Liatins, 118
Liberty Aircraft, 149
Liberty Loans, 54
Library, 123. *See also* Greenley Hall
Littledale, Harold A. *See* Johnson, Albert A. (investigations)
Location of College, selection of, 16, 18, 23, 24, 25, 26
Log Cabin, 100, **208**, 209–10
Long Island Agriculturist, 57
Long Island Agronomist, 5, 26
Long Island Rail Road, 3, 4, 5, 12, 26, 51
Long Islander, 18
Lupton Hall, **155**, 161, **174**, **190**, 226, 240, 251
Lupton, Edmund R., 82, 158, 161
Lupton, John M., xii, 2, 12, 13, 58, 161

Maguire, Captain, 54
Malcolm, James, 22
Mandato, Frank, 76, 92, 93
Manning. *See* State Architect
Manufacturing Technology, 225
Marino, Ralph, 226
Mark, Robert V., 231
Marra, U. J., 37, 43
Marshall, Frederick, 35, 93
Marshall, Reginald "Tye", 207
Mastroianni, Anthony, ix, 152, 186, 202, 221–22
Maybin, Arthur H., 171
Mayer, Ed, **154**
McEvoy, Judith, 247
McPherson. *See* State Architect
Mears, Sherman, 149
Mechanical Engineering Technology, 156, 204
Medesy, William A., 166–68
faculty petition for professional status, 167–68
Mehlman, Stanley, 237
Melville Road, 6, 8, 25
Memorial Oak, World War I, xii, 59, 60, 61, 62, 63 **61, 62, 79**, 101
Metal Products Designs, Production, and Inspection, 148
Michels, John, 37
Middle States Association of Colleges and Secondary Schools, 129, 173, 208
Milk, **188**
Miller, Governor Nathan, 67, 70
Mission of the college, xi, xiv, 1, 17, 23, 39, 55, 113, 118, 132, 140, 142–43, 177–78, 193–94, 202, 223, 225–26
Monaco, Joseph, 171, 198, 202, **222**
Morrill Land-Grant Act of 1862, 11
Morrisville, 2, 12, 13, 98, 141
Mortuary Science, 203, 224
Mott House, 8, 25, 41, 122
Mott, Richard S., 25
Mountain, Betty, ix, 108

Murphy, Henry A., 46
Murray, John F., 22
Murray, Michael, 171

Names, Changes in College, xi, xiii, xiv, 1, 2, 55, 98, 169, 228
Nassau Community College, 194, 224
National Collegiate Athletic Association Division III, 180
National Junior College Athletic Association, 180
Nazareth Trade School, 143, 146. *See also* Conklin St. School
New Deal projects, xiii, 35, 93, 94
New York American, 64
New York Evening Post, 67
New York Knickerbockers, 179
New York State Egg Laying Contest, 56, 57
New York State Federation of Farm Bureaus, 67
New York Tribune Farmer, 14
Nihan, James F., 171
Nissley, Walter B., 37
Nold Hall. *See* gymnasium
Nold, George E., 179
Northam, John L., 94
Nursing, 68, **184**

O'Brien, John, 211
O'Donohoe, Major A., 54
Old Westbury, 178, 194
O'Neill, Eugene, 171, 211
Open House. *See* Country Life Open House
Orchard Hall, 247
Ore, Ed, ix, 243
Ore, Edwin F., 49, 243–44
Orgelfinger Jr., Louis, 37
Ornamental Horticulture Department. *See* Horticulture

Pack, Charles Lathrop, 61
Palmer, Bernard, 159
Palmer, Noel, ix, 171, **189**, 202, 206–207, 214
Papp, Richard, 176
Pataki, Governor George, 216, 230
Patterson, Eric, 53, 58, **94, 185**
Perry, Alphonse, 149
Peters, Clayton, 60, 63, 64, 101, 102
Peters, Mary, 60, 63, 64, 101, 102
Peters, Ralph, 3, 4, 52
Petrella, Dashimi, 231
Phi Theta Kappa, 182
Physics Department, 149
Pilcher, Lewis F. *See* State Architect
Posillico, Michael, 230
Poultry Department, 57
Power Laundry and Dry Cleaning, 148
Power plant. *See* Conklin Hall
Pratt, Frederick B., 22
Purcell, John M., 171, 187
Pyenson, Louis J., 123
Pyne, Frank, 100, **154**

Radio and Communications, 148
Radio station. *See* WATI
Rakowski, Casimir, ix, 13, 153, **154**, 202
Ram Mascot, 76, 92, 93
Rambler. *See* Student newspapers
Ram's Horn Award, 211
Recreation Supervision, 203, 224
Reeves, Henry A., 22

Refrigeration, Heating, and Air Conditioning, 148
Republic Airfield, xiii
Republic Airport, 170, 218–21, **238, 239**
Republic Aviation, 149
Retrenchment, 227
Rockefeller, Governor Nelson A., 129, 152, 176, 194
Rodriguez, Raymond, 171
Roosevelt Hall, **175,** 178, 179
Roosevelt, Col. Theodore Jr., 58, 87, 245
Roosevelt, President Theodore, 4, 5, 13, 21, 38
Roukis, George, 171
Route 110, xi, 24, 25
Ruland, Judson F., 25
Rural Engineering building, 35

salaries
  of alumni, 251
  of faculty, 227
Santmann, Theresa Patnode, 256
School of Business building, 248
Seaman, M. A., 25
Senyk, Ann, ix, 156, **181**, 182, 211
Shortt, William A., 22
Silos, 35
Skyline Conference, 180, 249
Sloam, Myrna, x
Smith, Ezekiel K., 25
Smith, Governor Alfred E., xii, 57, 84–87
Smith, Terry, 231
Solar Energy Center, 248
South Side Signal, Babylon NY, 14
Sports Management Technology, 247
St. Killian's Parochial School, 130
State Architect, 22, 30, 31
State University of New York (SUNY), 1, 103, 106, 128, 129, 134, 194
Steffens, Emily, 123
Stockbridge, Robert, 211
Stony Brook University, 194
Stony Kill farm, 100
Student clubs, 119
Student newspapers, 43, 48, 208
Student strike. *See* Johnson, Albert A. (investigations)
Student Success Center, 240
Suffolk Community College, 194
Sweeney, Robert, 248–49
Swimming, 46

Taylor Law, 173
Taylor, G. A., 37
Technology Transfer and Utilization Center, 226
Tedesco, Peter, ix
Tedesco, Peter, 109, 110, 111
Telecommunications, 247
Televised courses, 182
Tennis, 46, 99
Tenure, 107
Thompson Hall, xii, xiii, 97, **105**, 118, 123, **125, 137, 219**
Thompson, George L., xii, 2, 12, 14, 46, 97
Thompson, Nancy, 231
Thomson, C. Dick, 49, 100, 120, 243
Time capsule, 215
Titus, Elwood, xii, 3, 12, 13, 71, 87
Tobin, William, **154**
Track, 46
Trimester schedule, 176–77
Trolley, Huntington cross-island, 24

Tuition, 247
free, 15, 26, 37, 122
increases, 228
non New York residents, 26, 71, 122, 247
Russian students, 66
televised courses, 182
Tuthill, Russ, ix
Tuttle, Ezra, xii, 3, 12, 22

Undeclared Majors, 247
Unigraphics, 155–56
Unions, 104, 106, 107, 134, 173
United University Professions (UUP). *See* Unions
Urban Center, xiii, 171, 207

Vairo, Dan, 59
Van Hoogenstyn, Parker, 187
Verplanck family. *See* Stony Kill farm
Veteran students, xiii, 59, 114, 126, 127, 150
Veterans Bureau, 67
Vietnam War, xiii, 171–72, 179
Vinciguerra, Michael, **222**, 226, 228, 233, 235–36
Visual Communications, 226

Waite, Donald, 149
Wall of Honor, **229**
Wallace, Raynor, ix, 49, 156, 182, 243
Walsh, Frederick J., 171
Ward Hall, 16, 35, **44, 45**, 68
Ward, Hilda, x, 67, **68**, 69
WATI radio station, 153
Watson, James, 209, 230
Watt, Tom, **111**
Weather station, 120
Weiners, William A., 25
Whitman Hall, xii, xiii, 123, 179
Whitman, F. L., 37
Whitman, Governor Charles S., 36
Willenbrock, B. D., 171
Williams, Ira L., 114
Williams, Patricia Hill, ix, 213–16, **234**
Williams, Robert, **154**
Wilson, Governor Malcolm, 194
Winter School of Agriculture and Allied Subjects, 13
Women's Land Army, 41, 43, 52, 114
Works Progress Administration. *See* New Deal projects
World War I, xii, 22, 51, 52
military training on campus, 39, **40, 41**, 42, 54
student cadets, **41**, 42
World War II, xiii, 113, 119
Casualties, 114
GI Bill of Rights, 113, 123, 128
World's Fair of 1939, 108
WPA murals. *See* New Deal projects
Wydler, John. W., 179

Yearbook-*NYSSA*, **75**
Yoakum, Benjamin F., 3, 22

Zimmer, Edward G. *See* Johnson (investigations)
Zipper, Herb, ix, 213, 251
Zulli, Mauro S., ix, 187, 190, 202, 205